Children's Mathematical Frameworks 8–13:
A Study of Classroom Teaching

Children's Mathematical Frameworks 8–13: A Study of Classroom Teaching

Kathleen Hart
David C. Johnson
Margaret Brown
Linda Dickson
Rod Clarkson

Edited by David C. Johnson

NFER-NELSON

Published by The NFER-NELSON Publishing Company Ltd.,
Darville House, 2 Oxford Road East,
Windsor, Berkshire SL4 1DF, England.

First published 1989
© *1989, Kathleen Hart, David C. Johnson, Margaret Brown, Linda Dickson, Rod Clarkson*

British Library Cataloguing in Publication Data
Children's mathematical frameworks 8–13.
1. Great Britain. Schools. Curriculum subjects: Mathematics. Teaching
I. Hart, Kathleen II. Johnson, David C. (David Carlton), 1936–
510'.7'1041

ISBN 0-7005-1211-X
ISBN 0-7005-1212-8 pbk

Phototypeset by David John Services Ltd, Slough
Printed by Billing & Sons Ltd, Worcester

ISBN hardback: 0 7005 1211 X; softback: 07005 1212 8.
Code hardback: 8326 02 4; softback: 8327 02 4.

Contents

Authors' Note

Selected interview items for use by teachers, teacher trainers and/or other researchers are available from the research team based at King's College London. These items were developed for use in following the progress of the interview sample for each of the seven mathematical topics. The selected items have been identified by the researchers as being of particular value in disclosing misconceptions and/or in providing information on the nature of the understanding of an individual child. This set of materials can be obtained by sending a stamped self-addressed envelope (or enclose payment for postage) to the CMF Project at the following address:

Mathematics Education Unit
Centre for Educational Studies
King's College, University of London
552 King's Road, London SW10 OUA, England.

(*Note*: Most of these materials already appear in the book. However, the materials indicated above also provide additional information on the specific questions asked at interview and the format and presentation of the materials and questions. Permission is also given to copy as necessary, with the condition that the CMF Project be acknowledged in the event any of the material is used in, or serves as the basis for, publication.)

Preface

This book reports the results of the investigation 'Children's Mathematical Frameworks: 8–13' (CMF). CMF was the third project in a programme of research based in the Centre for Science and Mathematics Education (CSME), Chelsea College, now part of the Centre for Educational Studies (CES), King's College London, University of London. The three projects span a period of over ten years and were all funded by the ESRC.

Each of the Chapters 3 to 9 in this book stands on its own in that it describes the teaching and learning of a particular mathematical topic. These chapters each have a principal author/researcher. The general methodology of the research however is the same for each topic, and is described in Chapter 2. Chapter 1 is an introduction to the work, and Chapter 10 a summary of the findings.

The directors of the research were Professor David C. Johnson, Dr Margaret L. Brown and Dr Kathleen M. Hart. The initial work, beginning in January 1983, was undertaken by Dr Hart and Dr Lesley R. Booth. Dr Booth left the project to take up a new post in January 1984. Dr Hart had to withdraw from direct day-to-day involvement with the project in August 1984 (to take up a new post), but she continued to participate as a director and also in the data analysis and writing phases of the work. The full-time research officer for the 16 months, September 1984 through December 1985, was Linda Dickson. Rod Clarkson, a Lecturer in the Mathematics Education Unit of the Centre, also participated in the work as part of his own doctoral research. His participation enabled the set of mathematical topics to be extended to include ratio (enlargement).

The work of CMF relied heavily on the good will of teachers who in addition to preparing for and carrying out the teaching allowed us into their classrooms to tape record lessons and to interview children. And, of course, it was the willingness of the children to talk about their experiences which provided us with the data from which we were able to draw what we feel to be important and useful insights on children's thinking/perceptions as they are learning school mathematics.

The researchers were also aided considerably by colleagues who helped with the work: D. Siemon, A. Hall, M. Dunkerley, P. Stockley, W. Butts, J. Matthews, D. Walters and N. Cawley.

Finally, the research team acknowledges the substantial contributions of Liz Cawdron and Linda Redmond whose dedication and hard work provided us with transcripts of the data (interviews and observations/tapes of lessons) and the many working drafts of manuscript for reports, articles and ultimately this book.

DCJ
MLB
KMH

Chapter 1
Background

'Sums is sums and bricks is bricks.'
'Somebody clever invented it.'
'I'd go find a fella who knows about that sort of thing.'
'The rules in maths say you can't do that.'

(Children aged 8 to 13 talking about their experiences learning mathematics)

Aims

Children's Mathematical Frameworks (CMF) was an ESRC-funded research project based at the Centre for Science and Mathematics Education, Chelsea College, University of London. The research was conducted in the period January 1983 to Autumn 1985. The aim of the project was to monitor children aged 8 to 13 years during their transition from concrete or practical work to the more formalized or symbolic mathematics commonly used in subsequent levels of the British school system, upper primary and secondary.

In the context of the research, 'formalization' can be considered to be a piece of standard notation, a rule, formula, algorithm or generalization, the adoption and use of which is expected of the child. The future mathematical experiences of the child are likely to be based on the assumption that these ideas which are usually expressed symbolically form part of his or her mathematical repertoire. No attempt is made to chronicle the entire development of an area of primary mathematics, the emphasis is on the brief crucial period when the child is expected to make the transition.

This book presents data from the observation of (i) teachers' planning of the work, (ii) their lessons designed to introduce a formalization deemed suitable for young children, and (iii) the responses of children in the classes.

Previous research

CMF was the third research project in a programme of research on children's understanding of mathematics based at the Centre for Science and Mathematics Education (Chelsea), and was a logical extension of the two projects carried out in secondary schools: 'Concepts in Secondary Mathematics and Science' (CSMS) (Hart, 1981) and 'Strategies and Errors in Secondary Mathematics' (SESM) (Booth, 1984; Hart, 1984; Kerslake, 1986).

CSMS

The CSMS project (1975 to 1979) formulated levels of hierarchies of understanding in 10 mathematical topics normally taught in British secondary schools. Word problems which embodied key ideas in the topic were used both for interview and in paper and pencil tests. The hierarchies of understanding were based on the results of testing 10,000 children in 1976 and 1977. The interpretation of the test paper results relied heavily on insights from interviews (n = 300) using the same questions. Items that were found easy by large numbers of children have often been solved correctly in the interviews by children using a naive or non-taught strategy. There was a marked difference in the success rate on questions where a counting strategy could be employed with success, even though the children had been taught a formula to solve such items.

METHODS USED BY CHILDREN

The methods of solution teachers present to children are usually applicable in all cases including the more complex, for example when non-integer measurements are introduced. Children have been found to use non-taught methods, referred to in the reports of CSMS and SESM as 'child methods'. The following example of a non-taught strategy is taken from the CSMS data on the topic of Ratio and Proportion. A high success rate (80 per cent plus) was achieved on the printed Ratio test paper question. If two pints of water are needed for soup for eight people, how much water is needed for six people? This question followed one which required the child to find the amount of water for four people and appeared to be at about the same level of difficulty. Very nearly all the children interviewed on this question (about 150) said 'Halve the two pints for four people then halve that amount again to find how much for two people, then add the two amounts together'. This is an efficient common sense method used in fact by most adults but *never taught*. It is only of use however if the ratio is n:2 and the halving process is straightforward.

ERRORS

The large amount of data produced in the CSMS testing revealed that certain incorrect answers to problems were given by as much as 50 per cent of the sample. If one takes the view that an erroneous response is indicative of a mode of reasoning and is not carelessness, then such wide scale errors or misconceptions were indicative of reasoning patterns belonging to large numbers of children.

In the topic 'Fractions' for example the CSMS data had shown that many children regarded non-integers as non-numbers, questioning whether they existed at all. When asked to divide 24 and 16 by 20 the pupils could, if they so wished, opt for the answer 'there is no such number' or 'impossible'. The data showed that 15 per cent of the 11- to 12-year olds said that 24 divided by 20 was 'impossible' and 50 per cent of the same group replied similarly to 16 divided by 20.

The work of SESM

The research project 'Strategies and Errors in Secondary Mathematics' (SESM) (1980 to 1982) used specific identified errors from the CSMS data on Ratio, Algebra, Fractions, Graphs and Measurement, as starting points. New samples of secondary school pupils were tested and those children whose work demonstrated the errors in question were interviewed in depth. From this information, ideas were formulated concerning the reasons for the error and possible methods of remediation. The corrective treatment was tried and revised by the researchers and finally used by a number of teachers with their classes. Results for some topics have been published (Booth, 1984; Hart, 1984; Kerslake, 1986).

The SESM investigation on Fractions (Kerslake, 1986) concentrated on the meanings children attached to a/b and a teaching programme was designed which attempted to expand their views to encompass 'fraction' seen as a result of division as well as being part of the region model which was already prevalent. The approach in this SESM investigation was therefore to push back the limits imposed on the children by their own restricted views.

In Ratio and Proportion the incorrect 'addition strategy' was investigated. This strategy uses the addition of a fixed amount to enlarge a figure rather than multiplication by a factor. The interviews with children who consistently used this method showed that their answers to 'easy' problems displayed:

(i)   an avoidance of multiplication even when whole numbers were involved. It was usually replaced by repeated addition or repeated halving.

(ii) a desire to work with pieces of the problem, collecting partial results together for the final solution.

(iii) an abhorrence of fractions other than one-half (they used the halving method on the soup question as previously described).

The existence of child-methods and the persistence of low-level skills when the demands of the questions asked required very different approaches, led to the formulation of the hypothesis that at the point of transition to formalization, that is the more generalized method (and symbolism), many children did not effect that transition and so were unable to use the formal method.

Children's mathematical frameworks (CMF)

For at least 20 years the future teachers of primary school children have been trained by mathematics educators according to beliefs which espouse the cause of practical or concrete experiences for young children. Books published as teacher resources (Williams and Shuard, 1970, 1973, 1980, 1982; Biggs and Maclean, 1969; Howell and Fletcher, 1978) tended to stress that classrooms should have a wide variety of equipment to support the learning of number or measurement. The work of Piaget might be considered to have been the major influence on primary school practice and the corresponding notion that if the children are within the age range suggested as the 'Concrete Level Stage' by Piagetian theory then their learning should be through 'concrete' experiences. At some time however in all British primary and junior schools, there takes place some symbolization and formalization of various aspects of mathematics. This may be because such an outcome is considered suitable for the children in question or it is seen as a requirement for the next levels of mathematics learning. The aim of the CMF research was to monitor both teacher and children during a sequence of lessons in which the teacher attempted to move to a formal version of a mathematical idea or relationship.

The research methodology is discussed in greater detail in the next chapter. It evolved over a period of time and produced data largely obtained from interviews with children and the observation of specific instances when the teacher and children were involved in 'formalization'. The analysis of the transcripts of the resultant tape recordings forms the subsequent chapters of this book. The intention is to provide information for teachers, gleaned from close observation of events in classrooms in 1983 and 1984 and not from some imaginary or ideal setting. In each chapter a topic is discussed, the emphasis being on points common to responses by children and not on the idiosyncrasies of a particular child. Each teacher's contribution is described and linked to the success or errors and misconceptions displayed by six children in the class being taught. The work is intended to cast light upon the reasons why children do not adopt formal methods taught by their teachers and instead cling to earlier learned strategies or invent new strategies.

Chapter 2
Methodology

The research project Children's Mathematical Frameworks (CMF) had three specific aims, each forming part of the intention to investigate the process by which the child becomes a user of mathematical formalizations. The aims were:

(i)   to investigate the development in children of formal mathematical methods and conceptual models with particular attention given to classroom experiences.

(ii)   to ascertain the connections between the information assimilated by the child and that given by the teacher.

(iii) to identify the nature, use and development of 'child methods' (see Booth, 1984, p. 37, or Hart, 1984, p. 79).

The data

The investigation was based on some classroom observation but mainly on the results of interviews, using carefully designed questions, with children in the classes being observed. The main components of the methodology were as follows:

(i)   recruitment of volunteer teachers of children in the age range 8–13;

(ii)   writing of a scheme of work or teaching plan, in some detail, by the teacher (these were discussed with the researchers);

(iii)   interviewing of six children in the class to be taught, before the specific teaching of the topic took place;

(iv)   reporting by the teacher of any changes to the lesson plan and the provision to the researcher of work-cards, assignment sheets, etc., used in class;

(v)   interviewing of the six children immediately before the formalization experience was planned to take place;

(vi)   observation and tape recording by the researcher of the formalization lesson(s);

(vii) interviewing of the six children (third time) immediately after the lesson(s);

(viii) interviewing of the same children three months later;

(ix)   transcribing of all tape recordings;

(x)   discussion and analysis of the transcripts.

The teachers

All the teachers who took part in the research were volunteers and all were experienced teachers. Many were recruited from courses leading to higher qualifications in mathematics education (Diploma or Masters degree). For these the research formed a focus for a long essay which was part of the course requirements. In their case it might be considered that the amount of time spent on the planning and dissection of the material to be taught was considerably longer than that usually spent by class teachers.

It was deliberate policy that the researchers did not seek to influence the way the teachers desired to present their chosen topics. They did however respond to the requests for help by providing books and materials to facilitate the preferred approach of the teacher. The teachers were not shown the interview questions until the investigation had finished.

The sample

The research was based in 25 classes from 21 schools. The classes were from schools mainly in or near London and in the Leeds/Bradford area. In some cases because of the teacher's individual style the entire class was taught as one unit, in other cases a small group of children was taught. One teacher taught six children on a one-to-one basis. The overall age band was from 8 to 13. However, for a particular topic the age was that at which the topic was typically taught in that school. For example, the age range for the topic 'equations' was 11 to 13, while in the case of 'place value: subtraction (three-digit)' the children were primarily aged 9. An interview sample of six children was selected from each class (four exceptions were interview samples of 4, 5, 7 and 8), giving a total interview sample of 150 children. Further details for each topic sample are given in the relevant chapter.

The scheme of work

The scheme of work was written by the teacher and contained as much detail as the individual teacher desired. It was given to the researchers in order that they might see the intended progression towards the formalization. The class textbook (when relevant) and workcards written by the teacher were shown to the research team. On a few occasions it was possible for the researchers to attend one or more of the lead-up lessons and the information obtained from these was also useful. Much of this information is included in the discussion (in the topic chapter) which summarizes the scheme of work for each class. The time taken to lead up to the formalization varied considerably from five days to nine weeks and this was at the discretion of the individual teacher.

The formalization lessons

Each teacher was asked to identify a time at which it was intended to move the mathematical topic being taught to a generalized procedure, often in a symbolic form, from the use of structural materials or diagrams. The occasion on which this move to a generalized procedure was to occur is called the 'formalization lesson(s)'. A brief summary of the 'formalizations' is given in Table 2.1. Flexibility was built in so that the teacher could change the date of the formalization if the introductory work was taking more (or less) time than originally planned and the researnh team would then be informed of the change. Each teacher chose a preferred format for the presentation. The teacher's words were tape recorded and any blackboard work or other non-verbal communication in the lesson was noted by the researcher. The tape recordings of the lessons were transcribed and analysed by the researchers.

If the teacher decided to continue or to re-introduce the formalization in another lesson the same procedure was used. Occasionally the second lesson's timing could not be accommodated by either team member so the teacher was asked to do the recording and this tape was also transcribed and analysed. When the teacher followed up the lesson by setting practice examples, this was noted but not monitored.

Note that the discussion or table (in the topic chapters) which presents an outline of the 'formalization lesson(s)' is a summary of the actual teaching/learning activity produced by the researcher/observer who was present at the time. That is, this is a record of what occurred rather than a repeat of what was planned in the scheme of work produced by the teacher.

The interviews

Each child in the research sample was interviewed four times and the evidence from these interviews forms the main content of this book. Each interview was for a different purpose and although some questions were repeated in order to provide a comparison of response, the

Table 2.1: Formalization(s)

Topic	Nature of Formalization
Place value: subtraction	Decomposition (changing the values in units, tens, etc.)
Equivalent fractions	Able to generate a set of equivalent fractions (ascertain whether two fractions are equivalent)
Circumference of a circle	pi as a constant ratio and the formula $C = \pi d$ or $C = 2\pi r$
Volume of a cuboid	The formula $V = l \times b \times h$
Area of a rectangle	The formula $A = l \times \omega$
Equations	Method of solution – 'doing the same to both sides'
Ratio: enlargement	Using a method for producing an enlargement (using scale factor, centre of enlargement, and 'pattern lines')

items were intended to reflect the purpose of the interview (see below). Each interview was carried out by a researcher with an audio tape recorder asking one child a series of questions in a room away from the rest of the class. The interview seldom took as long as 30 minutes but the time was dependent on whether the child's responses were understood by the listener or needed further questioning, or indeed whether the child wished to talk at length. The questions concerned what was being taught by the teacher and reflected the teacher's stated aims from the scheme of work as well as the researchers' views of what was fundamental to understanding the formalization. Paper and pencil were available and often the structural material used by the class together with any other aids thought to be of use, were nearby and could be seen by the child being interviewed. The intention of the interviewer was to ascertain the nature of the child's understanding and so if a word did not make sense to the child, it was replaced by another. Often the interviewing of a group of children was shared by two researchers so that discussion on responses and effectiveness of questions could take place. Full transcripts of the interview tapes were made and these were used for the later analysis.

The interview questions were written for each topic after discussion amongst the team and although some are the same for all the schools involved in that topic, others are written to reflect the intentions of a particular teacher or the stress given in the formalization lessons. The same type of question was sometimes asked using different models, e.g. the child being asked to find the volume of a real box, or of a box with the same dimensions shown in a drawing. There was usually an attempt to see whether the child had a preferred method of solution. The intention of the research was to monitor the transition to formal methods from a practical (with materials) introduction and therefore the children were asked if they saw any connection between these formats.

The first interview (I) was used to ascertain familiarity with prerequisite knowledge and to find out if the children (i) already knew and used the formalization about to be taught and (ii) had an available method to solve problems of the type for which the formalization would ultimately be used. It took place before the start of the sequence of lessons and for some groups the opportunity was taken to pose questions which explored ideas and language fundamental to the understanding of the topic.

The second interview (PreF) took place after the sequence of lessons and immediately before the 'formalization lesson(s)'. This was usually during the previous timetabled mathematics lesson and sometimes on the same day. The intention was to discover how close to the formalization the children appeared to be at this point. Questions were designed to see if the children (i) used the formalization, (ii) displayed proficiency on some of the prerequisite skills or understanding described by the teacher as necessary and (iii) showed any change in their response to some questions asked on the first interview.

The third interview (PostF) took place immediately after the 'formalization lesson(s)', sometimes on the same day but usually during the next mathematics lesson. The main intention was to see if the children had accepted and were using naturally the formalization just described or demonstrated by the teacher. The children were asked for their interpretation of what had been said by the teacher and diagrams or expressions used in the lesson were shown to them. Again some questions asked previously were used but this was not always appropriate since the pre- and post-formalization interviews might only be a day or hours apart.

The final interview (D) took place three months after the teaching and was designed to discover whether the children were working with the formalization, a method based on the structural material, or had invented or adapted a method. Often they had used a method of their own prior to the teaching and this was an opportunity to discover whether they persisted in using it. The formalization had sometimes been used over the intervening period for the solution of other mathematics problems but the teachers did not re-teach it from the beginning during this interval. The final interview was also an opportunity to find out whether the children could relate the formalization to what had preceded it. Often when children are having difficulty with a formalization the teacher may refer them back to the structural materials, so in (D) the pupils were asked to explain to the researcher the mathematical generalization using the materials.

Analysis

The research resulted in tape recordings of four interviews with each of 150 children and 30 tape-recorded lessons. The questions asked of the children were designed to find out to what extent they had adopted the formalization taught by the teacher and to monitor their performance throughout the period of the study.

The four sets of transcripts for any class, together with the transcript of the teacher's lesson, were read by at least two researchers who discussed what seemed to be points of importance within the teacher's lesson and children's statements. The children's responses to questions were tabulated and common strategies identified so that changes over time could be seen. These tables form the basis for the charts which appear in the topic chapters.

The teachers' presentation of a formalization after a sequence of preparatory experiences revealed their considered attempts at the most effective way of leading the children to this most important transition. The interpretation by the child of the teacher's statements was often not that which was intended – if this interpretation is sufficiently general, it is mentioned in the discussion of the results. Sometimes the research identified gaps in the prerequisite skills and knowledge stressed by the teacher (and textbooks). These are reported in order to alert teachers and textbook writers to likely causes of confusion experienced by the child when attempting to assimilate a new idea. Where possible the link between the practical work and the formalization is explored. Are the methods used on bricks necessarily transferable to symbols? If at one time the problem has been efficiently solved by using materials does the child always retain this skill and is it transferred to examples not previously met? Do we have any information on when children come to accept the formalization? The research did not test any particular method of presentation but did follow teachers who led up to a formalization through practical work and who had spent a considerable amount of time planning their approach.

In the description of each class and each topic an attempt has been made to highlight responses which have something in common with behaviour in other classes. However different mathematical topics have varied teaching requirements and so there are parts of each chapter which are not common to the others. Each topic chapter has been written by the researcher reponsible for that topic area and while there are variations of presentations any departures from the described methodology are noted.

Chapter 3
Place Value: Subtraction
Kathleen Hart

Introduction

The Hindu–Arabic numeration system enables us to deal with types of mathematics which were utterly impossible for those using Roman numerals. It is as Skemp says 'like the difference between walking and flying' (Skemp, 1971). Within the elegance of the system, however, there is considerable complexity. Number and Arithmetic form a large part of the mathematics taught to children under the age of 12 in British schools. 'Place Value' has come to be interpreted as (i) the meaning of the numeration system and then (ii) the use of the system in algorithms for the four arithmetic operations. Advice given on the teaching of the topic usually includes the suggestion of using structural material in activities where exchange is an important component although back in 1967 the authors of the Association of Teachers of Mathematics (ATM) publication, *Notes on Mathematics in Primary Schools* stated alternatives:

> There are a number of courses that can be adopted to try to lead children to understand it [Place Value]. One is to take the line that the rules of notation, like the rules for counting, can be told to the child, and that when he has, at a later stage, considerable familiarity with them, he can be led to analyse them and see how they work. (This must have been the path to understanding for most teachers.) A second method is to provide the child with structured material, like the Dienes Multi-base Arithmetic Blocks, which offers a physical model of the powers of the base, so that a considerable part of the job of structuring is already done by the material. A third method is to work through with the child, from the beginning, some of the decisions that are involved in making a suitable construction...

The authors further describe the development of an abacus which moves from a game in which the child pretends he is a merchant and records his stock with pebbles to using beads on needles, to numbers. The transition between the last two experiences is touched upon briefly thus:

> The next major step occurs when the recording on the abacus is transferred to symbols on paper. Children working with the abacus can transcribe directly from the beads on the needles. Some may need to have their paper pinned to the abacus in the early stages so that the direct correspondence can be seen.

Of considerable importance to teachers in training, when seeking advice on how to teach a topic is the work of Williams and Shuard (1970, 1973). They distinguished between grouping (where there is no limitation to only groups of ten) and the order of digits when written. 'But the introduction of some form of abacus is the occasion for deliberately establishing the reading and writing of numbers from left to right' (Williams and Shaurd, 1970). They stress that when a child can think of numbers without needing actual objects to guide that thinking then the child is ready for addition and subtraction with written symbols. The regrouping aspect of both operations is illustrated by structural apparatus such as Dienes Multi-base (base 10).

The relationship between columns is described thus:

When children use structural apparatus and diagrams to represent the ones, tens and hundreds that they write in columns, they become aware of the relation between the values represented by neighbouring columns. For example, they come to realise that a 3 in the tens place is worth ten times a 3 in the ones column, and conversely a 3 in the ones column is worth one-tenth of a 3 in the tens column. A ten is 10 times a one, and is also one-tenth of a hundred.

Subtraction is traditionally taught after simple addition and although it may be viewed initially as the removal of a certain number of objects, the number facts used are obtained from the addition bonds.

The teachers whose work is reported in this research, chose the algorithm for subtraction as the formalization they wished to reach during the teaching experiment. This algorithm (whether for two- or three-digit numbers) relies on the decomposition of tens or hundreds and quoting Williams and Shuard (1973) again:

Such operations with numbers greater than ten demand an effective understanding of the notation we use. If the recording of counts of sets in tens and ones has been done as suggested earlier in this chapter children will have little difficulty in carrying out additions and subtractions in which there has to be a carry over from ones to tens or vice-versa.

The availability of calculators brings into question the need for children to learn and use the subtraction algorithm. However the algorithm is at present taught in all primary schools and was the chosen formalization example of three teachers (four classes) taking part in the CMF research. The fourth teacher was teaching a class of eight- to nine-year-olds how to order numbers and this work is mentioned very briefly.

The sample

The classes which were observed being taught subtraction were mainly aged eight to nine years and for them it was their first introduction to the algorithm. One group of 12-year-olds was also taught as part of the research and their interviews are analysed after those of the younger children. Table 3.1 shows the sample.

Table 3.1: Place value sample

School 1 Class A, 8-year-olds (n=25) 2-digit subtraction algorithm
   (Primary school, Outer London, mixed ability)

School 2 Class A, 8- to 9-year-olds (n = 8*) 3-digit subtraction algorithm
   (Junior school, Outer London, mixed ability)

School 2 Class B, 8- to 9-year-olds (n = 8*) 3-digit subtraction algorithm
   (Junior school, Outer London, mixed ability)

School 3 Class A, 12-year-olds (n = 8*) 3-digit subtraction algorithm
   (Middle school, Surrey, remedial class)

School 4 Class A, 8- to 9-year-olds (n = 8*) Ordering numbers
   (Junior school, London, mixed ability)

---

* These children were selected by the teacher from a larger class and taught together as a group.

Analysis

Besides the particular formalization being taught all the teachers dealt with the exchange of ten units for one ten and except in School 1 they also worked examples on exchanging ten tens for one hundred. Across the schools an attempt was made to ask similar questions so that the answers could be compared. The explanation of the algorithm was one such question; another concerned the number of tens in a three-digit number.

The information obtained from each class is described in the following way. Firstly the scheme of work pursued by the teacher is quoted giving details where possible of the structural material used. Then follows a description of the formalization lesson(s) as witnessed by the researcher. The four interviews are recorded (i) by diagrams showing each child's response to questions involving subtraction and also tens and (ii) by excerpts from the interviews.

School 1, Class A (aged 8)

The first series of interviews described in this chapter concern the youngest children learning the subtraction algorithm for two-digit numbers. They were eight years old.

The scheme of work

The 25 children in the class were all given the same set of experiences although the teacher thought the aims of the work would be realized at different times by individuals. The six children chosen for interview were thought by the teacher to represent different ability levels. They were called Ann, Alex, Edith, Audrey, Tom and Andy. Table 3.2 shows the general aims of the teaching sequence as described by the teacher. The transition from straws to Unifix was not seen by the researchers and was simply stated by the teacher.

Table 3.2: Scheme of work – School 1, Class A

Prerequisites: It is assumed that the children know the meaning of take away. Practice with sentences such as 'Six cars, one driven away, how many left?' is seen as revision of infant school work.

Apparatus: Straws and Unifix.

Time taken: Three weeks, a lesson each day. Spread however over five weeks because of mid-term and teacher absence.

Scheme
The aim was to teach the children the meaning of subtraction as 'take away' and to provide learning experience culminating in them being able to successfully perform the decomposition subtraction algorithm with two-digit numbers, when represented in symbolic form. The teacher intended there to be initially only practical work, followed by practical and recording side by side. Free play with straws was followed by (i) the bundling of straws into tens and (ii) the representation of two digit numbers by bundles of ten and loose straws.

(22)

The Unifix was then used and the children were given accompanying boards on which the sum was written (see Formalization Lesson, Table 3.3). Examples which did not require decomposition were also mixed in with those that did. For decomposition the accompanying statement was stated to be of the form 'Can you take 9 units from 3 units? Take a ten to help. Take 9 from the ten. How many left? One add three' (see Formalization Lesson, page 11).

Formalization lesson

This teacher's approach to formalization using bricks (see Table 3.3) was different from others in the sample in two respects, (i) he drew a version of the structural material on the blackboard although he did not suggest that the children copied this practice and (ii) he suggested to the children engaged in working only with the symbolic form that they *imagine* the Unifix configuration.

The demonstration by the teacher of the use of the materials matched the steps of the algorithm, so that a ten was taken from the pile of tens and transferred to join the units. However, since Unifix was being used, the ten did not need to be exchanged but simply broken to provide the correct amount. This in fact corresponded in a straightforward manner to the method of subtraction stated by the teacher in the scheme on number bonds over ten, i.e. for $15 - 8$ take 8 from 10 and put 5 on. Note that this was not used in the formalization lesson.

Teaching outcomes

MAIN OBJECTIVE

The main objective of the lessons was for the children to arrive at a working use of the subtraction algorithm (with decomposition) for two-digit numbers. The children were interviewed four times: before the teaching started (I), then just prior to the formalization lesson (PreF), the day after the lesson (PostF) and three months later (D). Table 3.4 shows the type of response given by each child on the occasion of the interviews. There is no order of merit in these answers but 'no attempt', 'other wrong' and 'subtract smaller' are assigned to three unsuccessful actions. The responses designated (part (a) of Table 3.4) are as follows:

(i)   No attempt – the child says 'I can't do that' or something similar.
(ii)   Other wrong – the method employed gives the wrong answer but cannot be categorized under other descriptions. Usually these methods are idiosyncratic.
(iii)   Subtract smaller – when faced with a subtraction involving two-digit numbers the child takes the smaller digit from the larger irrespective of whether it is on the top or bottom line.
(iv)   Count on – to obtain an answer the child counts on from one number to the other.
(v)   Blocks used – the child given the opportunity to use Unifix to solve the two-digit subtraction does so in preference to a pencil-and-paper approach.
(vi)   Algorithm – the child uses the algorithm with success in a variety of examples.

The table is provided to show the variety of response patterns obtained from these eight-year-olds who were all taught in the same class. We know nothing of their performance during the time we were not in the class, particularly the three months between (PostF) and (D).

Part (a) of Table 3.4 shows that prior to the teaching no child in the group interviewed had a successful method for carrying out two-digit subtractions for problems requiring decomposition. Edith almost obtained the right answers but since all working was done in her head she managed to retain a ten incorrectly.

Given $37-$ she worked with the tens figures first:
      29

E: Well, I was trying ... I took away 2 um ... tens ... 2 tens out of 30, so I've got one ten left, and I took away the 9, and I had to add one on to make it. I mean, it's um ... 1 and 8, so you'd put ... you'd work out this one ... (*after repeating it again*) ... which would make 18, 'cos I've got 1 ten and 8 units.

(*Note:* There were no blocks available at this interview.)

Of particular interest are the three children, Audrey, Alex and Andy, who used the Unifix after the formalization. Andy tried to do a subtraction in written form but took away smaller

Table 3.3: Formalization lesson – School 1, Class A

---

(1) Each child had a pile of Unifix and a board labelled tens/units, large enough to accommodate bricks.

(2) All class faced blackboard on which teacher wrote $42-$.
$$19$$

(3) Children were asked what the top written expression meant and they responded with 42 units or 4 tens and 2 units.

(4) One child was asked how he was going to set it up with Unifix. On his reply, all the children were asked to set up 4 tens and 2 units in Unifix bricks.

(5) Children were then asked what question needed to be posed, corrections were made if the statement was the wrong way round (i.e. take 2 from 9).

(6) Taking a ten from 'tens' column was carried out physically by the children and with number symbols on the blackboard by the teacher.

(7) Mixed allusions to the role of the Unifix, from 'I don't think you need to use the Unifix, but...' to 'But perhaps you'd like to check'.

(8) Second example $50-$ had initial stress by the teacher on starting with the units. The route to solution
$$11$$
was through the children moving bricks and the teacher writing both number symbols and drawing the blocks on the board.

(9) If number bonds such as $9 - 3$ were not known then child was encouraged to count using Unifix.

(10) After three such examples the boards and Unifix were collected and the children were asked how to do $65-$.
$$29$$

(11) The teacher's comments and questions guided the order of events.

    (i)   where to start – the units column

    (ii) take something from tens column

    (iii) how much now in the units column?

    (iv) how much left when we have done $15 - 9$?

    (v) now deal with the tens column.

(12) Another two examples were done this way with the teacher demonstrating the crossing out and number manipulation at the blackboard with the children's comments being called for. The suggested recording was:

The accompanying statement being 'Can you take 9 from 3 units? Take a ten to help. Take 9 from 13. How many left?' (This is at variance with the scheme of work in which it is suggested that 9 be taken from 10 and 3 then added to the remainder 1.)

(13) One child caused minor diversion by commenting that in a question such as $20 - 10$ you do not have to bother manipulating the units and the teacher said 'In a way you start with your tens, don't you?'

(14) The class was then given sheets of subtraction questions to do, and the advice, 'If you get confused, it might be an idea to *think* of the Unifix you have been using. *Think* of where you would put your blocks'.

(15) The teacher walked round the class helping individual children and on occasions repeated the instruction to 'imagine' the blocks.

Table 3.4: School 1, Class A Responses

(a) Two-digit subtraction questions

Type of response	I	PreF	PostF	D
algorithm		A An / Au E T	An / E T	Ad* An / E T
blocks used			A Ad / Au	A / Au
count on				
subtract smaller digits	A Ad An / T	Ad		
other wrong	E			
no attempt	Au			
* variable answer	**I**	**PreF**	**PostF**	**D**

Key
A   Alex
Ad Andy
An Ann
Au Audrey
E   Edith
T   Tom
arranged

| A Ad An |
| Au E T |

interviews

(b) sweets question: two-digit number (68)

	I	PreF	PostF	D
6 tens		A An	A An / Au E T	A / Au E T
counts in tens				An
long division				
rule (cross off)				
14 (adds digits)				
60 (68 sweets)				
other wrong		Au		
no attempt				
data unavailable		Ad / E T	Ad	Ad
	I	**PreF**	**PostF**	**D**

interviews

(c) sweets question: three-digit number (367)

	I	PreF	PostF	D
36 tens				T
30 tens + 6 tens	Ad / T	Ad / T	T	Ad
counts in tens				E
long division				
6 tens				
90 (30 + 60)				
adds digits	A / Au			
360 (367 sweets)				
other wrong	An / E	Au E	E	A An / Au
no attempt		A An		
data unavailable			A Ad An / Au	
	I	**PreF**	**PostF**	**D**

interviews

digits as he had done before (PreF). He then used Unifix, decided his first method had been wrong and then was able to complete the question in written form (PreF). (PreF) the two girls had used a written algorithm although Audrey had said she wished she had Unifix but counted on her fingers instead. Unifix was not available on the table (PreF) so all three children might have *preferred* to use the materials (PreF), we simply know that two pupils were able to work with the written algorithm the day before the lesson and opted to do without it the day after.

The children who seemed to cope with subtraction of two-digit numbers were asked to try 307– . On the final interview Tom succeeded but he had in fact been asked this same type of 139 question before the teaching started and obtained an answer then. His responses show a development and are quoted here.

Initial Interview (I) (I: Interviewer; T: Tom) 306–
7

T: Is that three hundred and six? Yes...7 from 6, you can't do that so you have to borrow a ten.
I: It's 7 from 6, is it?
T: Yes, but you can't do that, so you have to borrow a ten, but there isn't one, so you borrow a hundred from there, so you've got 106 take away 7 is 99, and you put the 9 here, and put a 9 here, and 6 from 9 is ...yes, 6 from 9 is 3, then 2 from 2 is zero.
I: So your answer is...?
T: 39.

Delayed Interview (D) 307–
139

T: ...7 take away 9 can't be done, and you can't take 2 from there, so you take 100 from there, leaves you with 2 and you've got 10 tens there, cross that out and you've got 17, then you take 9, makes 8.
I: 9 from what?
T: 9 from 17.
I: Oh I see.
T: Then you take 3 from 9 leaves you 6, 1 from 2 leaves you with 1.

Alex, Ann and Audrey could not transfer the method to three digits. Edith's attempt (D) showed considerable insight although she had not been formally taught a method:

(I: Interviewer; E: Edith) (D)
E: Well first of all you can take 9 away from...actually you can take...you can't take 9 away from 7, so you take that, put the 2 there and I think...you can take it right into the units, although you're breaking it up into units. Put the 1 there.
I: Now hang on, you've crossed out the 3 and put 2, and you've taken the 1.
E: Over into the units.
I: And what does that one stand for?
E: Stands for...10 units.
I: But what was it when you took it from here?
E: Ah, it was 100. Um...
I: You see up here, when you first tried it, you put the 1 up here into the tens column.
E: Yes, but I only need ten so I could have left 9 over in the tens.

After further questioning which served to make her check what she was doing, she obtained the right answer.

DECOMPOSITION

The intention of the teaching for this class of eight-year-olds was that they should successfully complete examples of subtraction using the two-digit algorithm.

The overall investigation was however concerned with 'place value' and so a question which seemed to embody the significance of the placing of the digits in a number was asked of all children, in the guise of a problem about sweets: 'I have a pile (or a large jar) of 367 sweets and I want to put them in bags so that there are 10 sweets in each bag. How many bags can I get? Are there any sweets left over?' The number 367 was also written down if this seemed to be needed. It seemed likely that the knowledge of place value possessed by the children in School 1, Class A would not extend to three figures. Consequently on two or three interviews the same question but with a two-digit number was asked. The demand of this second question is very different since there is no need to do anything beyond selecting the figure already in the tens column. Table 3.4(b) and (c) show responses to the two questions. The labels mean:

(1) 36 tens. The child says immediately that 367 contains 36 tens.
(2) 30 tens + 6 tens. The hundreds are used to provide 30 tens and then the 6 from the tens column is added to give 36.
(3) Counts in tens. Counting in tens until the child thinks 360 has been reached.
(4) Long division. $10\overline{)367}$ carried out using the algorithm.
(5) Cross off last figure. The child quotes a trick which provides an answer.
(6) 6 tens. Only the tens figure has significance.
(7) 9 tens (90). The child adds 30 (from the hundreds) to 6 tens (60).
(8) Adds digits. Some form of addition of digits irrespective of their value, e.g. 16.
(9) 360. Only the 7 units is seen as not belonging to a count of tens.
(10) Other wrong. The answer is wrong but for none of the above descriptions.
(11) No attempt. The child does not know an answer to give (and says this).

None of the girls could provide an immediate answer to how many tens there were in 367 although Edith counted in tens eventually on the fourth interview (having provided herself with tally marks for each ten). She had used this method before and made a curious error which was in fact repeated by other children. Prior to the teaching she counted in tens but stopped at 130, rather than 300:

(I: Interviewer; E: Edith)
I: Now here I have 367 sweets, and I've written that down, and I'm going to put them in bags of ten. Now, I've got lots of plastic bags and I'm going to put 10 in every bag. How many bags can I fill?
E: ...Oh, I've got muddled up.
I: Never mind, start again, you've got plenty of time.
E: You can fill, um...13 bags and you've got 67 left over.
I: Now 13...how do you write 13, put 13 down so that I can see it.
E: (*Writes 13*)...
I: Now tell me how you got that, 'cos you were counting on your fingers, weren't you?
E: Yes, you count 10, 20, 30, 40, 50, 60, 70, 80, 90, 100, 120, 130 and then you work out how...and you can't fill another bag with another ten lots of sweets, so you've got 167 left over.
I: You said you had 67 left.
E: Oh yes, you do have 67 left.
I: Right, so I fill 13 bags from that 300, yes?
E: Yes.
I: And then how about these, can I fill any more bags of 10?
E: Another 6.
I: Why?
E: Because there's another 6 tens, and there's only 7 units left.

I: I see, so how many bags altogether have I filled then?
E: ...19.

(PreF) she again counted in tens to 130 and this time puts 'six' at the end to obtain a total of 136 bags. She used her fingers and said that when she needed to go past ten she just started all over again. A day later (after the lesson) she had another incorrect method:

E: Well what I was doing, I had a hundred, and then I added on my 3, so I had 100 and then I add on 3 then another 6, so that made, um...109.

Ann also mixed 'three tens' and 'three and ten' on her first attempt (I). She did not attempt the question at all on the second interview and three months later for two digits she counted in tens and for three digits said there were 300 tens in 367.

Those children who added digits arrived at varying results. Alex for example, said:

(I: Interviewer; A: Alex) (I)
A: Two.
I: Can you tell me why?
A: You have 7 and you add 3 on and you get 10 and there's 6 odd ones.
I: Ah...and one, that makes 1 packet then, does it, and the odd 6 make another packet.
A: Of...6 sweets.

Audrey (I) added 3 + 6 + 7 but initially thought the 3 in 367 was the number of tens, with 6 and 7 being units. (PreF) she could do neither the two- nor three-digit sweet questions. Tom and Amy worked from the written number and dealt with ten tens in a hundred first. Nobody immediately stated that the first two digits provided the number of tens although Tom gave an immediate answer (D).

PERCEPTION OF THE MATERIALS

Children in School 1, Class A sometimes asked for the Unifix materials so that they could proceed with a question. Audrey (PreF) said, 'I wish I had my Unifix here' when faced with 45 − 19 and the next day, after the formalization lesson, she used Unifix to solve the subtraction question. She said that she liked using the bricks and employed a mixture of algorithmic language and the materials.

In order to find out whether the children considered using bricks helped understanding (D) they were asked to explain subtraction to an imaginary 'new girl' so that she would understand. Audrey faced with 43 − 28 used Unifix but for the 'new girl' doing 65 − 29 she approached the question differently:

A: You can't take away 5 from 9, so you cross the 6 and put a 5 and then you put 15 and then you take a 9 from 15 which will be 6, so you put 6 like that...and then 5 from 2 which will leave 3.

Audrey was then persuaded to try an explanation using Unifix, which she did – in a different way to her own method on 43 − 28. This time when 'teaching' she modelled the algorithm.

I: So you've got 5 units all joined together, right. Now what would you do, what would you tell her. How would you tell her to take away 29?
A: Well...you could have 65 and you take away one ten and put it in the units column and then you'll have 15 there and you take away 9, which leaves 6...etc.

This is one of the few examples when a child appeared to be able to subtract algorithmically or with materials and generally preferred the materials. Alex (D and PostF) used the Unifix when faced with a subtraction. (PostF) she crossed off symbols on paper as she manipulated the materials. She too when explaining to 'a new girl' talked through the algorithm although initially she took smaller digits away in both tens and units.

Ann (PostF) said that she did not like using Unifix. 'Well I can use the Unfix but, um...I just like...I don't really like using it.' She did however three months later deal with the algorithm symbolically but showed 'the new girl' with Unifix. Her demonstration did not match the algorithm.

(I: Interviewer; A: Ann)   65−
                                                       29

A: ...well I would have got some...65 Unifix.
I: Now, Ann has taken six tens of Unifix, and she's taken 5 little ones, right.
A: Then I would have taken two tens and another ten, but on the other ten, the third ten, I would have taken one unit off, so I would have 29, oh!...oh yes, so then I would take the 29 away and add up all the others and see how much is left. And it's 36.
I: Yes, so you'd tell her to do this, you'd show her how to do that, okay. And then do you show her anything else?
A: ...No.
I: No. Now you haven't been using Unifix though, have you, when you've been doing these sums?
A: No.
I: No, well do you like using Unifix? Or do you prefer just doing the paper work.
A: I prefer doing the paper work.
I: I see. Well how is this poor girl going to get to the paper work if you don't explain to her?
A: I could...would write it down, and then I would show her how to do it, taking 5 from 9, you can't do it, so you borrow a ten from the tens column, so cross out the 6 and put a 5 'cos you've got 5 left and you put the ten into the units column, and then you work out 15 take 9, which is...6...and then I would show her to work out 5 tens take away 2 tens, would leave 3 tens, 36.
I: I see, now the 9 from 15 you did on your fingers, and the 2 from 5 you knew. Now is there any connection between that paper method and what you were doing with the Unifix? Are they connected in any way?
A: ...(*Pause*)...
I: Let's say I'm this girl and I say, well that's alright and that's alright, but why do you need two methods? Did you find it helpful when you did the Unifix?
A: Well it might have been more easier for...to understand.
I: Was it more easy for you to understand?
A: Well, um...well I find both ways quite...very...quite easy.

Andy (D) said that he preferred using paper to bricks and his attempt at 65 − 29 with bricks was rather confused. Tom also said he did not like using Unifix, he did however 'show the new boy' the method with the bricks when asked 65 − 29. He set out both numbers in Unifix blocks, using the '9' column to measure against a column of '15'.

Edith stated her aversion to using bricks:

(I: Interviewer; E: Edith)   45−
                                                    27

I: I see, now you prefer doing it this way, or do you prefer the Unifix?
E: I like doing it this way.
I: Now why is that, why do you prefer it?
E: Well, sometimes because its quicker and...I just...I don't like setting out the Unifix, 'cos you've got to move all the things about, and do lots of things, and I like this way better, I don't know why.

Edith's explanation of what she was doing was very good and three months after the teaching her explanation to a new girl was very clear. When she was encouraged to use Unifix, her explanation with the concrete materials was in fact a translation of the algorithm into bricks. The opposite way round to what would be normal teaching practice.

Child methods and misconceptions

Table 3.4 part (a) shows that no child could successfully subtract two-digit numbers with decomposition prior to the teaching. All of the interviewed group needed to count on their fingers to obtain remainders or sums.

When it came to order of subtraction Andy (I) successfully subtracted the tens digit first both when decomposition was needed and also in $28 - 16$. Faced with three-digit subtraction he subtracted the hundreds digit first but was unable to continue.

(I: Interviewer; A: Andy)
A: 306 take away 267.
I: Is there any way of doing that?
A: ...take away the 200 from the 300, which gives you one hundred, then you add, take away the 7 from there and then you take away the 6 from there, which gives you...

Working from left to right resulted in error just as it did three weeks later when (PreF) Andy was asked to try an addition question in which he again reversed the conventional order. The next day however after the formalization lesson he dealt with the units figure first. Edith (I) also subtracted the tens figure first, as reported previously.

It appeared that prior to any teaching on this type of subtraction the natural decision taken was to deal with the largest denomination first. The use of Unifix in no way contradicted this usage.

Sometimes incorrect ideas were expressed by the children which appeared to be directly linked to the work inaugurated by the teacher or the lesson seen by the researcher. One such misconception was demonstrated by Ann who (I) had been asked to try the addition of two-digit numbers, $35 + 17$.

(I: Interviewer; A: Ann)
   35 +
   17

A: Well, I was doing 7 add 5, and it worked out to be... it worked out to be 12, so I put the 2 there and carried the 1.

A conversation about subtraction then took place, returning eventually to the addition.

I: Um... shall we go back to that little 1 that sprouted up there. You said, put down the 2 and carry 1, and I said what... where did that 1 come from, what sort of 1 is it?
A: It's a carry one.
I: I see, is it the same, you carried it with that big one there, is it the same sort of value as that big one?
A: No.
I: Oh, it's different, is it?
A: Yes because it's smaller.
I: Because you drew it smaller.
A: Yes.
I: I see, what is this big 1 here worth then, 1 what?
A: 1 ten.
I: I see, and what's the little 1 worth?
A: Just 1... not 1 ten.
I: Not 1 ten, just a 1.

A: Yes.
I: I see, and is that...alright, how about the 3, what sort of 3 is that?
A: 3 tens.
I: I see. So you now start adding up 3 tens and 1 ten and a little 1, is that right?
A: ...41...
I: Oh.
A: Because um...because 30 and 1 ten is 40 and if you put the 1 there it's 41.
I: Well, you write out, write under here then what your answer's going to be.

Ann wrote 412 as the answer.
Although Alex's misconception did not seem to stem from the immediate series of lessons just described, it did arise from a generalization often heard in primary classrooms when odd and even numbers are concerned. The following conversation took place during the fourth interview (D).

(I: Interviewer; A: Alex)
I: I have 2 packets of Polo mints. There are 10 in each packet and then there are 5 spare. Two packets, 10 in each, and then 5 spares. How many children can have one sweet each?
A: ...Out of all of them?
I: Mmm...
A: ...24.
I: How did you get that?
A: Because a ten's an even number, so each child could have 10 out of one packet of Polo's and then there was 10 in the other packet so another 10 children could have another sweet each and then that was 20, but 5 is an odd number, so I could only...give...4 more children a sweet.
I: What did you do with the odd sweet then, the one that was left? Throw it away?
A: Yes.
I: (*Laughs*)...Well now, why can you only work with even numbers?
A: Because you can't share out odd numbers.
I: Oh I see, now how many children then altogether got one sweet each?
A: 24.

Even when the algorithm was successfully used (D), Ann thought the exchange process had changed the value of the top number.

(I: Interviewer; A: Ann)   ²₃₀₇
I: You don't need it any more, okay. Now you've done lots of crossing out, what's the number on the top of that sum? I gave you 307.
A: 307.
I: Yes, well is it still ²₃₀₇?
A: No.
I: No? What's it now then?
A: One thousand, ten hundred and seventeen.
I: Good gracious me, has it changed then?
A: Yes.
I: Well, has it got bigger, has it got smaller or is it just the same but in a different form?
A: It's got smaller.

General observations

School 1, Class A was the youngest group of children being taught subtraction and some of their reactions which appeared spontaneous and natural were at variance with the required order of events dictated by the algorithm. For example a number of children initially subtracted the tens figure first as indeed was the case when they were using the Unifix material. There was also no need to put a ten stick with the units prior to subtraction since one could remove the required amount directly by breaking another ten stick already in the display. The children still preferred using the bricks to solve subtraction problems three months after the teaching although four others used the algorithm.

The finding of the number of tens in a three-digit number gave rise to a variety of answers. Only two children found the result from the position of the digits.

The misconception that one wrote the figure 1 in smaller script when carrying because it was 'worth less' seems to be a perfectly valid conclusion to draw. Ann's answer took this lesser status into account and so was incorrect. Do we teach children to write their 'carrying' figures this way in order that their books should be neat – or are there other reasons, and if so should these be made explicit?

School 2, Class A (aged 8–9)

Children taken from two different classes (aged 8–9) but taught by the same teacher, are described in this section. Eight children in Class A were selected because they were considered to be at about the same level of readiness and similarly eight were chosen from Class B. The Class A set received slightly more time with the teacher than those in Class B. Each group was taught separately for two separate one hour sessions each week for approximately nine weeks. Among the groups discussed in this section on place value these two groups received the longest preparation for the formalization of subtraction of three-digit numbers. In addition the style of teaching was the most informal.

The scheme of work

The scheme of work for each group was the same and is shown in Table 3.5.

Table 3.5: Teaching scheme – School 2, Classes A, B

Prerequisites: Ability to record two-digit numbers, although not much experience of numbers over 20; some knowledge of addition with 'carrying'.
Apparatus: Pebbles, Dienes' Multi-base blocks (base ten), dice games, cords with knots.
Time taken: 16–18 hours spread over nine weeks.

Scheme
(1) Check and observe counting methods used by children when given containers full of pebbles (between 20 and 100+ in number).
(2) Game with Dienes' blocks – collecting and exchanging for longs (tens) on the throw of a dice.
(3) Recording using pebbles for units and sticks for tens.
(4) Game using pictures of pebbles and sticks showing numbers.
(5) Other material for collections.
(6) Forming chart of different ways of showing tens and units (e.g. 3 sticks, 5 pebbles for 35).
(7) Consider written numbers as a shorthand for the array of material.
(8) Abacus – physically moving tens.
(9) Game on ordering of numbers.
(10) Addition of hundreds, tens and units using an abacus, pebbles, etc.
(11) Subtraction by removal from the abacus, emphasis on decomposition.
(12) Recording the decomposition process in drawings.
(13) Given numbers, interpreting the subtraction with apparatus but recording the answer as a number.
(14) Formalization of process, including zero in tens column.

Formalization lesson(s)

In very nearly every lesson the children played a game to reinforce (i) their ability to exchange in sets of ten or (ii) their knowledge of ordering. The plans made by the teacher for the formalization lessons (each class had two such sessions) were the same but in actuality the two classes had slightly different experiences (see Table 3.6).

Table 3.6: Formalization lessons – School 2, Classes A, B

---

(1) Verbal review of past few weeks' work – materials and organization into sets of ten. Children read two- and three-digit numbers when written.
(2) Addition of two three-digit numbers with and without 'carrying' in written form on blackboard, emphasis on lining up like denominations.
(3) Emphasis on children saying three hundreds and not '3' for the digit in the hundreds column when it is used in addition.
(4) Subtraction question written in vertical form and children asked whether it can be done (children expected to answer that 'top number is bigger').
(5) Pupils suggest answers to subtraction 654 – 232 (written on board).
(6) 651 – 235 put on board, children asked to suggest how it could be done.
(7) Discussion on why rule is not 'always take smaller from larger'. [Omitted in Class B.]
(8) Teacher reminds group of the work with Dienes' blocks in which longs were changed. He used 'borrow' but crosses out tens digit and replaces by a figure one less. [No reminder of Dienes' blocks with Class B.]
(9) Group talks through question in which decomposition is required twice. [Not done with Class B prior to (10) below.]
(10) Group talks through 205 – 137. [Two questions of this type talked through with Class B.]
(11) Group given cards with subtraction questions and told to solve them. Teacher goes round talking to children individually asking them to 'talk me through it, tell me what you did'.
(12) Mention by teacher of surplus zeros in left-hand place in answer and their significance.
(13) Game played in which children seek to make lowest number with three cards.

2nd Lesson
(1) Subtraction question written horizontally but changed to vertical form for operation. [Reinforces the fact that top number must be biggest.]
(2) Deliberate mistakes made by teacher to alert group to placing of figures.
(3) Emphasis on starting with units. [Teacher corrects children who say subtractions wrong way round, e.g. 5 from 7 when 7 from 5 is meant.]
(4) Two subtractions talked through by group with teacher writing on board. [Teacher spends some time on significance of redundant zeros in answer with Class B.]
(5) Six questions written on board for children to do in their books.

The lessons given to Class A form the main part of Table 3.6, any modification for Class B is shown in square brackets.

In both the formalization lessons in School 2 there was no sign of the structural material which had been used in the previous lessons. In one class the exchange practice with Dienes' blocks that had been carried out some time before, was mentioned when exchange was shown symbolically. Both groups were reminded in a general way of the different apparatus and exchanging experiences they had had.

During the formalization lessons the teacher was adamant that children should say 'fifty' and 'thirty' rather than five and three when dealing with the tens column digits, e.g. the teacher explained:

(T: Teacher; P: Pupil)
$$654-$$
$$232$$

T: 4. Now, I made 2 big mistakes there. I said 4 take away 2, I'm happy with that, that's not a mistake, then I said 5 take away 3 ... what should that really have been in my mind? I know I said it, but what should I have been thinking?

P: 153.

T: No.

P: 50 take away 30.

T: Thank you, yes. I should really have been thinking 50 take away 30. We say 5 take away 3 for easiness ... it's twenty. But the same thing applies, as we looked at last time, although that comes out as 20, the nought doesn't affect that 2, so we don't bother to put it. And in this one I should have said.

P: 600 take away 200.

T: 600 take away 200, which leaves ...?

P: Four hundred.

He also displayed examples where the positioning of digits was incorrect, i.e. 'deliberate mistakes' which the children pointed out.

Teaching outcomes

MAIN OBJECTIVE

The teacher in School 2 had spent the longest time of all the teachers in the CMF research on the lead-up to the formalization of the subtraction algorithm with three-figure numbers. Three months after the teaching, five of the six children in Class A appeared to be successfully carrying out the algorithm. Table 3.7, part (b) shows the erratic nature of the responses given over the four interviews and how there is a wide range of child responses. Children were asked to try written examples and sometimes questions were read to them, including the variation 'take 45 from 73'. Table 3.7(b) lists typical responses (described earlier) to the subtraction questions asked, e.g. $45-$, $132-$, $307-$.
$$\qquad 19 \qquad 95 \qquad 129$$

The response patterns of Nina and Toni mirror the expectations of the teacher who would build up the experiences of the children until they could formulate the algorithm and use it confidently. Rene quoted the algorithm after the formalization lesson and Andrew and Kate were not successful users of the three-digit algorithm until (D). Andrew and Sally are discussed in some detail since their responses over four interviews give some indication of the reasons why children find place value so difficult. Andrew made no attempt to solve three-digit subtractions before or immediately after the formalization lessons.

(I) Sally tried to do subtraction of two-digit numbers in a commonsense fashion and wrote the question horizontally, so that faced with '37 take away 29' she said 'I take away 10 ... then 10, 11, 12 ... 19 ... so is it 19?'. The interviewer asked her to explain and she said that she took away 10 then 'so you've got 20, then you've got 27 ... so I need to take away something to make it ... 9, oh, I don't know ... oh dear'.

(PreF) she attempted $45-73$ but rejected it as impossible. She obtained the correct answer for $73-45$ by decomposition.

$$\overset{6}{\cancel{7}}\,\overset{1}{3}-$$
$$\underline{4\,5}$$
$$2.8$$

However, when asked what number was on top Sally said '613' and 'It's gone higher', but later said 'Um ... no, it doesn't change the answer, because that would be on there, you just changed it to the units'.

Table 3.7: School 2, Class A Responses

(a) Sweets question: three-digit number (367)

Type of response						Key
36 tens						A Andrew
30 tens + 6 tens	T	R	T	R	T	K Kate
counts in tens					K	N Nina
long division						R Rene
6 tens						S Sally
90 (30 + 60)						T Toni
adds digits	S	A	A N	A N		
360 (367 sweets)	K N	S	K*			arranged
other wrong	A R			R		A K N
no attempt		K N				R S T

* variable answer

(b) Subtraction algorithm questions

		45– / 19	132– / 95	307– / 129	
3-digit algorithm		N / S T	R*	N / T	A K N / R T
2-digit algorithm		K N			
count on	A	R			
subtract smaller digits	R				
other wrong			K / S	S	
no attempt	S T	A K	A		

* variable answer

I	PreF	PostF	D	Interviews
	9 weeks		3 months	

For 307 − 129 she correctly carried out the algorithm 'you have to change it, otherwise you couldn't do it' and then suggested that the top number had become 29 hundred and 17. (PostF) Sally was asked to do 304 − 178, for which she obtained the answer 036.

$$\begin{array}{r} {}^{1}\cancel{3}\ {}^{\times}\cancel{0}{}^{10}\,4 \\ -\ 1\ 7\ 8 \\ \hline \end{array}$$

Her reasoning is described on page 24.

'You can't take…8 away from 4, so you have to…and you can't borrow one from the tens, 'cos there's nothing there, so you have to borrow one from the hundreds and put it into the tens, borrow 1 from the tens and put it into the units and that makes that 14, and then it's nothing take away 7, so you have to borrow one from what you're left with in the hundreds, put it into there, change that into a one, that's ten, so it's ten take away 7, and that makes 2 …3…and 1 take away 1 is nothing.'

She used a separate hundred each time she needed to 'borrow'. When asked to describe what she had done she talked about '9' in the tens column even though the computation from which she was reading did not contain a nine.

(D) Sally was asked to do $305 - 97$. She wrote

$$
\begin{array}{r}
2\,3\,0\,5 \\
9\,7 \\
\hline
1\,8\,8
\end{array}
$$

She reasoned, 'You had to cross off the 3 to make it 2, and you had to cross one off the 2, so it's one'.

Sally's route to the successful completion of the subtraction algorithm was confused by the inaccurate use of the decomposition step in which she appeared to change amounts when not needed.

In order to show Andrew's progress we need to describe his responses to a number of items. At the first interview a question put to each child was how they would make the largest number they could with the cards from two packs each labelled 0–9. Andrew used 12 cards (more than any other child) but appeared to disregard the importance of putting big numbers at the front. His array read 5764587698…. Asked whether the first figure had to be five, he said 'it wouldn't matter' which card came first. (I) Andrew's response to how many bags of 10 sweets could be obtained from 256 sweets was '140, I'd say' and to 367 sweets he replied '240'.

Andrew's first attempt (I) at subtraction concerned counting back starting from the top number. (PreF) he tried $73 - 45$ and obtained 38 by 'Then I took away, um…40 of it because they're supposed to be tens, all of them, all of that, so it's…30, that came to 30, then I added that and that and that up and that made 8, so that makes it 38'. Faced with '$307 - 129$' he said '7 take away 9…can't do…you can't take…you can't take 9 from 7…take 9 away from 7' and proceeded no further. This response was after nine weeks devoted by the teacher to building up to the algorithm, concentrating on exchanging.

After the two formalization lessons Andrew interpreted the question 'Take 95 away from 132. It's a take away sum' as $\begin{array}{r}95-\\132\end{array}$ by taking the smaller digit from the larger each time, obtaining 163 as the answer. When it was suggested that perhaps he could try doing the question the other way round $\left(\begin{array}{r}132-\\95\end{array}\right)$ the following conversation took place:

(I: Interviewer; A: Andrew)
A: You can't do it like that.
I: Why not?
A: Because you can't take 5 away from 2.

(PostF) To $\begin{array}{r}304-\\178\end{array}$ he gave the answer '2'.

A: Say if you said, four take away 8, it's 4. You've got 4 and you can't take 8 from 4, so there's nothing there and…nothing take 7, you can't do that and 3 take away 1 gives you 2.
I: I see. So 4 take away 8 I can't do, right. So do I write anything underneath there or do I not bother?
A: Not bother.

(D) Andrew could complete the algorithm method of subtraction for 305 − 97 but thought with his crossing out that the top line had become 1915 (one thousand, nine hundred and fifteen). He tried 73 − 97 after hearing 'Take 73 from 97'. Andrew said, 'What happens, 3 take away 7, you can't do it, so you cross the 7 off, to carry a ten from there, so I put the one down and put the 6 up there, 'cos I've taken 1 away, so it's 13 take away 7 . . . 6'. He then said that '6 − 9' was impossible so wrote '0'. It seems likely that Andrew's understanding of the role of zero was faulty and his adaptation of the teacher's 'don't bother with the zeros' added to his confusion.

The games the teacher used all the way through the nine weeks' teaching stressed exchanging flats and longs in the Dienes' Multi-base material. However the essential sameness of the *value* of the material was not retained and we have three out of five children who were asked (PostF) insisting that the top number in a subtraction question has changed its value even though five could use the algorithm on the final interview.

DECOMPOSITION

The question which required the child to find how many bags each containing 10 sweets could be filled from a jar of sweets numbering 302, 256, 600 and 367 has already been discussed when used in School 1. Table 3.7(a) shows Class A's responses. Note that the only child in this group who could consistently tell how many tens there were in a three-digit number was Toni who could do so before the teaching started.

Kate's responses varied according to the number of sweets that one started with. Three children added the digits on one or more interviews, e.g. Nina's responses were different each time, e.g.

(I: Interviewer; N: Nina) 367 sweets (I)
N: Three hundred . . . three hundred and sixty.
I: Oh, 360. What happens to that odd 7 then?
N: Put them in a bag, but you don't have to put them in tens.
I: Why not?
N: Because you haven't got enough.

(PreF)
I: 367 sweets and I'm going to put them in bags of 10. How many do you fill? There are 10 in every bag.
N: 367.
I: They're in a great big jar and I'm going to put 10 in a plastic bag and 10 in another plastic bag . . . how many plastic bags can I fill?
N: (*pause*) . . . don't know.

(PostF)
I: how many bags of 10 I'd get out of 473?
N: . . . 50.
I: And how did you get 50, Nina?
N: Because . . . um . . . 7 and 3, and there's 400, and 4 tens make, um . . . 4 forties . . . that's 400, so I said 4 . . . 40 . . . and then added them, that made 50.
I: Well you've got an answer here, this one, you said . . . I can't do it − 256 sweets in bags of ten.
N: Oh . . . 70.
I: Tell me how.
N: Well, there are ten tens in 100, so that's two tens are 20 . . . oh, I can't explain it now . . . and 50 is 5 tens, so . . . 70.

On the same occasion as this last attempt however, Nina managed to obtain 30 bags for 307 sweets but said, 'It's hard to explain'.

(PostF) When the children were given the question with the numbers 473, 500 and 42, four children who gave incorrect answers for 473 were able to provide the correct number of tens for 500 and 42. The other two were correct on all three numbers.

PERCEPTION OF THE MATERIALS

The children in School 2 were not asked to explain to a 'new girl' how to do subtraction in order to see whether they automatically chose concrete materials as the easiest way. Instead they were asked more baldly if they remembered using blocks to help them with subtraction and whether they could draw pictures to show 452 represented in Dienes' Multi-base. Class A regularly used Dienes' Multi-base material in class and referred to the materials as Dienes' blocks.

In Class A all the children for the most part could remember using Dienes' blocks, three months after the lessons. Five drew pictures to represent 452 so that the different shapes of flats, longs and units were apparent. Although Andrew made all his shapes the same size he judged their relative values on the positions in which he had drawn them. The remembered usefulness of the Multi-base blocks varied from child to child and was by no means entirely positive. Two children stated that they did not know whether using the blocks helped them to do subtraction questions.

(I: Interviewer; K: Kate; R: Rene)
I: I see, and was it easier with the blocks, or is it easier with just the sums?
K: I think with just the sums, I found it easier with just the sums.
I: Easier than with the blocks?
K: ...than with the blocks.

I: And did it help you to use these blocks?
R: Yes.
I: Can you tell me how?
R: Well, because you don't need to use your fingers for big sums, and it's like using a sort of calculator.

Child methods and misconceptions

The teacher made a video of a games session with each group of children and showed the film to the staff of School 2. Besides the discussion on personality traits which were displayed during the game all the teachers commented on how often the children used their fingers to count rather than using number bonds. In the tape recorded lessons this method was accepted and reinforced by the teacher.

Andrew, asked to subtract 29 from 37, counted back from 37 until he had used up 29 and explained, 'Go through my fingers twice and then go through them 9 times after that'. The interviewer asked, 'Any idea how many it's going to end up, vaguely?' and Andrew said 'No'.

A question that was asked the children on the second and third inteview was 'Take 45 from 73'. This form of verbal question prompted all six of them to try to do a question of the type 45−.
73

Toni rejected the question since she thought it impossible:

(I: Interviewer; T: Toni)
I: Can you take 45 away from 73?
T: No.
I: You can't? Why not?
T: Because...if you write it like this, you can't. What number is it?
I: I said can you take away 45 from 73?

T: Well, you can do the 5 and 3 and that leaves 2 but you can't do the 4 and 7, because there's not enough numbers.

I: I see, well let me say it another way round then. Say if I said 73 take away 45, can you do that?

T: Yes.

Kate, when asked 'take 95 away from 132' said 'Is it alright if I put the biggest number on the top?'.

However she had difficulty with the algorithm and the interviewer as a final question referred back to 95− which Kate had written initially and left unfinished.

       132

(I: Interviewer; K: Kate)

I: Let's go back to what you wrote first of all Kate, you had the numbers like that, 95 take away 132.

K: That would probably be easier than this!

In the formalization lesson the teacher had made particular reference to which way round questions had to be written, although he did not read out the questions in the way quoted above.

The teacher, unlike the other teachers who taught subtraction, took some time requiring the children to say 'five hundred take away three hundred' rather than 'five take away three' yet three months after the initial teaching only two children were using this type of statement occasionally.

Sometimes misconceptions can be linked to the teaching. The teacher had, during the formalization lesson talked about the reasons why zeros need not be put in numbers if they came at the beginning:

(T: Teacher; P: Pupil)

P: And that would be 100 take away 100 is nothing.

T: Is nothing, so do I put that there?

P: No.

T: Shall I put that there? Who thinks I should put that there? Who doesn't think I should put that there? Well, I mean, you can, but if I was to ask you to write down 99 . . . in your books, just write down 99, you wouldn't write down 099 would you?

P: No.

T: You would just write the 99, wouldn't you? So we don't really need to put that there. 1 take away 1 leaves you with an empty space, so we might as well leave an empty space, okay?

The particular nature of the omission was lost on Andrew who generalized for 304− as

                                                               178

quoted earlier (p. 24) to say zeros need not be bothered with and if you could 'not take it' you put nothing, giving finally the answer '2'.

School 2, Class B (aged 8–9)

Class B was composed of eight children drawn from a parallel class to Class A in School 2. They were taught by the same teacher as Class A but for marginally less time. The teaching scheme and formalization lessons have already been described and are outlined in Tables 3.5 and 3.6. All eight children were interviewed at some time but three were absent for two interviews.

Teaching outcomes

MAIN OBJECTIVE

Table 3.8 shows the performance of five children who were interviewed four times. The labels are as described previously.

Table 3.8: School 2, Class B Responses

(a) Sweets question: three-digit numbers (256 and 367)

Type of response	I	PreF	PostF	D
36 tens				
30 tens + 6 tens	No	A* W	No W	A No W
counts in tens				
long division				
6 tens				
90 (30 + 60)		No		
adds digits	W		A*	
360	M	M*	M Ni	Ni
other wrong		Ni		M
no attempt	Ni			
data unavailable	A			

* variable answer

Key

A   Adam
M   Mike
Ni Nigel
No Noreen
W   Winnie

arranged

A M Ni
No W

(b) subtraction algorithm questions   45−19   132−95   307−129

	I	PreF	PostF	D
3-digit algorithm	No		A M W	A M Ni* No W
2-digit algorithm				
count on				
subtract smaller digits	A M Ni	A Mª		
other wrong		Ni	Ni	
no attempt	W		No	
data unavailable		No W		

* variable answer
ª 'own rule'

I   PreF   PostF   D   **Interviews**

9 weeks   3 months

Four of these five children could successfully (D) repeat and apply the subtraction algorithm for three-digit numbers (including a zero in the middle) whilst Nigel could do so for some questions. As Table 3.8 shows, however, the path to this successful conclusion was by no means straightforward. Noreen seems to have been able to do the subtraction prior to the teaching sequence but then made little attempt at any question which required decomposition, until (D) when she was again successful. (PostF) she started the algorithm correctly for $132 - 95$ but could not cope with the tens although successfully decomposing for the units. (PreF) she had been unable to do two-digit subtraction which was all that was asked of her. Mike and Adam could use the algorithm after the formalization lessons but not before, but Adam was not always correct. Mike's own method of subtraction on the second interview is described later. Nigel had a far from straightforward set of responses. His replies are described in detail below.

Part of Nigel's problem when dealing with subtraction was that the basic number skills he had available were very limited. On the first interview he was asked to try $37-$ which was

$$29$$

written down for him. This he did by putting up nine fingers and then folding down seven of them and afterwards said $3 - 2$ is one, answer 12.

(PreF) he was asked to try $73-$. The responses were revealing.

$$45$$

(I: Interviewer; N: Nigel)

N: You've got 3...take away 5 and you end up with nothing...7 take away 4 leaves...7 take away 4...that'd be 3.

I: Okay.

N: 30.

I: Right, now, when you said, 3 take away 5 is 0, why is that nothing, Nigel?

N: 3 take away 5...you can't do it...it's 3...you've got 3...take away 5.

(PostF) Nigel volunteered the information, 'I'm not good at take aways', and subtracted the small unit digit even though it was on the top. When he was given $304-$ which was closer to

$$178$$

what he had just been taught, Nigel said, 'Borrow one, 14...6, 7, 8, 9, 10' and used his own and the interviewer's fingers. The interview continued:

N: Take away 7, that'd be nothing. 2 take away 1 is 1.

I: Smashing, now would you like to explain why you crossed that 3 out and put a 2 above it?

N: Because I borrowed 1 for the units.

I: Oh, borrowed 1 what?

N: Hundred.

I: I see. So when you put that in the units, was it 100 then?

N: No.

I: Changed, did it?

N: It became ten. The 14.

I: Is that fair?

N: Yes.

I: I see, alright. So it went in the units, then you took 8 from 14, and then what did you do in the middle?

N: Nothing take away 7 is nothing.

I: Oh, why?

N: Because you can't take 7 away from anything.

I: I can take 7 away from 9.

N: Mmm...you can't take nothing away from 7.

I: Oh I see.

N: You've got nothing, you can't take away 7 unless you've got 7.

I: Unless you've got 7 there to take it away.

N: Yes, or more.

Three months later Nigel could do $305 - 97$ and drew 15 small circles to help him do the subtraction in the units column. However when asked 'I want you to take 73 from 97' he wrote:

$$\begin{array}{r} 73 \\ \underline{97} \\ 06 \end{array}$$
    000000000000000

and described his work

N: I've got it wrong...because you can't really do that...
I: I see.
N: You can't go back and borrow from there.
I: So you're taking the bigger number away from the smaller number...and that's difficult is it?
N: Yes.
I: Let's see how you started it anyway...you've got 7...you were trying to take 7 away from 3 right? Now I see you've got a little 1 down there alongside the 3...where did that come from?
N: The 10s.
I: I see. And how did you take it away from the 10s?
N: Put a line there.
I: That's through the 7?
N: Through the 7 and then you put a 6 and the 10 near the 3 and it ends up as 13.
I: I see, and what does this 6 mean there?
N: It's 60 tens.
I: Six tens 60. Fine, okay, now you've put a whole lot of little circles down on the line here. What was the idea of that?
N: 13 and you can take away 7 and what number you're left with is there and you just count them up.
I: I see...is the 6 you put down...you counted them up I see, but the problem is that you've got to take 9 away from 6.
N: You can't do that.
I: 9 tens from 6 tens. Why don't you put them round the other way? Would it make any difference? If you put 97 on the top and 73 underneath.
N: No.

Nigel's misunderstanding that zero is a replacement for 'impossible' compounded the poor knowledge of number bonds he had. Nevertheless he could apply the algorithm to some questions on the final interview (D).

DECOMPOSITION

A question asked (PostF) in order to ascertain the child's view of the action of decomposition was whether the top number in the subtraction had changed its nature or was just another way of writing the same value. To illustrate four points of view on this we quote from Adam, Alan, Angela and Noreen.

$$\begin{array}{r} \overset{2}{\cancel{3}}\,\overset{9}{\cancel{0}}\,\overset{1}{5} - \\ 9\ 7 \\ \hline 2\ 0\ 8 \end{array}$$

(I: Interviewer; A: Adam; Al: Alan; An: Angela; N: Noreen)
I: ...what number is now on the top line?
A: Two.

I: You're quite right, absolutely on the top line and if you look at the top line of the sum, as opposed to the top line in the writing down, what number?
A: 29.
I: 29...and is that what you started with?
A: No
I: Does it make any difference?
A: ...(*pause*)...
I: What did you start with?
A: 305.
I: I see, what number do you have now?
A: 29.
I: 29. So what's happened? Has it changed?
A: Yes.

I: ...Is it still 305 take away 97?
Al: No.
I: Well, what's happened?
Al: I've changed it.
I: Well, what's the answer to...208's the answer to which sum?
Al: 211 take away 97.
I: I see. I didn't ask you that did I? I asked you 305 take away 97.
Al: Shall I do it again?
I: Have you got any other ideas? How to do it?
Al: ...I could try and see if I could do it another way. 5 take away 7...you can't do that... 300s...take away nothing would be 3, so I put 3 down 'cos if I put 3 down I won't be able to (*poor tape*)...them to, so I have still to borrow 1 off and put 2...and then put it there, or it's 200 now...put...still going to be the same thing there. I could borrow 2 off there and make it 1, shall I do that?

I: Well, you see, the sum I gave you was 305 take away 97. Now you've done a lot of crossings out, is it still 305 take away 97?
An: No.
I: What is it now?
An: Two hundred and nine...two...two thousand, one hundred and 15, take away 97.
I: Well, would that give you the same answer as 305 take away 97?
An: No.
I: Well, what is your answer to? Which sum?
An: Um...305 take away 97.

I: Now, I'm saying is it still 97 from 305, or is it 97 from something else?
N: 97 from something else.
I: I see, and what is the something else?
N: 29.
I: Ah, can you take 97 from 29?
N: No.
I: I see, well how did you manage to do it?
N: I don't know.
I: Has the top line changed then, has the top line of the sum changed?
N: Yes, because of the bits I crossed out.
I: Oh, I see. Does that give it a different value?
N: Not really, because you're still giving it to the thing to help the sum...you're just really passing it down the line.

The sweets question again received very mixed responses (see Table 3.8). (D) Nigel and Mike still did not obtain the number of tens and yet Mike was successfully working the algorithm for subtraction (see Table 3.8b). In the sweets question we can see that each child's responses formed a different pattern although some types of answer which had appeared in other classes did not occur at all. (PostF) Mike, when asked how many bags of ten in 473 marbles drew without prompting the diagram shown in Figure 3.1 and mentioned the use of Dienes' apparatus.

Figure 3.1: Mike's diagram: 473 marbles in bags of 10

(I: Interviewer; M: Mike)
M: Um...4 hundred...1, 2, 3, 4...no...I won't draw out all those um...
I: Oh, you were going to draw out some.
M: I was going to draw the tens, but that would be a bit hard...I'll just use little Dienes like that, it'll be 1, 2, 3, 4...

Mike attempted to fill one of the squares with strokes, 'I was going to try and put ten', but he still said that there were 470 bags of 10 sweets.

Two other interesting attempts at the sweets question were from Alan and Paul. Each (PreF) was asked how many bags of 10 in 600.

(I: Interviewer; A:Alan; P: Paul)
A: Sixty.
I: Now can you explain to me what you were doing...you were doing it quietly.
A: Counting. I...like...um...10 in one, and that's one bag and 10 in the other and that's another.
I: Right, so what did you do to yourself, then...did you say 10, what did you put for the next one?
A: Um...20, 30, 40.
I: And then you went all the way up to 600 did you?
A: Yes.

P: None.
I: None? Why not?
P: 'Cos...um...there's 6...um.
I: Why did you say 'none'?
P: 'Cos I never knew how to put...'cos I don't know what...you have to put 10 in one bag...and I've only got 6.

Adam's responses depended on the number of sweets in the question. (PreF) he was correct for 600, 423 and 31 but not for 48 and 367. (PostF) he was correct for 500 but not for 473.

It is quite apparent that finding how many tens in a three-digit number is not a trivial task and is seldom solved by recourse to the position of the digits and their values.

PERCEPTION OF THE MATERIALS

The use of Dienes' Multi-base materials, stones, string with knots, etc. made up a large part of the teaching sequence of the classes in School 2. We have seen that Mike spontaneously drew his version of the Dienes' representation of 473 when asked about the sweets, Nigel drew circles as a step beyond counting on his (and the researcher's) fingers. Winnie referred to the Dienes' blocks but drew strokes to help her with computation. No child, however, asked to use bricks or other concrete aids at any time.

At the three-month interview the group was asked (a) whether there was any connection between using bricks one day and doing sums another, (b) whether they could show what a three-digit number looked like when represented by Dienes' Multi-base. Six of the group could draw a representation of 452 which showed the distinction between flats, longs and units. Sarah drew the tens and hundreds so that they looked the same and Angela could only remember that there were tens and units; Paul alleged that he had never heard of Dienes or played games with small blocks. Most of the group also considered that the structural material had been useful for understanding, e.g.

(I: Interviewer; S: Sarah; A: Alan)
I: And when you were using Dienes' blocks, did that help you to work out some ways for yourself?
S: Yes, . . . subtract, and I had to use them because every time I done some I got it wrong.
I: I see, and when you used the Dienes' blocks, you got it right?
S: Yes.

I: One day, you see, you were using bricks like this and another day you were doing subtract sums or take away sums like that. Is there any connection between them?
A: They're easier.
I: What? These bricks? Did they help you do the other sort?
A: Yes, they are much easier. They help you a lot because if I use them . . . if I use these . . . I get the right answer.

Note however that the usefulness appeared to be in the past. None of them asked to use Dienes' blocks whilst being interviewed.

Child methods

We have further evidence in Class B of children spontaneously subtracting the tens number first – Mike did this even after the teaching sequence when faced with $73-$. We have already
$$45$$
seen that Nigel had little success with subtraction problems, his attempts at number bonds were based on counting on fingers and he was not prepared to work hard at it.

(I: Interviewer; N: Nigel) (I)
N: I was just going . . . I had my hands under there. I was just going 10, 20, 30 . . .
I: I see, so why did you stop then?
N: I couldn't, it would've taken too long.

Discussion

The teacher in School 2 spent longer on laying the foundations for the three-digit subtraction algorithm than any other teacher although the actual formalization was only two lessons. He taught two small groups of children using Dienes' Multi-base and other materials and encouraged the children to play exchange games each time the group met. The video and transcripts of the lessons show him to engage in lively conversation with the children. The children can also be seen to be discussing the work with each other. If we look at Table 3.8 we can see a marked difference in the time taken by the two groups to come to the successful use of the algorithm. Class A had three children who used the algorithm (PreF), whereas Class B had nobody who appeared to be at this stage although Mike could do so the next day immediately after the lesson. In each class there were pupils who seemed to be using the method only on the fourth interview, three months later. We do not know what was happening within this period although their teachers said subtraction had been used when it naturally occurred but was not retaught.

Most teachers would expect the child to start from no knowledge (or if taught previously, from a knowledge of the two-digit algorithm) and then after the initial teaching be ready for the formalization, i.e. the child is 'almost' able to state and use the algorithm symbolically. The schemes of work clearly make this assumption. The formalization is then verbalized and the children are given written subtractions, so that the algorithm can be practised. The interviews show that these expectations are not always realized.

The decomposition of hundreds and tens in order to complete the subtraction had been based on a large number of exchange activities and yet when those children who were asked (eight from both groups) whether the top number of the question had changed in size, all said it had. A point worth considering is whether in our attempts to show children how they can change tens, hundreds, etc. we sufficiently emphasize the invariance of the number itself. This seeming acceptance of the capricious behaviour of numbers is further shown by the dismissal by Nigel of zero, since it has no value. The teacher had unfortunately in a different context told the children 'not to bother with zero' and Nigel had generalized this statement.

The children were very hesitant to use number bonds and relied heavily on counting – fingers, strokes or dots. This became very cumbersome when, for example, they needed to count in tens up to 300 and it is not surprising that the children gave up the struggle and did not finish the task.

There is evidence that the translation of a subtraction statement into symbols is not straightforward since most of the children wrote the first number stated, at the top, for sentences such as 'take 45 from 93' and some thought the order of writing made no difference to the result.

School 3, Class A (aged 12)

The oldest children observed learning some aspect of place value were 12 years old and formed a small 'remedial' class of nine in a middle school. They were being retaught subtraction with three-digit numbers. All had been taught the algorithm at some time but the teacher thought that a new introduction using Dienes' Multi-base would result in a better understanding of the algorithm.

The scheme of work

Table 3.9 shows the teaching plan suggested by the teacher.

Formalization lesson

The teacher attempted to bridge the gap between work with structural material and the formal subtraction algorithm performed symbolically by having the children work with the bricks and then talk through a symbolic form whilst he demonstrated the use of the algorithm on the blackboard (see Table 3.10). Only one question involving tens and units was done this way however and only one which involved hundreds.

The algorithm written in symbols and discussed in terms of 'exchanging' was intended to be represented physically by the child moving and exchanging one denomination of bricks for others. The translation was intended to be direct and yet both teacher and children tended to remove or deal with bricks on the left hand side of the display whilst the written algorithm requires a systematic use of the digits (i) first on the far right and then subsequently the next on the right, etc.; e.g. the teacher said in the lesson (for $62 - 19$): 'I want you to take away from that supply you've got there, one 10, well that's easy enough to do, isn't it? Just take that one 10 away, get that off your sheet, now we've got to take away 9 units as well.'

Table 3.9: Scheme of work – subtraction algorithm – School 3, Class A

Prerequisites: Exchange, collection, ordering in size, counting.
Apparatus: Dienes' Multi-base 10, dice, abacus, counters, calculators.
Time taken: Eight periods of 35 minutes each, over eight days.

Scheme

(1)	Dienes Multi-base (10) used for ordering exercise in terms of '9 less than' as well as '10 times as big'.
(2)	Exchange units, longs, flats. Games with dice in which child collects face value or face value times 10 units and exchanges for more convenient blocks.
(3)	Counting in tens.
(4)	Introduction of zero as space filler.
(5)	Breaking down numbers into composite parts, e.g. $2567 = 2000 + 500 + 60 + 7$.
(6)	Using calculator to find effects of multiplying by 10, 100, etc.
(7)	Subtraction using Multi-base and exchanging.
(8)	Recording in formalization lesson.

The removal of a set of bricks according to an instruction enables a child to utilize the most advantageous method for bricks since the child does not necessarily connect actions with the need to have a formalized written algorithm. Thus George, in the formalization lesson, when asked to subtract nine, said correctly:

(T: Teacher; G: George)
G: I'm going to take one of these tens and put it in the tens and take one.
T: Let's see if George can do it.
G: Put it out of the tens and get one unit and put it in the units column.
T: ...Come on, right, you told me you were going to pick up one unit and swop it for that. Well, I'm not sure myself.
G: Well, you're taking 9 away from 10.

(Another child is then asked to do the question and he exchanged a long for ten units before removing 9 of them – as in the written algorithm.)

Here, George has recognized that to take away nine units is the same as taking one ten and returning a unit to the unit column of 'the top'. This is easy to do with bricks. The teacher however was concentrating on the exchange of the 10 transferred from the tens column to 'help' the units and misinterpreted George's method which was indeed quite different from the algorithm being taught.

Teaching outcomes

MAIN OBJECTIVE

Table 3.11 shows the responses to subtraction questions on the four interviews. A two-digit subtraction was asked on the first interview and after that both two- and three-digit questions requiring decomposition were asked.

All the members of the group had been taught the subtraction algorithm before the series of lessons described and all could perform the computation adequately on two-digit numbers. Four members of the group could use the algorithm for three-digit numbers just before and after the formalization lessons and three months later all were still able to obtain the correct answer most of the time. Chris performed the algorithm correctly but was under the misapprehension that when a 10 was decomposed it immediately became '9'. This is discussed in more detail later. Ian had not been interviewed before the teaching started but (PreF) had

Table 3.10: Formalization lesson – School 3, Class A

---

(1) 62 – Written on blackboard (symbols).
    19

(2) Children instructed to put down 6 longs, 2 units
    and underneath   1 long, 9 units
    (using Dienes' Multi-base on a sheet of paper marked with columns).

(3) Remove 19 in bricks from sheet (so only top number was shown).

(4) From 6 longs and 2 units take 1 long.

(5) Do we have enough units to take away nine units?

(6) Exchange one long for units and put with other units.

(7) Teacher records in symbols on board and talks while recording as if moving bricks.

(8) Teacher writes 62 – on board and children talk through the algorithm when called upon.
             19

(9) Teacher emphasizes that number on top line has not changed but has been rewritten: 6 tens and 2 units is the same value as 5 tens and 12 units. Children are asked to demonstrate this by exchange.

(10) Computations put on board. Children asked to do the questions initially, without using structural material but this is available if they need it.

(11) Teacher talks through one question with help from children. (Note: corrects first child who subtracts tens digit first.)

(12) Teacher talks through questions after written attempts by class.

(13) Question with hundreds, tens and units written on board 123 – .
                                                            76

(14) Children place 123 in flats, longs and units on sheet.

(15) Child explains he will exchange 1 flat for 10 longs as a first step. Child then removes 7 longs from the pile of 12 longs.

(16) Teacher then asks another child to take away the 6 units. When child talks in terms of written work he is told to use bricks instead.

(17) Another child asked to explain in terms of written symbols. He starts with hundreds column and is told to start with units. Child explains in terms of 'can't take' and 'borrow'. The teacher talks of 'exchanging'.

(18) Questions written on board, children asked to attempt them and told to use bricks 'if you get stuck'.

(19) Teacher goes round class and if child does not seem to be performing adequately the bricks are brought into play again.

(20) At the end of lesson teacher talks through (without bricks) the questions, written on the board, which the children have attempted.

Table 3.11: School 3, Class A Responses

(a) subtraction algorithm questions: 137–   400–   600–
                                            19   38   236

Type of response		137– 19	400– 38	600– 236
3-digit algorithm		D G / P V	D G / P V	D G / P V
2-digit algorithm	C D G / P V			
count on		I		
subtract smaller digits				
other wrong		C	C	C / I
no attempt			I	
data unavailable	I			

Key

C Chris
D David
G George
I Ian
P Peter
V Vera

arranged

C D G
I P V

(b) number of tens in 367

	I	PreF	PostF	D	
36 tens	G				
30 tens + 6 tens	P	P G	D G	I P G	
counts in tens			I		
long division	V	V	V	D V	
6 tens					
90 (30 + 60)	C	D / I			
adds digits			P		
360					
other wrong		C	C	C	
no attempt	D				
data unavailable	I				
	I	**PreF**	**PostF**	**D**	**Interviews**

used 'counting-on' to obtain answers. After the lesson he made no attempt to do subtraction questions but (D) although he managed to decompose for the units he then said 0 – 9 was 0 but changed later to 9. Table 3.11 (a) shows what could be considered a successful outcome of a sequence of lessons with four of the children's responses matching the teacher's expectation.

DECOMPOSITION

A crucial part of both practical work and verbal description of the subtraction algorithm is the exchanging of tens to units when needed, without changing the value of the number involved in the exchange.

The teacher had emphasized during his formalization lesson that when digits were crossed out to show that they had been exchanged for a more convenient form, the value of the number had not changed. This message was not accepted by a number of his class; after three months four pupils thought their crossings out had changed the number and even earlier in the teaching the unchanging value of the numbers was in doubt.

(I: Interviewer; V: Vera) (PostF)
I: Somebody was doing a take away sum and on the top line there was this

Now what was the number they started with?
V: They started with 63.
I: 63?
V: 3 units and 6 tens.
I: 3 units and 6 tens. I see. And what number have they got written down now?
V: 13 in the units column and 5 in the tens column.
I: I see, 13 in the units column and 5 in the tens column, and is this the same number as that . . . as the number they started with?
V: No.

David when asked (PreF) to do 137 – 19 wrote $1\,\overset{2}{\cancel{3}}\,\overset{1}{7}$ and said, 'It's 2 hundred and . . . no, it's 1 thousand, two hundred and 17'.

At each interview the children were asked to state how many bags each containing 10 sweets could be obtained from a pile of sweets, e.g. 367, 452, 600 (the number varied). Table 3.11 (b) shows the varied success children had on this question. (D) three of the pupils were able to correctly answer the question by appealing to the value of the digits, two others could solve it by recourse to other than 'place value' methods and Chris failed to obtain a correct answer.

Chris three times gave the answer as 306, taking 30 from the hundreds and just putting 6 on the end. Vera consistently carried out a long division question (as shown her by her father)

$$
\begin{array}{r}
36 \\
10\overline{)\,367} \\
30 \\
\hline
067 \\
60 \\
\hline
07
\end{array}
$$

When asked to try the question in her head she could not do it and confessed that she was imagining a long division question in her head.

PERCEPTION OF THE MATERIALS

The teacher had stressed the importance of structural materials during the formalization lesson as well as in the lessons preceding it, e.g.

> Teacher: Now, we've actually done it, in front of ourselves, with the material, we've seen it work – you've done it. There shouldn't be any mystery about it because you're the ones who've actually moved the bits and pieces around.

And of their experiences in the past:

> Teacher: ... and some of you grasped the idea what to do, probably a lot of you didn't and even those of you who did understand, well you probably didn't understand, you could do it mechanically, you could take 1 there, put it there, you didn't really know what you were doing. Alright, well let's hope today, with the work you've done with the materials, you're going to be able to.

We asked the children three months after the experience: (i) whether they could show what 452 looked like when translated into Dienes' Multi-base and (ii) what was the connection between the use of bricks one day and the 'sums' they had done on another day. David, Peter and George described the bricks accurately as being of different shapes and made up of ten longs or ten units, etc. Vera showed 452 as four squares, five squares and two squares all of equal size but spaced out in the correct order.

> (I: Interviewer; V: Vera)
> I: Well, haven't you got on your table now just a pile of little blocks?
> V: Yes, in each column.
> I: Ah, you need columns, do you?
> V: Yes.
> I: Say if you didn't have the columns?
> V: You wouldn't know where to put them.

Chris drew a very similar picture but described his marks as boxes into which things are put.
    Ian drew two types of picture, one for Unifix (not used in this class), and Dienes' Multi-base. The Multi-base picture showed a distinction between the shape and size of the blocks whilst the pictures of Unifix for '452' had four columns of ten, five single bricks and two circles.
    Asked about the connection between the experience with blocks and the sums, Peter could not remember what the connetion was in the past but thought he could not use bricks to do subtraction now:

> (I: Interviewer; P: Peter)
> I: Could you take away the 97, if you made 305?
> P: Well you could do it in your mind, but I don't think I could do it using them.

David however could describe how he would do a subtraction using the blocks. George insisted he never used the blocks. 'I always done them like that' but thought one could do subtraction with numbers or blocks.
    These children do not appear to use the opportunity of returning to the structural materials if they found the subtractions difficult although Chris had done this in the past:

> (I: Interviewer; C: Chris)
> C: Say ... there's a sum and you can't do it, you go and get some blocks and it helps you a bit more.

I: Do you usually do that?
C: Not now.
I: No?
C: I did in my old school though.
I: But now you...you just do the straight sum like this, do you?
C: Yes.

Child methods and misconceptions

The children in Class A, being 12 years of age, had already been taught methods of subtraction, so besides their invented methods they also retained parts of algorithms. George had a flexible approach to number and could cope with subtractions before the teaching sequence.

(I: Interviewer; G: George) (PreF) 45 − 19
G: I put... I subtracted the 10, left me 30, subtracted 5 out of the 9, that left me...30, and subtracted the 4, what was added to the 9, that left me 36.
I: ...Do you think you could explain that again to me?
G: I took away the 10 from the 19, that left me 35.
I: I see.
G: And then I took away 5 out of the 9, that left me 30, and I took away the 4 out the 9, left me 26.

(When asked to 'write down' what he had done, George produced the standard decomposition algorithm.)

(PostF) For 123 − 58 George did not follow entirely the suggested algorithm since he decomposed the hundred first.

G: 3 take away 8, you can't do, so you have to cross that one out, which brings that to nought, cross out the hundred, add it on to ten...makes it 12, and then take away 1 from that, cross out the 12, ...leaves that 11 and add 1 on to there, so that's 13, take away 8...5. 11 take away 5 is 6...and there isn't no hundreds.

The teacher always talked about exchanging but Vera had been taught this algorithm before and she used 'borrow' and when asked to explain how the loan was repaid she humanized the action:

(I: Interviewer; V: Vera)
I: ...isn't that going to make it all rather peculiar, if you start borrowing and not paying back?
V: Oh yes, right. Five you can't so the units column goes to the 4 and asks him can I borrow one from you.
I: I see, one what?
V: Can I borrow one tens please, one tens?

Vera was seemingly unaffected by the teaching sequence which used Dienes' Multi-base bricks and she was clinging tenaciously to the algorithms she knew. In the interview just before the formalization she said when doing 137 − 19, 'You can't say 9 take away 7, because it's not ...the rules in maths say you can't do that'.

The successful use of the subtraction algorithm depends on manipulation of addition bonds. At least, the teacher explained in terms of number facts known but the children used various other strategies. For the most part these gave the correct answer but the amount of work and memory involved was disproportionately high and what to the teacher may have seemed a lesser aspect of the operation was to the child the most time consuming part. All the children in this sample counted on their fingers at some time. Vera (PreF) used tally marks and, for example, for $137 - 19$:

> V: ...7 take away 9 you couldn't do so you went to the tens column and borrowed a 1, and you crossed out the 3 and made it 2, 'cos you borrowed it for the ones column. So 17 take away 9, can I use the paper clips please?
> (*She draws* | | | | | | | |\| | | | | | | | | .) Which is 8.
> I: Can you tell me what you did there?
> V: Oh yes, I put 17 on.
> I: You put 17, and then you counted back.
> V: Yes, I counted 9 and then I crossed it out where I was up to and then I counted all of them, which came to 8.

Paul did not use tally marks and so for $45 - 19$ he said:

> P: 10, 11, 12, 13, 14, 15...6...write down 6.

This number of fingers can be seen whilst the counting on proceeds but should the question require more than ten then the need to record in some way is apparent. Ian counted in tens, 10, 20, 30, 40...to find how many tens in a hundred and later did $100 - 19$ by writing:

10 10 10 10 10 10 10 10 (10 10)

He reasoned, 'Yes, 19 from 20 is 1, then it's 10, 20, 30, 40, 50, 60, 70, 80...81'.

As the children talked through the subtractions they often stated the question the wrong way round.

> David: 13 from 8...5, right, 11 from 5...um...6.
> Vera: 0 from 6 you can't do.
> Chris: 3 from 8 you can't, so you cross...

In order to test whether the group could set out a subtraction problem the pupils were asked (D) to 'take 73 from 97'. David and Peter wrote the question in vertical form with the largest number at the top. George and Chris tried $73 - 97$, Vera did it both ways as did Ian, who said $(73 - 97)$ was 30.

> (I: Interviewer; Ia: Ian)
> I: ...if I write it down like this...does that make any difference? $(97 - 73)$
> Ia: No, it doesn't.
> I: That doesn't make any difference?
> Ia: No, not to the answer, no. You could have it any way round. You could have, 97 take away...no, you couldn't, no...it would make a difference, I should think, er...'cos that is the highest of the both...so that should come to er...zero, I should think.
> I: That comes to zero, does it? $(97 - 73)$? Why should that come to zero?
> Ia: 'Cos this is higher than that, and that hasn't got enough to take away that, so that would be zero.

To a teacher the emphasis in teaching subtraction by decomposition is usually placed on the need to exchange. Bricks are often used for the child to physically carry out the exchange. To the child the reasons why certain actions take place in the algorithm are more to do with layout, space or rules and not the single necessity of exchange.

Vera was a stickler for the way things were done. She for example reasoned that carrying takes place because there is insufficient space.

(I: Interviewer; V: Vera) (PostF) 347 + 95
V: So I put the 2...2 in the units column under the 5 and I carry the 1.
I: What does that mean? What does the 1 stand for?
V: The left over, because you can't fit 12 in there.
I: Is it 1?
V: One unit.
I: It's 1 unit, is it?
V: Yes.
.
.
.
So I couldn't fit the 12 together because it gave me...it would look like it was...it was 10 units and you can't squeeze them together, so I put the 2 and just carried the 1...
.
.
.
V: It's under the...um...tens column.
I: Does that mean it's a ten?
V: No.
I: It's not a ten.
V: No, it's just the number from the units...the units column...it's just that I carried it.

At some time the children have been told to exchange when they have more than nine rather than when they have ten. They now remembered the nine as crucial which in some cases led to error.

Peter (PostF) explained for 347 + 95:

(I: Interviewer; P: Peter)
I: And then you got 14, so you said you put 1 in the hundred column?
P: Yes.
I: Why did you put 1 in the hundreds column?
P: Well, you're only allowed 9 and it will be 14, you're only allowed 9 in one column...so you have to carry the one.
I: Why are you only allowed 9 in one column, Peter?
   Any idea?
P: Not really.

(I: Interviewer; Ia: Ian) (PostF)
Ia: Once it gets past the 9, it turns into a ten.
I: Oh, I see.
Ia: And there's more than...say there's more than 9 in that column, so it goes straight to a hundred.
I: Oh I see, you exchange them up?
Ia: So once that turns past 9...say 9 hundred, it can either...it can be...um...a thousand.

Unfortunately the belief that a column (HTU) can contain no more than 9 led to error in Chris's case.

(I: Interviewer; C: Chris)
I: Can you do 600 take away 236? (*Repeats*)
C: Nought take away 6 you can't do, so you cross out that, and you put a 9.
I: Oh, where did that come from?
C: Because once you go down to nought, that's the highest one you can go up to for 9.
I: But if I had no tens, how can I take 1 and get 9?
C: Because when you cross out the 1, it goes from...

I: But there's no 1 there.
C: When you cross out the 0, it goes directly to 9.
I: Does it?
C: Yes.
I: So from nothing, I suddenly have 9?
C: Yes, because it's the highest number you can go up to, that's the way I do it.

Discussion

Although these 12-year-olds were regarded as in need of new teaching of the subtraction algorithm, they could for the most part accurately use the rule on two-digit numbers before the teaching and on three-digit after the teaching. Their knowledge of exchanging may have been deficient initially but unfortunately it appeared to have improved little and three months after the teaching they alleged that the top number in a subtraction was changed in value by the decomposition.

School 4, Class A (aged 8–9)

The work done in School 4 with eight 8- to 9-year-olds was different from that already described in this chapter in that it concerned rather more basic ideas about place value. The ultimate aim was for the children to be able to order three-digit numbers written symbolically having previously worked with an abacus and other materials.

The teacher's interpretation of formalization was to verbalize and have written what had previously been shown on an abacus or with Dienes' Multi-base. She did not have the structural material available at the same time as the verbalization nor did she write the digits on the board as she talked about them. The children were given a sheet of questions, e.g. 'put 121, 131, 145, 211 in the right order with the smallest first'. When the children had tried the questions the teacher verbally went through the required responses.

Conclusions

All the teachers taking part in this phase of the research were planning to teach a series of lessons which led up to a formalization relating to place value following experience with practical work and concrete materials. In one case, quoted only very briefly in this chapter, the children were expected to be able to order a series of written numbers. The other four classes described were being taught the subtraction algorithm for two- or three-digit numbers. The decomposition model was used in each case and so questions were asked not only about the algorithm but also the relationship between hundreds, tens and units.

Differences between teaching approaches

There were three stages in the process: (i) the build-up through other experiences, in the case of the reported research, through practical work; (ii) the transition period; (iii) the use and acceptance of a generalized, usually symbolic form of mathematics. The first stage was described quite clearly in the schemes of work and varied in length, the transitional stage was the formalization lesson(s) which lasted at most two hours and the third stage was expected to be sufficiently established to be the working format for the child from then on. The time spent on stage (i) varied from two hours a week for nine weeks to 40 minutes a day for eight days. The formalization lessons were those observed by the researchers.

The techniques adopted by the teachers, to bridge the gap between work with materials and a formalization varied. We had two teachers who preserved the materials and the written form side by side for around a quarter of a lesson, then the materials were put away. One teacher started the lesson by referring to the various concrete aids used but introduced the formalization without them. A fourth teacher used a kind of written test which was talked through with the children after they had been told that materials were not to be used. One teacher asked the children to imagine the physical display as they wrote their computation although this advice seemed more for those who might have trouble in the transition rather than an advocated and rehearsed strategy. Two teachers drew pictures of the bricks on the blackboard but did not advocate this as a step for the children to copy. This 'bridging' was seen as momentary and not needing to be generally available.

Competence in using the subtraction algorithm

The tables which show the responses given on four occasions to questions which were chosen to illustrate the declared objective of the teaching, show very varied patterns. The 12-year-olds' pattern is perhaps the closest to what might be called teacher expectation but it must be remembered that this group had already been taught the algorithm at least once before. For young children the path to success on an algorithm was by no means smooth although at the end of three months most were performing the computation adequately. Although performance was generally good many children demonstrated their tenuous hold on what was happening, when asked whether the top number in a subtraction had changed, after decomposition had taken place. Indeed all those asked the question stated at least once during the three later interviews that the top number had changed to become bigger or smaller.

Decomposition

An understanding of 'place value' involves both a knowledge of the significance of the position of a digit and also the relationship between digits in the same number. The subtraction algorithm taught by teachers in this research relied on decomposition which for example entails that 83 can be thought of as 7 tens and 13 units. Similarly 304 can (and sometimes must) be written in its equivalent form of 2 hundreds, 9 tens and 14 units. None of the children who were asked how many bags of 10 sweets could be obtained from a jar holding 367, could immediately give 36 although some came to this answer in two steps – how many tens in 300 and how many tens in 60. A large number of those interviewed however sought an answer from adding or manipulating the digits in some inappropriate way. This demonstrates little understanding of the system of representing whole numbers with which they will be expected to work throughout their lives. It can be seen from the tables that the children can adequately complete the subtraction algorithm without knowing the interconnection between the digits in the numbers involved. For many of them there is little transfer between one aspect and another.

Very few children could attempt a three-digit subtraction having successfully completed a two-digit version unless they had been specifically taught the techniques. The logical transfer seemed to be that adopted by Tom (School 1) who ended up with 99 in the units place but managed to cope.

Child methods

The interviews which took place prior to the teaching of subtraction showed that the children tended to work from left to right i.e. take away large denominations first (e.g. in 76 – 39, remove 30 first). This is contrary to the order demonstrated in the algorithm but is perfectly acceptable when Unifix or Dienes' blocks are used to obtain a result. In fact the teacher in Class 4 took away longs before blocks when demonstrating subtraction. Some children prior to teaching obtained a difference by counting on or counting back. This provided an answer but required that information be held in the head and a tally kept in some way. Note that some pupils graduated from informal but successful methods to failure (e.g. taking away smaller digits irrespective of their position) when the teaching took place. Very few of any class knew their number bonds and there was a heavy reliance on counting on fingers. This is cumbersome and time consuming and indeed daunting as Nigel illustrated: 'I couldn't, it would have taken too long.' One might consider whether the introduction of an algorithm presumably to provide a straightforward and foolproof method can be based on primitive and far from foolproof tools.

Language

A large number of the children described the manipulation of numbers incorrectly, e.g. take 7 from 9, rather than the other way round. One teacher did correct this in the formalization lesson but some of his group persisted. Few children recognized the meaning of 'take 73 away from 97'; the first number spoken was the one they wrote on the top line of the subtraction. We perhaps do not take sufficient note of the number of different ways we have of verbalizing a unique symbolic statement in mathematics. Possibly we expect children to generalize from a narrow usage of language without exploring with them the meanings.

Misconceptions

We often in mathematics expect children to generalize from a number of specific instances. They do however often generalize in a way we do not expect. We have given a number of instances of statements made by the teacher which have been interpreted by the child in an entirely different way. School 2 teacher's throw-away line on the importance of zero in 099 was interpreted by at least two children as 'never bother with the zero'. Such misunderstandings would seem to need rectifying before an algorithm involving numbers can be successfully assimilated.

Ann's (School 1, Class A) interpretation that the reason for writing small 'carrying' figures was due to their lack of importance has considerable sense behind it. Similarly Chris's (School 3, Class A) carefully putting 9 in a column each time he decomposed a 10 has some justification in that he had been told 'a column cannot hold more than nine'. Many children described the reason for moving tens into another place as lack of space, which is of course not true if one has a large amount of paper on which to write. Providing simplified but not quite adequate explanations does not appear to help some children but on the contrary confuses.

Materials

Concrete materials are used in schools in a number of ways. They can be used in their own right so that the child can adequately work mathematically within that mode. In the cases described in this chapter, experience with materials has been seen as a basis for generalization and then formalization of the generalization. In many cases however what the children were doing with the materials although often an appropriate use of concrete aids, did not immediately model the algorithm or formalization. With Unifix if one wishes to remove 9, an easy way is to remove a ten, break off one unit, and return it to the minuend. This is not the same as appreciating that more units are needed in order to take away 9, exchanging a ten into ten ones, adding it to the units we already have, etc. If the formalization is to be a symbolic representation of what has previously happened with materials then the match needs to be considered very carefully.

It is thought that children find it easier to work with materials than with symbols, yet some of those interviewed stated their aversion to the bricks, particularly three months after the teaching when they were working symbolically. It is often thought that if a child is unable to work a particular question with symbols then a good teaching strategy is to provide the concrete materials again and this will provide 'success'. This is by no means obvious from the answers received on interview. The child may be able to set up materials to model the formal subtraction question but it is doubtful that (re)invention of the other stages of the process and improvement in the use of the algorithm (the intended outcome) will follow.

Chapter 4
Fractions: Equivalence and Addition
Kathleen Hart

Introduction

The topic of Fractions appears in the mathematics curriculum for both primary and secondary schools. Children are for example expected to know the terms 'half' and 'quarter' from a very early age. Later they are taught to deal with fractions of the form a/b and considerable time is spent practising the four rules.

This chapter describes the teaching of the multiplication rule for generating equivalent fractions, and for one class, the further extension to the use of equivalent fractions in addition. In the case of the primary school class the transition from work with discs and bricks to the statement and use of the rule, was monitored. The two secondary school classes in the sample were observed and interviewed when equivalent fractions and, in one case, addition of fractions were introduced.

Reports such as that produced by the Cockcroft Committee (1982) question how much work on fractions needs to be done in school, particularly when one considers the research reports commissioned by the Committee on the use of mathematics in the adult world (Sewell, 1981; Fitzgerald *et al.*, 1981). The hierarchies of the Concepts in Secondary Mathematics and Science (CSMS) research show that some aspects of fractions, such as recognition of the fractional name given to a region are correctly reproduced by most children of secondary school age whereas both addition and multiplication are very much more difficult. On the CSMS Fractions test papers (now the *Chelsea Diagnostic Tests*, Hart *et al.*, 1985) word problems requiring fractions were matched by computations which seemed to be appropriate for solving the problem. Often the same sample performed more successfully on the word problem than the computation, suggesting that the methods used by the children were different for the two contexts.

The scrutiny of all easy CSMS items (across topics) suggested that many secondary-aged children worked entirely within the set of whole numbers and any CSMS item which required the manipulation of non-integers was done incorrectly by over half the sample. Responses to questions on the CSMS Test 'Place Value and Decimals' (Brown, 1981, and see Chelsea Diagnostic Tests, Hart *et al.*, 1985) suggest that children do not appreciate that fractions are numbers which enable the operation of division to be extended beyond integers. Kerslake (1986) further researched the meaning given to fractions by children and found the children were most familiar with a region model. Kerslake's work included the provision of learning experiences designed to convince children that fractions could be seen as numbers resulting from division. This teaching scheme was only partially successful.

Among books to which teachers turn for advice, *Primary Mathematics Today* (Williams and Shuard, 1982) suggests that 'halves' and 'quarters' arise through measurements and can be extended in paper-folding activities. Later work on fractions includes 'part of a set' as well as 'part of a whole' and the authors repeatedly underline the value of presenting division and fractions of a set alongside each other. Fraction strips are advocated and the need to allow children to work with non-unit fractions emphasized. These authors also note that that ratio is an 'aspect of the fraction concept which deserves more attention than it often receives'. The suggested ways of gaining experience relevant to the discussion of equivalence are

(a) matching divisions of shapes, (b) examples in money, (c) fraction strips, (d) tabulating equivalences found from these practical experiences and (e) plotting graphs of fractions.

Towards Mathematics (Glenn and Sturgess, 1980) states 'the practical activity of measuring provides the experience from which vulgar or decimal fractions can be abstracted'. Glenn and Sturgess suggest the making of fraction strips for 1 whole, ½, ¼, ⅛. These authors use the term 'fraction family' for a set of equivalent fractions, so (½, ²⁄₄, ³⁄₆, ⁴⁄₈) form a family which has the name ½ ('head of the family'). Although most of the activities mentioned concern 'parts of a whole' the authors state that rational numbers as number pairs illustrated by work with two number lines or graphs are important.

Textbook series for primary schools usually contain an introduction to equivalent fractions. The rule tends to be an outcome of tabulating results gleaned from matching fraction strips. It is often practised with pairs of fractions which can be formed one from the other by doubling or addition. The Nuffield Primary Maths 5–11 (1982) scheme positively defines fractions both as regions and as the result of division and explains the rule for equivalence as multiplying a fraction by unity in the form ²⁄₂ (this despite the fact that multiplication of fractions is not introduced until later in the series). The Howell and Fletcher (1978) series introduces a fraction as part of a set of discrete objects first rather than by a shaded region and equivalence is explained as multiplication by one.

Fraction names can be seen to come from a variety of models, the region, part of a set, result of division, etc. and equivalent fractions can thus be based on any of these.

The sample

The investigation of a small part of the topic of fractions described in this chapter involved three classes. One was the final year group (School 5, Class A), class size 33, aged 10–11, in a primary school. The other two were the bottom (School 6, Class A) and top (School 6, Class B) first-year sets (of five), each with class size 25, aged 11–12, in a secondary comprehensive school which takes children from the primary school. Thus, there is an aspect of continuity, from the younger children's experience to the secondary school's review and teaching of 'equivalence' and 'addition' of fractions.

The research

The multiplication rule for obtaining a fraction equivalent to another was the generalization intended by the primary school teacher. She led to this by providing practical experiences to demonstrate the equivalence. In the secondary school one class was observed when being taught the equivalence rule whilst the other covered both equivalent fractions and addition in the teaching period under consideration so that other aspects of fractions had already been formalized prior to the observed lesson.

There were interviews on four occasions: (a) just before the start of the teaching sequence denoted by (I) for 'initial'; (b) immediately prior to the lesson in which the rule was verbalized, denoted (PreF); (c) just after the formalization lesson, denoted (PostF); and finally three months later, denoted (D) for 'delayed'. The children chosen for interview in each class were asked questions on different models for fractions, i.e. regions, subsets, number on a number line, and they were asked about equivalent fractions. Specific examples of the questions used are shown in Table 4.4.

School 5, Class A (aged 10–11)

The first series of interviews described in this chapter are those with the 10- to 11-year-olds who were in their final year in the primary school. Their teacher was introducing them to the rule for obtaining equivalent fractions. She had already analysed a number of suggestions and schemes concerning this topic and had decided not to use the presentation in the class textbook but to adapt it.

The scheme of work

Table 4.1 shows the type of activities engaged in by the class which the teacher hoped would lead up to the children adopting the rule 'multiply top and bottom (or "divide top and bottom") by the same number to obtain an equivalent fraction'.

Table 4.1: Scheme of work leading to equivalent fractions (9 lessons over 2 weeks) – School 5, Class A

(1)	Construct 'whole' from eight interlocking cubes. Revise fraction names.
(2)	Terminology ²⁄₄ – two of four equal pieces that make up a whole one.
(3)	Cutting and folding variety of shapes for half, quarter, eighth.
(4)	Expressing fraction as ½ of 8 cm or 8 cm ÷ 2.
(5)	Shading fractions, including shapes not already adequately subdivided.
(6)	Halves, quarters, eighths from cutting strips of paper. Making fraction board for ½, ¼, ⅛.
(7)	12 cubes used as 'whole' ¹⁄₁₂, ⅙, ¼, ⅓, ½.
(8)	³⁄₆ and ½ referred to as members of the same 'family'.
(9)	Number line and the placing of fractions on it. Ordering.
(10)	Addition and subtraction of fractions with same denominator.
(11)	Tenths and fifths with cubes, strips and number lines.
(12)	Cuisenaire rods to make fraction strips, 'Families of fractions' found from the rods and symbolized.
(13)	Diagrams of fraction strips to find equivalence. Use of 'other members of the family'.
(14)	Two formalization lessons to verbalize the multiplication rule for generating equivalent fractions (see Table 4.2).

The 33 children in the class were all taught together although they sat in groups around tables. A large amount of the work leading up to the formalization lessons involved the use of worksheets and construction activities such as making fraction boards, or cutting circles into eighths, etc., so children could be allowed to work at different rates. The seven children interviewed were regarded by the teacher as being at different levels of attainment. They were called Terence, Warren, Ann, Brian, David, Sally and Ellen.

Formalization lessons

The teacher chose to have two long formalization lessons of about an hour each. The rule was introduced in the first lesson and in the second lesson the teacher returned to the use of materials and built up the equivalences again.

The materials were used essentially to build up a set of equivalences which could be seen to match in size or number and from these patterns the children were invited to generalize a rule. Table 4.2 provides a summary of the lessons as recorded and observed by the researcher.

The teacher wished to provide experiences which involved both regions and sets of discrete objects and also to go beyond unit fractions. In order to provide many fractions she used 12 as the base. The two formalization lessons involved the use of counters and rods. The definition of a fraction known by the class was based on regions – this led to some confusion in language, e.g. the teacher, in the context of six apples, said

> 'Say I wrote up ⅙, that's writing it in numbers. On your sheet I wrote it in words. Now what does that actually mean...'

Table 4.2: Formalization lessons (2) – School 5, Class A

(1) Set of 12 drawn objects and questions asking 'how many in half, quarter?' had been given for homework and were now discussed by the teacher. Sentences '2/4 of 12', '1/2 of 12' written on board and children asked to state what they noticed about the two answers.

(2) Set of six circles on worksheet from previous nights' homework. Half of 6, one-sixth of 6, three-sixths of 6?

(3) The teacher follows up suggestion that to find a quarter of six apples, they would need to be cut into pieces, this leads to language difficulty of half apples, and half of the set of apples.

(4) The teacher follows up child suggestion that 1/4 and 3/6 of six apples give the same amount.

(5) Same example but children asked to note (3/6. 1/2) and (2/6. 1/3) when set of six objects investigated.

(6) Children given 12 counters between two pupils. Class asked for how many in half the counters. How many in each of four equal groups, six groups, three groups?

(7) How many sixths of the counters to make half the counters. Thirds and sixths. On blackboard is now written 1/2 = 2/4 = 3/6 = 6/12.

(8) Verbal review of activities which have led to the making of fraction families.

(9) 1/2 = 3/6. What must you do to 2 to obtain 6?

(10) Teacher writes $\dfrac{1}{2}\overset{\times 3}{\underset{\times 3}{}}\dfrac{3}{6}$

(11) $\dfrac{1}{2} = \dfrac{6}{12}$ $\dfrac{1}{2} = \dfrac{2}{4}$

(12) The teacher says that a child has said, 'Both the top and bottom are multiplied by the same number'. Teacher goes through written pairs asking if this is true.

(13) Collective practice of rule on $\dfrac{3}{2} = \dfrac{?}{18}$

(14) Child suggests a whole one is 6/6, 12/12. Rule for equivalence is not applied by teacher, who says this can be 'seen straight off'.

(15) Fractions which were not found from the 'counters' demonstrations are now converted by the rule and stated to be members of the same 'family', e.g. 3/9.

(16) Demonstration of the rule using configuration above $\dfrac{a}{b} \overset{\times}{\underset{\times}{=}} \dfrac{c}{d}$

(17) Worksheets given out and explained; (a) multiplier, and diagram $\frown$, (b) one fraction and part of equivalent in diagram $\dfrac{1}{3}\overset{\frown}{=}\dfrac{\square}{12}$

(c) series of equivalent fractions to be continued; (d) pairs of fractions, one with part missing.

Second lesson (next day)

(1) Cuisenaire or Colour Factor rods given out to pairs of children. The purple rod is a 'whole' in the Colour Factor set. Two reds make a whole in the Cuisenaire system.

(2) Class asked to find two rods to match the 'whole' then 4, 6, 12 pieces.

(3) Class asked to set up matching lengths for one-half.

(4) Pairs are called out by children and teacher writes: $\dfrac{1}{2} = \dfrac{2}{4} = \dfrac{3}{6}$ on blackboard.

(5) Thirds 'family' set up using bricks; $\dfrac{1}{3} = \dfrac{2}{6} = \dfrac{4}{12}$ on board.

(6) Child suggests 24ths even though no bricks match these. This is used as a start for revision of 'rule'.

(7) Teacher tries to elicit a response of 'division' when she asks how many halves there are in 3/6 but a child says 6 becomes 2 by subtraction so this is followed up by repeating 'What is done to top must be done to bottom' and showing that a negative number results.

(8) Teacher writes $3 \div 3 = \square$ on board, questioning children on divisors for other pairs. $6 \div 3 = 2$

(9) Pairs which have not been illustrated by the use of bricks.

(10) Pairs found by division and checked with bricks $\left(\dfrac{3}{12} = \dfrac{1}{4} \right)$

(11) Examples on work sheet involving multiplication and division, e.g., $\dfrac{3}{9} = \dfrac{1}{?}$; $\dfrac{3}{5} = \dfrac{6}{?}$

Children reply: 'One of the six equal pieces that makes up a whole one.'

Teacher: 'Now if you look at our whole one this time, it's this group of apples...'

Later a child suggested that a quarter of the six apples be found and a discussion ensued in which apples were supposedly cut in half so 1 and ½ apples was one-quarter of six apples and there was 'half an apple' as well as 'half of the apples'.

The rule came about after the children were asked, 'What sorts of things did you notice between those, those answers? Surely everybody noticed something, didn't they?' James replied, 'Each answer goes up 1, 2, 3'. The discovery of 'multiply' and 'both the top and bottom are multiplied by the same number' was attributed to a child, but was in fact heavily led and stated by the teacher. The teacher appealed to the evidence applied by the bricks when a child suggested that ³⁄₆ = ¼: 'No. So it won't work. We won't get back to what we know is true from using the bricks...'. Later she said, 'So ³⁄₁₂ equals ¼. Would you just like to check that with your bricks...?' The conversion of sevenths to 28ths was done by the rule and the new denominator was suggested by the teacher, so that the children were at no time required to prove equality of unfamiliar fractions from materials set out by themselves, although they were encouraged to think this might be possible; 'You may leave the sticks out in case you need to use them or look at them at all'.

Teaching outcomes

FRACTION EMBODIMENTS

The main objective of the teaching was for the children to arrive at and subsequently use the rule for generating equivalent fractions 'multiply (or divide) the top and bottom of the fraction by the same number'. The teaching scheme mentioned different embodiments of fractions, so on interview the children were asked to demonstrate their knowledge of the conventions for fractions in three ways: (a) using shaded regions (b) being shown part of a set and (c) being asked to point out the position of a fraction on a number line. Table 4.3 shows the performance of the seven children on items for assessing these ideas (prior to the formalization lessons).

Using the region model some errors occurred when the child wrote the ratio of shaded/unshaded or used the number of squares (or triangles) shaded as the denominator. Terence however, unlike the others, interviewed on the first occasion (I) wrote his fractions using a different convention, so that two-thirds was written 2_3 and correctly shaded, whilst one-quarter was written 1Q. At (PostF) he used the generally accepted notation. All the children marked ¾ on a number line at a point greater than one, usually at the point 3 but sometimes between 3 and 4. When asked whether ¾ was more or less than one most said 'less' but did not mark the point thus. Warren when asked to distinguish between three-quarters of the line and the number ¾ at interview (I) did so by marking both points, e.g.:

(I: Interviewer; W: Warren)
I: You see this line here, with the numbers on it, can you mark in on that line, where would the number ¾ be?
W: What...you mean...before the 1?
I: Well, ¾...where does that go?
W: Here.
I: Right, okay. Well what have you done there, then? Why have you marked it there?
W: Because um...there's 4...4 digits and 3...would be ¾.
I: I see, so have you marked in the number ¾ or have you marked in ¾ of the line?
W: ¾ of the line.
I: Okay. Right, you've marked in ¾ of the line, jolly good. Now, can you mark in the number ¾?

Table 4.3: Children's understanding of conventions for fractions at interview, School 5, Class A

	Interview	T	W	A	B	D	S	E
Region Model (a) (b)								
What fraction	I	×	√	×	√	×	×	×
shaded?	PreF	√	√	√	√	√	×	×
Shade 2/3; 9 squares given	PostF	√	√	√	√	√	√	√
Set Model								
5 of 12 eggs are cracked. Fraction?	I	×	√	√	√	√	0	×
Number on number line								
Mark the number 3/4 (with an ×) on the number line	I	×	√	×	×	×	×	×
0 1 2 3 4	PreF	×	?	×	×	×	×	×

Key
0 not tried   T Terence   B Brian   E Ellen
× at least one example wrong   W Warren   D David
√ all correct   A Ann   S Sally

Region Model. 4 items (I), 4 items (PreF), 1 item (PostF)

At (PreF) he marked ¾ correctly if the line segment was marked 0 to 1 but chose the point marked '6' when the segment was marked 0 to 8. The children tended to view the number line as another region model and marked ¾ as a length of the line.

EQUIVALENCE

The questions asked on equivalence varied between interviews but can be typified by the items listed in Table 4.4

In question 3b, finding fractions equivalent to ⅔, the interviewer mentioned pattern but awaited an explanation in terms of equality and multiplication. However, five of the seven children on the two post-formalization interviews, (PostF) and (D), interpreted the question solely in terms of pattern and used multiples of two for the numerator and multiples of three for the denominator. This means that some had to count on in twos until they reached the numerator 20 and then use the number of intervening terms to find the new denominator. Some of those interviewed in fact interpreted each of the dots (. . .) as standing for a term. On the third interview only Brian mentioned equality as an afterthought (and when asked):

(I: Interviewer; B: Brian)
I: Do you think those fractions are worth the same?
B: Yes.
I: How do you know?
B: If they're in the pattern, they are the same as well.
I: Are they? How do you know?
B: 'Cos if...like half equals ¾ or ⅜ and ⅛ and 5/10. That is a sort of pattern.
I: I see. And what are all those fractions worth?
B: They're all worth ⅔.

Table 4.4: Interview items for equivalent fractions

(1a) What fraction is shaded? Can you give another name for the shaded part?

(1b) Shade two-thirds (given 9 squares).

(2) Two boys have equal amounts of pocket money. One decides to save 1/4 of his pocket money, the other to save 5/20 of his pocket money. Compare 5/20 and 1/4. (Given as multiple choice, with different distractors on different interviews.)

(3a) Choose the fractions which are worth the same:
$$\frac{3}{8} \quad \frac{6}{12} \quad \frac{6}{11} \quad \frac{6}{16} \quad \frac{10}{26} \quad \frac{9}{24}$$

(3b) Here is a pattern, fill in the missing figures:
$$\frac{2}{3} \quad \frac{4}{6} \quad \frac{?}{9} \quad \frac{?}{12} \quad \frac{10}{?} \quad \ldots \quad \frac{20}{?}$$

(4a) Is $\frac{3}{7}$ the same as $\frac{21}{49}$? Why?

(4b) Complete $\frac{3}{12} = \frac{1}{?}$

A too rigid adherence to seeking for a number pattern led Ellen (PostF) to produce $\frac{9}{19}$ as an equivalent to $\frac{9}{16}$ even though the triangle (see 1a, Table 4.4) was shown.

The results for 3b are not included in Table 4.5 which shows comparative performance on each of the four interviews. Although items may have been slightly different on each interview the performances are shown as fractions of the number of questions asked.

Brian and Warren could on the first interview give fractions equivalent to $\frac{9}{16}$ and $\frac{9}{9}$ when diagrams were given. Each of them continued to correctly answer the equivalence questions they were given on subsequent interviews. Warren was the only child to look at the relationship between numerator and denominator in fractions belonging to a series (PostF). David could provide no equivalent fractions until (D) when he knew that $\frac{5}{20} = \frac{1}{4}$, for example, although he provided an invented rule for other fractions (more on this later). Sally and Ellen also failed to answer even half the equivalence questions correctly at interview (D) (note however that Sally had some success at (PostF)). Ellen, (D) when asked whether $\frac{5}{20}$ was more or less than $\frac{1}{4}$, said that $\frac{5}{20}$ was bigger 'because I think that the two top numbers...5 is bigger than 1 and 20 is bigger than 4'. She further continued the numerator pattern in question 3b (Table 4.4). Ann and Terence are shown as giving some deficient replies (PostF) because they failed to recognize all pairs of equivalent fractions.

The profiles shown in Table 4.5 indicate that even after the work with discs and bricks, the essential nature of equivalence was not understood and that the rule was not easily accessible to many of the children.

Table 4.5: School 5, Class A, performance on equivalence items

	I	PreF	PostF	D	Key
All correct	B W	B W	B W	B W	A Ann
Half < × < all	A			A T	B Brian / D David
Half correct	T	A	A S		E Ellen / S Sally
None < × < half			E T	D S	T Terence / W Warren
None correct	D E S	D S	D E	E	arranged

Interview

NB: Terence was only asked one question at PreF

Key
A Ann
B Brian
D David
E Ellen
S Sally
T Terence
W Warren

arranged

A B D E
S T W

PERCEPTION OF THE MATERIALS

The teacher based the recognition of the multiplication rule on the identification of patterns seen in matching regions or subsets. The children's attitude to, and use of, the materials were of interest and so questions concerning these aspects were asked in the interviews.

During most of the interviews the questions were either given diagrammatically or symbolically, it was only on the three-month interview, (D) that discrete objects were provided for the children. Some children tried to demonstrate the veracity of their symbolic answers however by drawing a picture of the bricks or fraction wall. If one knows the answer it is relatively simple to decide upon the divisions, if however the picture is needed to provide a clue to the size of the denominators, the drawing must be accurate to be helpful and even then one must have a reason for choosing a particular partitioning. Just after the two formalization lessons (PostF), Terence was asked whether there was another name for $\frac{6}{10}$. He drew the picture shown in (a) in Figure 4.1 and said the following:

(I: Interviewer; T: Terence)
I: You see those little sausages you are drawing, what are you doing?
T: I'm breaking them up, like we did in class.
I: I see. They're supposed to be the bricks?
T: Yes, measuring up... tenths. How many? How many times this...
I: $\frac{6}{10}$...I asked was there another name you could give to $\frac{6}{10}$, that fraction?
T: It's more than half.
I: Yes.
T: $\frac{1}{3}$.
I: Why should it be $\frac{1}{3}$? Are you just guessing or is there a reason?
T: I'm just guessing.

Undaunted Terence tried again when asked the next question (his diagram is (b) in Figure 4.1).

(I: Interviewer; T: Terence)
I: Now, in this list here, I've got a whole series of fractions. Now, are there any of them worth the same? Could you write down any which are worth the same? (*Interviewer shows the set* $\frac{3}{8}$ $\frac{6}{12}$, $\frac{6}{11}$, $\frac{6}{16}$, $\frac{10}{26}$, $\frac{9}{24}$)
T: (*Draws b*).

Figure 4.1: Children's diagrams

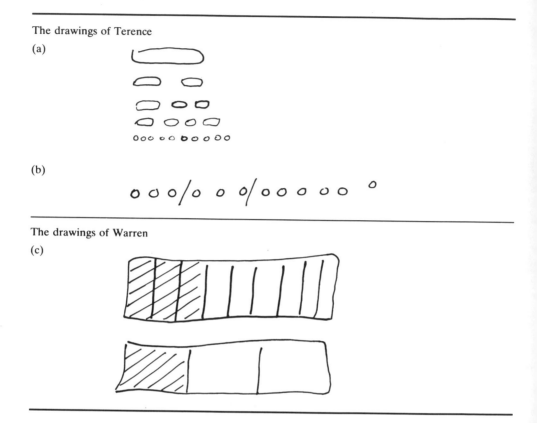

The drawings of Terence

(a)

(b)

The drawings of Warren

(c)

I: Tell me what you are doing. You've done a whole set of little circles there.
T: Yes, twelve.
I: There's twelve of them, yes.
T: So...er...12, 6. They would be up to there, see [*marks halfway*]...six twelfths.
I: You've drawn 12 circles.
T: I marked in ⁶/₁₂. Three-eighths...1, 2, 3, 4, 5, 6, 7, 8. So the whole one would be there [points to a break 00000000 ↑ 0000] and 3 would be in between. These two are not the same.
I: They're not the same, right. ⅜ and ⁶/₁₂...we've knocked out because...now what did you do? I have to tell the machine what you did. You put your hand over the last four of those circles.
T: Yes, because there's 12 here, but if I put my...hand over there to show that was 8 and ⅜ would be there and it isn't the same as that [*pointing to 6 circles.*] Try ⁶/₁₁, is the same (*counts from left hand side of circles and gets to same point*).
I: As what...
T: Er...⁶/₁₂.

The diagram (a) in Figure 4.1 might have been of use if drawn accurately but in order to use discs as in (b) Terence would need to know how many discs to draw initially in order to test out ⁶/₁₂ and ⅜.

Warren drew the diagram shown in (c) in Figure 4.1, to show that $\frac{3}{9} = \frac{1}{3}$ but as can be seen, the pictures did not actually show the equality as the inaccuracy in drawing could have led him to another answer. Warren already knew that $\frac{3}{9} = \frac{1}{3}$ and the diagram was for the interviewer's information, which is different from Terence's use of a picture. Terence's comments indicate that he thought the diagram might provide the answer.

On the three month interview (D), the children were also asked:

(a) If they remembered whether the materials were useful and
(b) to demonstrate the equivalence of $\frac{2}{14}$ and $\frac{1}{7}$ by using discs or bricks.

Brian thought the bricks were useful when introduced in the lessons but Warren found the blackboard work preferable (and easier to follow). Ann thought the counters had been useful, 'Because when we were using the counters we were learning how first to work them out. We worked them out with counters and then the next time we worked them out we wouldn't need counters.' Sally said she could not remember doing equivalent fractions at all and Ellen who had no success said she thought she could demonstrate something with bricks but having taken ten bricks said, 'I was going to say try and halve it into six but it doesn't go because there are only 4 left – it won't halve properly'.

On interview (D) the children were shown discs and bricks (the same materials as those used in the teaching sequence) and asked to demonstrate that $\frac{2}{14} = \frac{1}{7}$ using concrete materials. The responses of Brian, Terence, David and Ann are given below.

Brian had many tries; eventually he used the discs and attempted to explain in terms of subsets (remember the ratio aspect had played no part in the teaching).

(I: Interviewer; B: Brian)
B: Yes, there would be one little group with 7 in it and if you cut them in half there would be two little groups which equal 14.
I: Could you physically put in my hand $\frac{2}{14}$ths?
B: $\frac{2}{14}$ is both of them.
I: $\frac{2}{14}$ths is both of them?
B: $\frac{1}{7}$th is only one of them.
I: Right, put in my hand $\frac{1}{7}$th then.
B: Here you are.
I: Right, I have in my hand then 7 little bricks. Now put in my hand $\frac{2}{14}$ths.
B: 14 little bricks.
I: Well one of those feels very much heavier than the other one and you tell me they are equal.
B: They were as $\frac{1}{7}$th but then I cut them in half; I do see now what I've done wrong... this is $\frac{1}{7}$th.
I: Show me $\frac{1}{7}$th. Now you are putting them back in pairs so you now have 7 pairs.
B: That's $\frac{1}{7}$th and if you cut them in half we would have $\frac{2}{14}$ths but they would be the same.

Terence took a set of discs and the interview went as follows:

(I: Interviewer; T: Terence)
I: How many have you taken?
T: Not too many... I'm taking 1, 2, 3, 4, 5, 6, 7, 8, 9, 10, 11, 12, 13, 14.
I: Right, now you're going to show me why $\frac{2}{14}$ equals $\frac{1}{7}$.
T: Equals $\frac{1}{7}$?
I: Well that's what you've got down there, haven't you? Now you've got 2 piles of bricks.
T: Yes... there's one there... there's 7 there and there's 14 here... um... I can't work it out with these bricks... it's easier to work out...
I: With the circles?
T: Yes.

He then proceeded to draw circles which however could not have shown the equivalence since they were of different sizes and haphazardly partitioned.
David used a pile of discs and said:

(I: Interviewer; D: David)
D: Equals...2 times 7 equals...
I: We've got a little pile of two and a pile of 7, yes.
D: 2 times 7 equals...14.
I: Right, so let's see what we've got. We've got 2 and then another pile...a pile with two and then a pile with seven and a pile with 14.
D: That's all I can think of to use them.
I: Oh, I see.
D: Unless I do um...2, 14, 7 and 1.
I: Oh good, so now we've got 2 discs and then underneath them 14 discs, and then a 1 disc, and underneath them 7 discs. It's a bit difficult to see why they should be equal. Can you show me why they should be equal? Because that's what it says, doesn't it?
D: Well...14 times...2 times 7 would equal 14. 14 times 1 would equal 14 as well...and 7 times 2 equals 14.

Ann tried to connect the numbers in the numerator and denominator with the bricks:

(I: Interviewer; A: Ann)
I: That's a pile of 7 is it?
A: Yes – and another 7 – because this is $\frac{2}{7}$ths. And 2 times 7 make 14. I think that's it.
I: Well, where is the $\frac{2}{14}$ths?
A: I don't know how to do it.

Sally tried to show $\frac{1}{2} = \frac{4}{8}$ but chose a set of twelve discs and then found a half of the set (6). She could proceed no further. Ellen gave up when half of ten did not prove to be six.

The materials had been used by the teacher to make the rule seem reasonable, but in setting up equivalences she had known how many of each type of material she needed since she already knew the two fractions she desired to match. At the three-month interview none of the sample was able to demonstrate a given equivalence using the material with which they were familiar. It therefore seems unlikely that they could benefit by building the model themselves when they found understanding difficult as suggested by the teacher's statement, 'You may leave the sticks out in case you need to use them'.

Child methods and misconceptions

The rule for obtaining equivalent fractions depended on the use of multiplication or division but on interview some children were found to be using addition or subtraction.

Table 4.2 which details the steps which occurred in the formalization lessons, shows that at one stage one of the children suggested that the method of obtaining one numerator from another should be subtraction. The teacher asked, 'What have I done to 6 to end up with 2' and David said, 'Take 4 away'. The teacher endeavoured to explain that this was incorrect by recourse to an example which if following the rule 'do the same to the top and bottom' resulted in a negative number. David appeared to be unconvinced by the teacher's demonstration since on (PostF) he tried to solve $\frac{3}{12} = \frac{1}{x}$ by subtraction of two from the 12 to find the new denominator.

(I: Interviewer; D: David)
D: 3 take away 2 equals one. Put that number...take away one. Put that down there. 12 take away...12 take away 2, equals 10. So 10 would be in there.
I: I have to do the same to the bottom as I do to the top, do I?

D: Yes.
I: And then you took away 2 at the top and then you took away 2 at the bottom.
D: Yes. You have to do the same both ways.
I: And is there any other way we can go from 3 to 1?
D: ...(interrupts)...not that I know.
I: You started off by telling me you could divide somehow.
D: Um...But I was wrong.

Three months after the teaching, (D), David had invented yet another method(s) when asked to choose equivalent fractions from a list which included ³/₇ and ⁹/₂₁:

(I: Interviewer; D: David)
I: How do you tell? What are we looking for?
D: Try to get something like 7 times something...like 7 times something to put under there, so 7 times...so 7 add something so you can make it...make it like that then put something under there, and it could be the same. Put it over the top, and see what the answer is.
I: Well I think 7 times 3 is 21...
D: (*Pause*)...I know it's 21 but...it's got nothing to do with it.
I: Oh, hasn't it...I thought you were looking for a number that you could times 7 by.
D: I know, but it has to be on the top.
I: As well.
D: Yes, it has to be on the top, not um...one on the top and one on the bottom.

Terence (D) used the conventions in writing, demonstrated by his teacher but substituted subtraction for the operation, i.e.

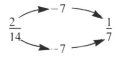

Sally (PreF) suggested that an equivalence she already knew had resulted from addition:

(I: Interviewer; S: Sally)
I: It's half of a circle. Is there any other name I could give to that ½?
S: (*long pause*)...¾.
I: ¾, good girl. What makes you think it's ¾?
S: You add on another one for that one and add another 2 for that one.
I: You added on one there, did you, to 1 on top, and you added on, how many, to the bottom?
S: 2.
I: 2 to the bottom. What made you do that? Or did you just know it was ¾?
S: I just knew it was ¾.

These three examples tend to show that the relationship was not necessarily remembered as multiplicative and that some children suggested addition or subtraction as the operations used to obtain a fraction from its equivalent. This same adherence to addition was evident in the children's reliance on pattern (PostF) and (D) when asked to find another equivalent fraction in a set. Five of the seven interviewed counted or added on to the numerators and denominators separately. This suggests that the fraction was not seen as formed from two parts which make sense only when interpreted together. In both the pattern and the pair questions quoted, the children were using a generalization which was faulty.
    Misconceptions should probably also include the use of inaccurate diagrams to provide information on subdivisions (as shown for Terence in Figure 4.1). As a picture to accompany a

known fact such inaccuracy is unimportant but if it is vital in obtaining the fact or relationship then accuracy may be crucial.

Discussion

The conventions used to show fractions were not well understood by the children prior to the teaching but each child improved during the teaching sequence, at least on giving the correct label to a region. It was not so obvious that the sample thought of ¾ as a number in its own right, since most children marked the fraction of the whole line rather than a point showing a number less than one.

The main objective of the teaching was that the children should be convinced of the truth of the generalization for obtaining equivalent fractions and be able to use the rule. Table 4.5 shows that some children were unable to interpret equivalence at all whereas others were only sometimes successful. The only pupils who were consistently successful three months after the teaching were those who were actually able to produce equivalent fractions in symbolic form prior to the teaching.

The materials, although appealed to by the teacher, as strong proof that the equivalence relationship existed, were of little use to the children when they tried to reconstruct the model themselves. If they drew circles to illustrate equivalence, only congruent circles accurately subdivided would give a convincing picture to a learner who did not know the result. Using bricks and counters one needs to know how many objects to choose before a demonstration of equality can be set up.

We have evidence that for five of the seven children the existence of an additive pattern was more dominant than a multiplicative relationship when a set of equivalent fractions was given to them. After the teaching, three of these five children opted for addition or subtraction to find an equivalent fraction.

Finally, even after building up patterns with materials, a number of children did not appreciate that the relationship was multiplicative.

School 6, Class A (aged 11–12)

The scheme of work

Class A was the fifth and bottom set in the same boys' comprehensive school as School 6, Class B. The teaching sequence as prepared by the teacher was based on the same textbook chapter as that used for Class B and is shown in Table 4.6. The points mentioned in the table are taken from the textbook examples and headings. There were five lessons of 45 minutes each which were the first experience of fractions the children had in the secondary school. The observed lesson, i.e. the formalization lesson, concerned the multiplication rule for finding equivalent fractions.

Formalization lesson

A summary (prepared by the observer/researcher) of the steps taken in the lesson by the teacher to come to the rule for generating equivalent fractions is given in Table 4.7.

The teacher drew circles on the board and marked half and its equivalents ¾, ³⁄₆, ⁴⁄₈. All these were drawn free hand and there was no mention made of accuracy in drawing. The circles were referred to as 'cakes'. The link between the diagram and the rule, was the teacher's question concerning 'how many times as many pieces' in the sharing of the second cake as in the first. This number then became the multiplier.

Table 4.6: Scheme of work for addition of fractions [Five lessons, each 45 minutes] – School 6, Class A, Class B

(Taken from class textbook, chapter called 'A quick look at fractions')

Classes A and B

(1) Parts of whole (circular, squares, other shapes)
(2) Different ways of partitioning a region, some 'by eye'
(3) Mixed number and improper fraction versions shown by
    (i)   partitioned discs
    (ii) length on a line
(4) Fractions with same denominator shown on number line for comparison

---

Class B Only

(5) Addition and subtraction shown by pictures of discs

Teaching outcomes

Six boys (chosen by their teacher to represent a range of attainment) were interviewed. At the time of interview they were in their first term at secondary school. The boys were called Gary, Bill, Larry, Brett, Mark and James.

FRACTION EMBODIMENTS

On the initial interview (I) the boys were asked questions concerning the conventions used in naming regions and a position on a number line, very similar to those asked the primary school children. Table 4.8 shows the responses given by the sample. It seems likely that Brett had very little knowledge of fractions and he in fact said that he had not met fractions in his primary school. All the boys failed to mark the number ¾ at the correct point on the number line. Brett, when asked 'is ¾ less than one?', changed the mark for ¾ from a point just after '3' on the number line to a point less than half way between 0 and 1. Brett and Bill referred to a clock face when shading a quarter of a circle. Prior to the teaching only two of the boys could shade two-thirds of nine squares; Mark, Brett and Gary shaded just two squares in a row of three whilst James did this initially but when reminded that two-thirds of the whole diagram was needed, shaded a further two squares.

EQUIVALENCE

The equivalence questions asked the boys in Class A are shown in abbreviated form in Table 4.10.
    The question concerning the equivalence of ⁵⁄₂₀ and ¼ of the same amount of pocket money was asked on all four interviews. Table 4.9 shows the results, i.e. the children's decisions (in note form).

Table 4.7: The formalization lesson – School 6. Class A

---

(1) Teacher draws a circle on board free hand and shades in half of it, referring to diagram as 'a cake'. Emphasis on parts being equal. Draws second circle and shades two-quarters saying one is getting exactly the same amount of cake.

(2) Teacher draws a circle free hand and shows it cut into sixths and another circle cut into eighths, saying that the same amount of cake is given each time and how much is that in sixths and eighths?

(3) Teacher asks class 'how many times as many' parts in the second shared cake as in first. Writes 1/2 and refers to multiplying bottom by two and top by two. Similarly, for 3/6.

(4) The multiplications are written on board as $\frac{1}{2} \times \frac{2}{2}, \frac{1}{2} \times \frac{3}{3}$ at first and then as $\frac{1 \times 2}{2 \times 2}, \frac{1 \times 3}{2 \times 3}$.

(5) Child asked to state number of pieces if cake split into 14 sections and he receives the same amount as in a half cake.

(6) Children interject with what would happen if the cake was split into an odd number of pieces. The teacher gave the example of seven pieces and says we would have three and a half pieces, but the children are told not to worry about this point.

(7) Teacher writes 2/4, 3/6, 4/8 and says they are equivalent. Teacher states that, 'we had 1/2, times the top number by 2 and times the bottom number by 2'. Asks child to provide fractions equivalent to 1/4.

(8) Children provide fractions and teacher tests them out by asking which number has been used to multiply the top and bottom.

(9) Class set to write out five fractions equivalent to 1/3 and then 1/5.

(10) Teacher goes round class looking at the boys' work. He stresses that the multiplier for the top and bottom must be the same.

(11) Teacher takes example 3/4 and states that equivalence results from multiplying the top and bottom by the same number.

(12) Examples on equivalence given to class to do, including the type $\frac{m}{n} = \frac{?}{b}$.

(13) Children told that the 'golden rule' is to multiply top and bottom by the same number.

(14) Boys ask whether the denominator could be turned into millions. Teacher says, '...I could if I wanted to...times the top number by one million and times the bottom number by one million. So I'd have 3 million over 4 million but its still the same fraction. But very large numbers.'

Bill (I) followed the context of the question and asked how much pocket money was at stake and then proceeded to carry out various divisions, e.g. 'Quarter of £10 is...4 into 10 is...8 remainder 2'. He then changed his mind and chose the equality statement because 'if you divide that 4 into 10, it only goes twice remainder 2, so that's why I think they are the same'. James gave no reason for the equality he chose and Gary gave the same reason for choosing first one inequality, then the other. Brett always guessed wrongly whilst Mark always gave the correct answer which might be because he knew it was so. Larry gave reasons for equality which appealed to the use of multiplication and division, but he admitted that he did not know whether $5/20$ was five times $1/4$ as well as equal to it.

Table 4.8: Conventions of fractions, School 6, Pre-teaching interview (I) responses*

		Class A						Class B					*Key*
	Bi	Br	G	J	L	M	H	J	L	M	R		*Class A*
(i) Shading required fraction:													Bi Bill
¼ of ○	✓	✓	✓	✓	✓	✓	✓	✓	✓	–	–		Br Brett
⅔ of ▭▭▭	–	×	✓	✓	–	×							G Gary
⅔ of (figure)	✓	×	×	×	✓	×	×	×	✓	✓	✓		J James
													L Larry
													M Mark
(ii) Stating fraction for region shaded.													
													Class B
(checkerboard)	✓	×	✓	✓	✓	✓	×	×	✓	×	✓		H Henry
(triangle)	×	×	✓	✓	×	✓	×	×	×	×	✓		J Joe
													L Lane
(iii) Stating subset of set of discrete objects as a fraction.													M Matt
5 eggs in a box of 12 are cracked.													R Richard
What fraction cracked?	✓	×	×	×	✓	✓	×	×	×	✓	✓		(Mi Mick)*
uncracked?							×	×	×	✓	–		
(iv) Fraction as a number. On the number line mark the number ¾													
(number line 0 1 2 3 4)	×	×	×	×	×	×	✓	✓	×	×	✓		

Entries: ✓ correct, × incorrect or no attempt, – not asked
* Mick (Class B) was absent on first interview.

This ambiguity concerning two equivalent fractions when one is obtained by multiplying was further demonstrated by the ¹⁰⁄₁₄, ⁵⁄₇ relationship. The boys were asked on interview (D), 'Are ⁵⁄₇ and ¹⁰⁄₁₄ equal or is one double the other?' Only James and Mark chose the correct option and although James drew a circle with 14 sections, ten of which he shaded, he did not produce a similar picture of ⁵⁄₇. Gary chose 'double' and 'larger'; Brett chose the 'double' option having firstly rejected it, and Larry believed ⁵⁄₇ was double ¹⁰⁄₁₄. Bill's reasoning was consistent throughout this interview (D) but incorrect.

(I: Interviewer; B: Bill)
B: 'Cos of... 10 into 14 goes 1 with 4 left over, and 5 into 7 goes 1 with 2 left over.
I: So, which one did you decide was the smallest?
B: ⁵⁄₇.
.
.
.
B: Because there's more wholes and fractions in that one than there is in that one. There's 1 and 4 fractions – there's one and ⁴⁄₁₀ in that one, and there's 1 and ⅖ in that one.

These results are included with others in Table 4.10 which shows the children's responses on the four interviews.

Asked the question concerning the set of equivalent fractions which also formed a pattern (PreF) and (D) Bill and Larry referred to the equivalence as well as the pattern although Bill's (PreF) explanation used the division of the numerator into the denominator resulting in some

Table 4.9: Summary of responses to the question: Is 5/20 the same as 1/4?

Child	Interview	Responses
Larry	(I)	√ : 4 goes into 20 five times. One-fourth goes into 20, five times.
	(PreF)	: Absent
	(PostF)	√ : Because one times 5 is 5 and 5 times 4 is 20. (He says he does not know whether 5/20 is 5 times 1/4 as well.)
	(D)	√ : Because 5 goes into 20 four times.
Bill	(I)	× : Confused divisions of 10 (see page 60).
	(PreF)	× : 5/20 is more than 1/4 because there's 5 fifths in a whole and if there's 20 on the bottom then there's got to be more.
	(PostF)	√ : If you times 4 by 5 it gives you 20 and if you divide 20 into 5 it gives you 4, and if you divide 1 into 4, it gives you 4.
	(D)	√ : Divide 5 into 20 and it goes 4 times.
James	(I)	× : 1/4 > 5/20, one half is more than 1/4 so 1/4 is more than 5/20.
	(PreF)	√ : 1/4 = 5/20, I just think it is.
	(PostF)	√ : 1/4 = 5/20, I don't know why.
	(D)	√ : 1/4 = 5/20, it was a guess.
Mark	(I)	√ : Because if you had a square, or a round circle of...split up into 5...up into 20, and you shaded 5, that would make 1/4. (Does not draw diagram.) Equal.
	(PreF)	√ : 1/4 = 5/20 Don't know why.
	(PostF)	√ : 1/4 = 5/20 If you had a cake and you split it up into 4...split it up into 20 bits...then eat 5 of them...that would be 1/4, so that's the same as that, 1/4 of something is that so 5/20 is 1/4, must be the same.
	(D)	√ : No reason given. Not probed but correct.
Brett	(I)	× : 1/4 > 5/20 no idea why.
	(PreF)	× : 5/20 > 1/4 5/20 is bigger.
	(PostF)	× : 5/20 is 5 times as big as 1/4, no reason.
	(D)	× : 1/4 > 5/20, I just had a guess.
Gary	(I)	× : 1/4 > 5/20, no reason.
	(PreF)	× : 1/4 < 5/20, because it's only one part of 4 and 5/20 is 5 parts of 20.
	(PostF)	× : 5/20 > 1/4, because 1/4 is only four parts and it's only 1 part out of 4, and 5/20 is only 5 parts out of 20.
	(D)	√ : 5/20 = 1/4...5/20 is one part of 20...one-fifth of 20 and...1/4 is one part of 4.

Key √   correct
       ×   incorrect

cases in 'remainders'. All the other boys referred only to the pattern and the increase in the numerator with a corresponding increase in denominator. The task set by the teacher at the end of the formalization lesson was for the class to provide five fractions equivalent to $\frac{1}{3}$ and then five equivalent to $\frac{1}{5}$. Four of the five children who were asked this question on the Monday after the formalization lesson (on Friday) could produce fractions equivalent to $\frac{1}{3}$ although Gary said, 'You're making the bottom bigger by three...adding one to the top numbers all the time'. This method led to disaster when the starting fraction was $\frac{3}{9}$ (or $\frac{3}{7}$):

(I: Interviewer; G: Gary) (PostF)
G: $\frac{4}{18}$.
I: Mmm...
G: $\frac{5}{27}$.
I: Any more?
G: ...$\frac{6}{36}$.
I: Okay, how did you...how did you know that?
G: Because I added it on to the number...I added 9 with itself, and I added 3 with itself.

Mark wrote '$\frac{1}{3} = \frac{2}{6}, \frac{3}{9}, \frac{4}{12}, \frac{5}{15}$' and described the step $\frac{1}{3} = \frac{2}{6}$ as 'Well, I just...I went up to 2 and then I doubled the three'. When faced with $\frac{3}{7}$ he wrote '$\frac{3}{7} = \frac{4}{14}, \frac{5}{21}, \frac{6}{28}$' and said:

(I: Interviewer; M: Mark)
I: So you've got $\frac{3}{7}$. Right, how did you get this first one?
M: Well, I added one again, and times'd it by 2 again.

.
.

M: So then...(*pause*)...if you draw a cake again, and you done $\frac{3}{7}$, it'd make $\frac{1}{4}$ and if you done it again, you made 4, cut it into 14, you made 4, and so that'd be another $\frac{1}{4}$, the same as $\frac{3}{7}$.

Finding the five equivalents to $\frac{3}{7}$ (PostF) was not as well done as finding them for $\frac{1}{3}$ which had been asked in the lesson, although three of the boys were able to do this.

PERCEPTION OF THE MATERIALS

The textbook used by Class A had diagrams of circles and rectangles and the teacher had not only referred to cakes but drawn circles on the blackboard to show a piece which was one-half and its equivalents.

Mark on interview (I) appealed to the idea of having a cake cut up but he did not draw it; on (PostF) he volunteered to draw circles to show $\frac{10}{26} = \frac{6}{16} = \frac{3}{8}$. He drew a number of pictures but very few conclusions could be drawn by attempting to match parts. Mark on interview (D) also attempted to show with diagrams that $\frac{3}{7} = \frac{2}{5}$ and that $\frac{3}{4}$ did not equal $\frac{6}{8}$. His circles were drawn free hand, and were unequal in size as were the sevenths into which one of them was partitioned. He did however feel that diagrams were helpful. James, interview (D), thought that drawing diagrams helped and tried to compare $\frac{10}{14}$ and $\frac{5}{7}$ by drawing unequal circles partitioned into slices and triangles subdivided by smaller triangles. When asked whether when doing examples he thought of numbers or a diagram, Gary (D) said 'Think of them as numbers'. Bill was the only boy who asked how much pocket money was involved in the $\frac{1}{4}, \frac{5}{20}$ comparison. When shading a quarter of a circle (I) he marked the circle as a clock face with 3, 6, 9, 12... On interview (D) he thought (D) that diagrams helped, 'Because you can shade in...$\frac{6}{8}$ on that and $\frac{3}{4}$...and it would just be the same'. Brett (D) stated 'The diagrams make it easier' but tried and failed to draw a circle which showed $\frac{3}{4}$ equal to $\frac{6}{8}$.

Both teacher and children attempted to show equivalent fractions by partitioning circles which were drawn free hand and unlikely to be congruent. The partitioning was not superimposed on an already cut circle. Some children appealed to this method for verification that fractions were equal but the demonstration was inadequate.

Table 4.10 contd

Table 4.10: School 6 performance on equivalence items and addition of fractions

Class A

Interview	Bi I	Bi PreF	Bi PostF	Bi D	Br I	Br PreF	Br PostF	Br D	G I	G PreF	G PostF	G D	J I	J PreF	J PostF	J D	L I	L PreF	L PostF	L D	M I	M PreF	M PostF	M D
Shade 2/3 of 9 squares	✓	×	—	—	✓	×	—	—	—	×	—	—	—	×	—	—	a	a	—	—	—	—	—	—
Compare 1/4 and 5/20	✓	×	✓	✓	✓	×	×	×	✓	×	✓	✓	✓	×	✓	✓	✓	a	✓	✓	✓	✓	✓	✓
An equivalent ◭ (6/16 shaded)	×	×	—	—	×	×	✓	—	—	×	—	—	—	×	—	—	a	a	—	×	—	×	—	—
Another name 6/9																		a						
Equivalents 3/8 6/12 6/11 6/16 10/26 9/24	—	×	×	×	—	×	×	×	—	×	✓	✓	×	×	×	—	a	✓	✓	✓	×	✓	✓	✓
Fill gaps 2/3 4/6 5/9 10/12, 10, 20	✓	p	—	✓	✓	p	—	p	p	p	—	p	p	—	—	—	a	—	✓	✓	p	—	p ×	p ×
Compare 10/14 5/7	—	—	—	×	—	—	—	×	—	—	—	×	—	—	×	✓	a	—	×	×	—	—	✓	✓
3/12 = 1/□	—	×	—	—	—	—	—	×	—	—	—	—	—	—	×	—	a	✓	✓	—	—	✓	✓	—
5 fractions equivalent to 1/3	—	—	✓	—	—	—	✓	—	—	—	✓	—	—	—	×	—	a	✓	✓	—	—	✓	—	—
5 fractions equivalent to 3/7	—	—	✓	—	—	✓	—	—	—	×	×	—	—	—	×	—	a	✓	—	—	—	×	×	×

Table 4.10: cont'd

Class B

Interview	H I	H PreF	H PostF	H D	J I	J PreF	J PostF	J D	L I	L PreF	L PostF	L D	Ma I	Ma PreF	Ma PostF	Ma D	Mi I	Mi PreF	Mi PostF	Mi D	R I	R PreF	R PostF	R D
Shade 2/3 of 9 squares	×	–	–	a	–	–	–	a	–	–	–	–	–	–	–	–	–	–	–	–	–	–	–	–
Compare 1/4 and 5/20	×	×	√	a	×	×	√	a	×	√	√	√	×	√	√	√	√	√	√	√√	√	√	√	√
An equivalent (6/16 shaded)	–	–	–	a	×	–	–	a	×	√	–	×	×	√	–	a	–	–	–	–	–	–	–	–
Another name 6/9	–	×	√	a	–	×	√	a	–	×	√	–	–	×	√	–	a	–	√	a	–	–	√	–
Equivalents 3/8 6/12 6/11 6/16 10/26 9/24	–	×	×	a	–	×	√	√	×	×	√	√	×	×	√	√	a	√	√	√	–	√	√	√
Fill gaps 2/3 4/6 _/9 10/_ 20/_	–	p	–	a	p	–	–	√	–	√	–	√	p	√	√	p	p a	p	–	p	–	p	–	–
Compare 10/14 5/7	–	–	–	a	–	–	–	√	–	√	–	√	–	√	√	×	a	–	√	√	–	√	–	√
Same denominators	–	√	√	a	√	√	–	√	–	√	–	√	–	√	√	–	a	√	√	√	–	√	–	√
Denominators multiples 3/5 + 1/10, 2/8 + 3/4, 9/10 + 3/5	×	×	√	a	×	×	√	× a	×	√	√	×	×	×	√	×	× a	√	√	×	–	√	√	√
Different, non-multiple 2/7 + 1/3	–	–	√	a	×	×	–	–	–	×	–	×	–	√	√	–	a	–	√	√	–	–	–	–
Baker's word problem 3/8 + 2/8	–	–	√	a	–	–	–	√	–	–	–	–	√	√	√	–	a	–	√	√	–	–	√	√
Symbols 5/8 − 2/8	–	–	–	a ×	–	–	–	–	–	–	–	√	–	–	–	–	a	√	√	√	–	–	–	–
Pie pieces and word problem 5/8 − 2/8	–	–	√	a	–	√	–	–	–	√	–	√	–	–	–	×	a	√	√	×	–	√	√	–
Is there an error? 3/4 + 1/2 = 4/4, 2/3 + 3/5 = 5/8	–	×	√	a	√	–	×	–	–	√	–	–	–	–	–	–	a	√	√	–	–	√	√	√

Key

	Class A					Class B
Bi	Bill		H		H	Henry
Br	Brett		J		J	Joe
G	Gary		L		L	Lane
J	James		Ma		Ma	Matt
L	Larry		Mi		Mi	Mick
M	Mark		R		R	Richard

√ correct
✗ partially right, e.g., one equivalent pair / instead of two
× wrong
– not asked
p pattern only reason given
a absent

Child methods and misconceptions

We have already discussed the use of a pattern in forming a series of equivalent fractions and generalizations made by children which resulted in error. Bill divided numerator into denominator which worked sometimes but if there was a remainder, left him comparing remainders. Larry's criteria, on interview (D), for judging equivalence of two fractions had two parts:

(I: Interviewer; L: Larry)
L: 'Cos you see...the 2, it should be an even number...on top because the two's an even number...like...then I look for the 3, then I look for the 9, oh yes, there's another one.
I: Which one?
L: $\frac{3}{7}$ and $\frac{9}{21}$.
I: So you looked for...what sort of number there then?
L: Odd.
I: Okay, and what else did you do?
L: Looked at the bottom to see if it was odd or even...then I said if the one...that was on the top was an odd one...
I: You see 7 is odd as well and so is 19.
L: But 7 don't go into 19.
I: Oh, that 7 on the bottom doesn't go into 19 on the bottom?
L: No.
I: I'm with you, that's another test you apply?
L: Yes.

This same boy however, was the only pupil who referred (PostF) to the multiplier of two on the top and two on the bottom as 'a whole'. Often the rule had become 'double top, halve bottom'. Mark declared that $\frac{6}{15} = \frac{3}{30}$, and when asked 'How did you decide that?' replied 'Well, half that and double that'.

Larry had said $\frac{2}{3} = \frac{1}{6}$ on the same occasion 'Because you can take one away from that...half that, then just...double that and it will be $\frac{1}{6}$'. Brett (D) declared $\frac{2}{5} = \frac{1}{10}$ but later changed his mind. He had thought immediately after the lesson that $\frac{3}{9}$ equalled $\frac{6}{18}$ but that $\frac{6}{18}$ did not equal $\frac{9}{27}$, since his method was to try to multiply 6 to obtain 9.

The method for obtaining equivalent fractions taught in the observed lesson was to multiply top and bottom by the same number. Table 4.11 shows that only Larry consistently used this method (PostF), i.e. just after it had been taught, and that nobody had retained the method for consistent use three months later (D) although Larry used division of top and bottom as a replacement.

James on the last interview, (D), said $\frac{1}{2} = \frac{2}{4}$ (spoken) because on a clock two fifteens made 30 and 30 was half an hour. Gary (PostF) had misremembered a rule and stated the following:

(I: Interviewer; G: Gary)
I: 3 over 12 equals 1 over what?
G: 1.
I: 1 over 1. And how did you know that?
G: Because whatever the top part...whatever the top number is, the bottom number has got to be exactly the same.
I: Mmm...so that...what has it got to be the same.
G: Because it's got to be the...same amount as each other.
I: Mmm...
G: Because like if it was 2 over 1, it would be a top heavy fraction.

Table 4.11: Multiplicative methods used to generate equivalent fractions – School 6, Class A

	PostF	*D*	
Brett	× ? ? × 0 √ √ √ √	× × × × ×	
Gary	√ √ × × × × × × × ×	× × 0 √ √ ?	
James	× × × 0 0	× × × × × × ×	
Mark	√ × × × × × × × ×	? × × × × × × ×	
Bill	× × × × √ √ √ √	× × × × √	
Larry	√ √ √ √ √ √ √ √ ?	× √ × × × ×	(3 are division of top and bottom.)

Multiplicative method interpreted as 'multiply top and multiply bottom'.
Key × Signifies non-multiplicative methods including guessing.
    0 Omission by child because he cannot attempt the question.
    ? The method is unknown or the interviewer's questions prompted the response.

Discussion

On the initial interview (I), the boys could show the region corresponding to a fraction if the denominator was the same as the number of sections available, but only two could show ⅔ if 9 squares were given. The formalization lesson demonstration of equality was based on circles drawn and partitioned free hand and showing the 'fraction family' for one-half. We have seen before that this use of circles does not provide the equivalence although it might illustrate a fact already known. The teacher made no mention of the boys manipulating materials or cutting regions and the diagrams in their textbooks were the embodiments used. The results show that immediately after the teaching (PostF), only one child consistently used a multiplicative method to obtain equivalent fractions and that three months later (D), he had changed to a division method. The boys invented many ways of getting one fraction from another and some of these methods, although perhaps working for one pair, fell down when applied more generally.

School 6, Class B (aged 11–12)

The scheme of work

Class B was the top set of five in the first year of a London comprehensive boys' school. The six boys interviewed were Matt, Richard, Joe, Lane, Mick and Henry. The teaching sequence was planned to lead to addition of fraction rules and was the first work on fractions the boys had done since they left primary school. The teacher kept very close to the sequence of events outlined in the textbook (see Table 4.6). The scheme entailed no manipulation of objects, discs or bricks, but there were many diagrams in the textbook.

There were five lessons of 45 minutes each in the teaching sequence. The formalization (observed) lesson, lesson 5, concerned the methodology to be used by the boys when required to add two fractions with different denominators. The questions asked in the interviews however were used to cover a wide range of fractional ideas: (a) models used to display the meaning of fractions, (b) equivalence and (c) three types of addition of fractions.

Formalization lesson

During the formalization lesson (see Table 4.12) the teacher reviewed a number of fractional ideas which appeared to have been formalized previously by the teacher during the teaching sequence or they were assumed to have been completed prior to the boys' arrival at the school.

The lesson could be considered as the one which provided a general rule. This fact was not pointed out to the children who during the course of the lesson also reviewed how to add fractions (a) with the same denominator and (b) when one denominator was a multiple of the other.

Table 4.12: The formalization lesson – addition of fractions – School 6, Class B

(1) Review of cancelling – fractions in their lowest form are recommended as most useful. Check by carrying out opposite operation.

(2) Review of addition of two fractions with same denominator (teacher says this was 'done' the previous week, i.e. during teaching sequence). Child quotes rule as 'you add the other two numbers' and this is accepted.

(3) Review of addition of two fractions with different denominators – 'which fraction did we decide last week needed to be altered? . . . The one with the smaller bottom number.' The example is 3/4 + 1/8 and doubling is suggested. The children quote the rule 'whatever you do to the bottom one you have to do to the top'.

(4) As a review of the rationale behind changing 3/4 into eighths, the teacher talks of a cake being cut into slices – no diagram is drawn. When adding fractions the two numerators are joined above a line with the denominators written below, e.g. $\frac{6 + 1}{8}$.

(5) Introduction of a method where one denominator is not a multiple of the other.

(6) The teacher appeals again to the idea of a cake in order to elicit how many twelfths there are in 3/4. Then he asks for a multiplication method.

(7) To find the equivalent fraction the child is told to divide old denominator into new and to use this number as a multiplier. The resulting fractions are written as $\frac{9 + 10}{12}$ (from $\frac{3}{4} + \frac{5}{6}$, without an intermediate step of $\frac{9}{12} + \frac{10}{12}$).

(8) Children are encouraged to cancel and to change the results into mixed numbers.

(9) A new example is illustrated by reference to a cut cake and to multiplication by a found factor, then a line is drawn and the common denominator put in place.

(10) Examples from the textbook are set for the class to do.

The teacher talked of equivalent fractions and required the class to state the value of the multiplier which would give an appropriate equivalent fraction. The setting out of the answer however had a line drawn and a number underneath, i.e. $\frac{9 + 10}{12}$ rather than $\frac{9}{12} + \frac{10}{12}$. For most answers the teacher preferred the fraction to be given in its lowest form. He used expressions such as 'Easier to undersand', 'It's quicker', 'I still don't like it' (of non-cancelled fractions), 'What is a better way of writing it?'. To provide a more convincing demonstration of equivalence the teacher referred verbally to the cutting of a cake into pieces, but he did not draw a cake and show a matching of pieces. This use of a region model was different to that quoted for School 5 where the 'cake' was always drawn and sections matched by size.

Teaching outcomes

FRACTION EMBODIMENTS

As with the primary aged children the boys were asked on the first interview to name fractions, as shown in Table 4.8 (page 61). Three of the boys thought that the name of any fraction was three-quarters and were likely to further add that $2/3 = 3/4$. Henry wrote three-quarters as 3 and similarly 2 for $2/3$. Note that Joe and Henry were only able to recognize and draw a quarter of a circle and yet could mark the number $3/4$ on the number line. Richard distinguished between the two uses of $3/4$:

(I: Interviewer; R: Richard)
R: Oh, it's about there.
I: Right, now what's the difference?
R: I thought it was $3/4$ of it.
I: Is there a difference then between the number $3/4$ and $3/4$ of it?
R: A lot of difference, yes.
I: Ah, good can you explain to me what?
R: $3/4$ of the whole thing would be 3 places out of 4, whereas this is only 3 places out of 1 little piece.

At interview (D) all the boys could name the fraction of the triangle which was shaded (shown in Table 4.4) but at (I), the initial interview, only Richard and Peter could do so.

EQUIVALENCE

The teacher alluded to equivalence prior to teaching the rule for addition of fractions with different denominators. Since this relationship forms a cornerstone of operations upon fractions the boys were asked the type of question shown in Table 4.4. Table 4.10 (page 64) shows the performance at each interview on items which concerned equivalent fractions. The profiles for Mick and Henry are incomplete because they were absent on one or more interviews. Four profiles show a deficient understanding of the principle of equivalence prior to the formalization lesson, which was on addition of fractions and in which equivalence was used. Joe, Matt, Henry and Mick tackled the series of equivalent fractions ($2/3$, $4/6$, $6/9$, etc.) by looking at the increments in the numerator and denominator, whilst Richard said they were all $2/3$ and Lane eventually after tortuously obtaining $8/12$ given $2/3$, $4/6$, said '$2/3$ in all of them'. Matt further (PostF) stated $9/24 = 10/26$ because the pattern was continued in this way.

All the boys present at interview (D) were asked whether $10/14$ was double $5/7$ or equal to it. Four children declared the two fractions equal, appealing to the fact that two times five gave ten, etc. Mick thought saying they were equal was a better answer but one could be double the other. Matt however thought that $10/14$ was both equal to and double $5/7$. His reasons were interesting in that they did not include multiplication:

(I: Interviewer; M: Matt)
I: So they are both true are they: $10/14$ths is double $5/7$ths and $10/14$ths is equal to $5/7$ths?
M: Yes.
I: What about this one? $10/14$ths is more than $5/7$ths?
M: That's false.
I: How do you know that?
M: Because that can't be the same as that. If that is true then that would be false.
I: What about this one?
M: $10/14$ths, you just add them: add that and you get 10 and add that you get 14.

Matt (PreF) had produced a rule to justify the equivalence of $3/8$ and $6/16$ appealing to one-half as a standard amount to which they approximated 'Because if... that was two more than would be eight, which would be half of sixteen...

ADDITION OF FRACTIONS

On the first interview (I) the boys were asked verbally to find the total fraction of a bag of flour used in a bakery when three-eighths had been used for bread and two-eighths for cakes. Of the four who were asked the question three answered correctly (see Table 4.10, page 64) although when extended to a word problem requiring the subtraction of $\frac{2}{8}$ from $\frac{5}{8}$ Joe initially gave the answer $\frac{3}{0}$:

(I: Interviewer; J: Joe)
J: Just, um... like... $\frac{5}{8}$ take away $\frac{2}{8}$ is... $\frac{3}{8}$.
I: Super.
J: No, I mean... just 3.
I: It's just 3... or is it $\frac{3}{8}$?
J: 3... 3 nothing... 3 over nothing.

Table 4.10 shows the varied performance on the addition questions included in each of the four interviews. Matt's attempts at addition were marred by inconsistent strategies. On the second interview (PreF), for example, he added $\frac{3}{4}$ and $\frac{1}{2}$ correctly but for $\frac{2}{8} + \frac{3}{4}$ he obtained four different answers, $\frac{5}{12}$, $\frac{6}{12}$, $\frac{11}{12}$ and finally $\frac{8}{8}$ 'equals one'. Three months later (D), he had adopted the popular but erroneous rule for $\frac{3}{5} + \frac{7}{10}$, i.e. that of adding numerators and denominators to result in $\frac{10}{15}$ – 'I just added both, I added those two and that came to ten, and added the bottom two and that came to fifteen'. The question $\frac{2}{8} + \frac{3}{4}$ belongs to the type of addition problem in which one denominator is a multiple of the other. When asked to try this example Joe (PreF) adopted the rule which he remembered as 'take the larger':

(I: Interviewer; J: Joe)
I: Let's look at another one then. $\frac{2}{8}$ and $\frac{3}{4}$. What do we do with that one?
J: 1 bar of chocolate... $\frac{2}{8}$ and you add $\frac{3}{4}$, that'd make it $\frac{5}{8}$.
I: Okay, write that down, Joe.
Good, and how did you know it was $\frac{5}{8}$?
J: Because 2 add 3 is 5 and you're adding the 2 onto the 4 and you don't mind about the 4 ... you've got 8.
I: You don't mind about the 4? You don't worry about the 4?
J: Leave it, and then you write $\frac{5}{8}$.
I: Right, okay, well how do you know what number to put at the bottom then, how did you know to put the 8 at the bottom.
J: 'Cos it's the bigger number of the two.

At the final interview Joe drew diagrams (referred to later) to demonstrate that $\frac{10}{15} = \frac{7}{10} + \frac{3}{5}$.

The formalization lesson dealt with addition when the denominators were different and not multiples of each other. Immediately after the lesson all the boys gave the correct answer to $\frac{2}{7} + \frac{1}{3}$. This particular question was not asked on the three-month interview (D), but on that occasion Richard was the only boy of those present who could add $\frac{7}{10}$ and $\frac{3}{5}$. Mick for example chose the common denominator 5 and then obtained the answer $\frac{13}{5}$.

PERCEPTION OF THE MATERIALS

The secondary school boys described in this section had not cut out shapes or used structural material in the lessons leading to addition of fractions. The textbook they used had contained diagrams of circles and rectangles and their teacher had referred to the cutting of a cake into pieces. The pupils were reminded on the final interview (D) that they had used circles and regions in class and then subsequently they had simply said '$\frac{3}{4} = \frac{6}{8}$'. They were then asked if there was any connection between these two activities and if they could show $\frac{3}{4} = \frac{6}{8}$ by using circles. Lane drew two circles (freehand) and in one shaded $\frac{4}{6}$ saying '$\frac{3}{4}$' was the same as $\frac{6}{8}$. The following conversation ensued:

(I: Interviewer; L: Lane)
L: $\frac{6}{8}$ is the same.
I: Well did you draw $\frac{6}{8}$?
L: No...
I: What have you drawn?
L: $\frac{4}{6}$.
I: $\frac{4}{6}$, okay. How would you draw $\frac{6}{8}$.
L: $\frac{6}{8}$... you... it's the same as $\frac{3}{4}$ because you take 6 of them out of 8. 1, 2, 3, 4, 5, 6... and it's the same as $\frac{3}{4}$... it's just cancelled down.
I: When you think of doing it, do you think of the numbers or do you think of the diagram?
L: I think of the numbers.

Richard, who had been successful on all the questions asked, demonstrated using one circle that $\frac{3}{4} = \frac{6}{8}$ but added generally that he did not like using diagrams:

(I: Interviewer; R: Richard) (D)
I: Now, you say you can't get that shape in your head.
R: It... really, numbers picture best in my head... not shapes and um... drawings and things, or diagrams.
I: Don't they help you at all?
R: Sometimes... they do. In um... bar graphs... I... and then they're good but, the pie, the pie charts and things like that I don't really like because, I can't really, you know, it's not a thing that you can see offhand how much unless you've a figure inside. You've got to measure it, you know, with a protractor, to see how much of the whole thing is being used in each segment, so I prefer bar graphs, but really figures... I prefer figures because I can remember them better, than having all these numbers.

We could bear in mind the phrase 'it's not a thing that you can see offhand how much unless you've a figure inside', when considering Matt's attempt shown in part (a) Figure 4.2. He knew $\frac{3}{4} = \frac{6}{8}$ and was illustrating the fact (inaccurately) for the interviewer. In the lesson the teacher had similarly provided an inaccurate sketch of 'a cake' to accompany a known fact. Mick and Lane referred to 'a bar of chocolate' when attempting to illustrate equivalence and Joe (D) who thought that using diagrams had helped him understand, volunteered to demonstrate the result of '$\frac{3}{5} + \frac{7}{10}$' (shown in part (b), Figure 4.2). He thought the answer was $\frac{10}{15}$ as indeed the diagram showed and Joe explained:

(I: Interviewer; J: Joe)
I: So you've drawn a diagram and shaded $\frac{3}{5}$ths, is that right?
J: Yes. Then I'll make it up to 10 now.
I: You're adding on more squares to that diagram.
J: Yes.
I: What are each of those little rectangles worth?
J: 1.
I: They're worth 1 are they? What are you doing now?
J: Shading in 7.
I: 7 what?
J: $\frac{7}{10}$ths...
I: So they're 10ths now are they?
J: Oh yes... shades... and that makes it $\frac{10}{15}$ths.
I: Why are they 15ths?
J: Because it is 5 add 10.
I: I see, and where did the 10 come from, from 3 and 7?
J: Because 3 and 7 is 10.

Figure 4.2: Children's diagrams

(a) Matt's diagram for 3/4 = 6/8

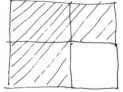
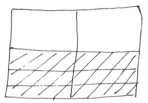

(b) Joe's diagram for 3/5 + 7/10 = 10/15

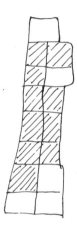

Mick volunteered (PreF) and (PostF) to demonstrate equivalence by drawing bars of chocolate (unequal sized pieces) and on the final interview he attempted to show equivalent fractions using different sized and badly drawn circles. He was initially enthusiastic 'when the question is a little bit hard, and you do a diagram, or if it's sort of easy, then you do it in your head', but eventually had to admit, 'I don't know how you'd put that on the diagram though ...it's not right...but that's equal...half is equal to that and that is equal to that, 'cos it's double'. His diagram did not show the equivalence which he already knew through symbols.

Between the teaching and the final interview the boys did some work on plotting (numerator, denominator) pairs on graph paper, this they also volunteered to show, as a demonstration of equivalence.

Child methods and misconceptions

The various misconceptions concerning fractions displayed by the children have been reported in each section. There were various adaptations of the rules of addition, i.e. (a) take the larger denominator (true only for multiples), (b) forget the other denominator. Equivalent fractions were found by adding the numerator to itself, the new denominator was found by the same method. As with the other two classes, given a series of equivalent fractions new ones were found from the pattern of numerators and denominators by adding a constant difference. The method gives correct results as long as the gap between terms is not large. A drawback of this reasoning however was demonstrated by Mick (D) who rejected the idea of any equivalent pairs in $\frac{3}{7}$, $\frac{2}{5}$, $\frac{5}{8}$, $\frac{7}{19}$, $\frac{9}{21}$, $\frac{20}{50}$ because there was no obvious pattern of numerators or denominators.

Discussion

Just prior to the start of teaching only one of the boys in the interviewed group could give more than one model for a fraction. In fact four of them could not consistently give the conventional name for a region. The teaching period was of short duration and relied on few diagrammatic representations of equivalence before the presentation of the rules for addition of fractions. These were presented as three distinct algorithms when (a) denominators were the same, (b) one denominator was a multiple of the other and (c) a common denominator was needed.

The boys tended to look for an addition pattern when faced with a series of equivalent fractions and at least one child rejected fractions which were equivalent because they did not form such a pattern. When they were asked to demonstrate equivalence, the diagrams they drew simply illustrated facts they knew and were inadequate for showing the equivalence if it was not already known.

Richard, the boy with the best success rate on each interview, admitted that he did not find most diagrams very useful. The others stated that they thought that pictures were useful but then failed to use diagrams in any useful way. Their 'cakes' and rectangles were appealed to for giving extra weight but were always drawn inaccurately and so did not clearly demonstrate relationships about fractions.

Performance after three months on the matching of individual pairs of fractions was quite good. The answers to addition questions tended to be correct on the third interview, immediately after the observed lesson, but only one boy was obtaining correct answers three months later. Adaptations of the algorithm had taken place and the method of addition being quoted was generally incorrect.

Summary

The three classes described in this chapter were trying to learn the general rule for obtaining equivalent fractions; one group, a top set in secondary school, went further and was introduced to the addition of fractions. The primary school class spent two weeks on the topic whilst each secondary class spent only one week. The use of materials was different for each age group.

The use of materials

The primary class spent time in cutting and colouring region models to represent a fraction, finding subsets of sets of objects and making fraction boards on which parts of a whole were matched. From these examples of familiar fractions, statements of equivalence were made. During the formalization lessons two embodiments were used and symbolic statements written to demonstrate 'families of fractions'. From these the teacher obtained the rule which was stated in terms of both multiplication and division. The secondary classes (first year) had no experience of manipulation of objects during the teaching sequence but they were given examples which used diagrams. The boys did not draw the diagrams themselves and when during the formalization lessons the teacher provided an illustration it was always of a circular 'cake' drawn freehand. All three teachers appealed to the evidence of the materials or rough diagrams as being particularly noteworthy or more convincing than a verbal statement. The primary school teacher offered to leave the material available after practice on the rule had been given, so that it could be used if a child 'needed' it.

During the interviews the children demonstrated their use of diagrams and the primary school children were asked to demonstrate the use of materials to show the equivalence of two unfamiliar fractions. In all three interview samples there were children who volunteered to demonstrate the truth of a statement by producing a diagram. These were drawn freehand and illustrated only in a very general way what the child already knew. When diagrams were used to actually produce the equivalence they were inadequate (see for example Terence in Class A, School 5). In order to produce the evidence of equivalence from drawn diagrams one must have (a) accuracy in drawing and (b) a knowledge of how many subdivisions are needed.

Three months after the teaching the younger children were asked to demonstrate that $\frac{1}{7}$ equalled $\frac{2}{14}$ using materials. None of those in the interview sample were able to do this. There is thus evidence that it is not a straightforward task to set up a diagram or a physical model to demonstrate an equivalence one does not already know or which is unfamiliar. When asked about diagrams the secondary school children often said that they found these visual illustrations useful but in fact they did not demonstrate this use.

When asked to reflect on their learning experiences three months after the teaching some children denied ever having used materials. One (successful) secondary school boy indicated that he preferred working with figures over working with diagrams.

Teaching outcomes

In two clases the intention of the teaching was that the children should be able to use a multiplicative rule for obtaining a fraction equivalent to another. In the primary school, the two children who could give another name for a region prior to the series of lessons, were the only pupils (of the seven) who successfully produced equivalent fractions after the lesson (PostF), and three months later (D). Two others were able to produce some equivalent fractions after the lessons. However three of the children were unable to obtain correct answers to half the questions set, three months after the teaching. A notable feature of the sample from Class A in School 6 (secondary) was that only one boy consistently used multiplication to obtain equivalent fractions just after the teaching, and three months later even he had adapted the method. No boy in the interview sample from this class obtained correct answers to all the equivalence questions asked on the final interview (see Table 4.10). The other secondary school class was asked questions on equivalence and only two consistently gave the correct answers to these questions just prior to the lesson on addition (which was based on the use of equivalent fractions). The interview samples from all three classes preferred an approach which involved an additive or table pattern of numerators and denominators when given a series of equivalent fractions.

The interview sample from the group of children who were taught a rule for addition were successful immediately after the lesson when given fractions to add, but only one boy was still successful three months later.

Most of the children in the three classes demonstrated a lack of understanding of equivalence three months after the teaching.

Fraction models

Prior to the teaching all three samples (n = 19) were asked to name regions, give a fraction name to a subset and mark the fraction $\frac{3}{4}$ on a number line. Fifteen children out of the 19 interviewed marked a length equal to three-quarters of the line segment rather than $\frac{3}{4}$ as a number between 0 and 1. Not all the children (at the initial interview) could name a shaded region and some had their own notation. The primary school children improved their performance in naming a region, over the teaching period during which time, of course, they were using this model.

Conclusion

In each class most of the children did not adopt the multiplicative rule for generating equivalent fractions. Although the sample investigated was small the distinction between the approach of the primary teacher and the secondary teachers to the problem of presenting a valid reason for the rule is noticeable. Many of the primary school children go on to this comprehensive school and their second attempt at understanding equivalence is likely to be that as described for School 6. In all the classes success in generating or testing equivalent fractions was only guaranteed if the underlying principle of two fractions being equivalent was already understood (or at least demonstrated) prior to the lessons – so in the situation described, there is a group of children who end up failing on both occasions.

Of general interest and worth consideration by teachers is the use children made of diagrams and materials when they wished to show (or find) a pair of equivalent fractions. Strategies on how to set up the materials or how to draw a diagram were not available to the children and what was produced was of use only if the child already knew the answer to the problem.

Chapter 5
Circumference of a Circle
Kathleen Hart

Introduction

Throughout their years in the primary school children see and use circular objects. They draw circles, initially by tracing round a lid or a cylinder and then with a pair of compasses. They are aware that discs can be rolled and when area is introduced the fact that circles do not tessellate is a point of interest. Perimeter and area of a rectangle are usually studied before the comparable measurements of a circle and so children have met formulae prior to that used for the circumference of a circle.

The general statement that the circumference of a circle can be expressed as $2\pi r$ or πd and the approximate length found from that calculation, is the formalization discussed in this chapter. The understanding of the general statement requires the child to recognize that there is a multiplicative relationship involving the radius and to accept the existence of a factor π which they cannot evaluate.

The sample

The teachers of classes in two coeducational middle schools (age range 9–13) volunteered to provide the sample which studied the circumference of a circle and the realization of π. The class sizes were 25 (School 7, Class A) and 28 (School 8, Class A) and interviews were with six children, aged 11–12, from each class.

Both teachers used worksheets during the teaching sequence and in each case the class was taught as one unit. Each group of children interviewed was chosen to represent a range of attainment.

Analysis

The intention of the research was to monitor the transition from using materials to the accepted use of $2\pi r$ (or πd) as a method of finding the circumference of a circle. The children were interviewed four times, before the teaching began (I), just before the formalization lesson (PreF), just after this lesson (PostF) and three months later (D). On each occasion the samples were asked a number of questions related to ideas that had arisen in the scheme of work or in the formalization lesson. They were also asked how to find the circumference of (i) a cylinder and (ii) a drawn circle. The two problems vary in that a cylinder can be rolled or circled with string whereas both these aspects are difficult to achieve with a drawn circle. The diameter of a drawn circle is easier to measure however since folding will produce it as a line of symmetry.

School 7, Class A (aged 11–12)

School 7 was a middle school in a London suburb and the children interviewed were Ellen, Ronald, Don, Ann, Nigel and Tracy who were aged 11–12 years, at the time of the teaching. There were five lessons of about one hour each.

The scheme of work

The teaching scheme rewritten from the teacher's notes is shown in Table 5.1. It uses many of the suggestions made in *Curriculum Bulletin No. 1* (1965). The recognition of the multiplicative relationship is a generalization within the teaching sequence. The formalization at the end of the series of lessons concerned π and the formula $C = \pi d$ or $C = 2\pi r$.

Table 5.1: Scheme of work for School 7, Class A

Prerequisites

It was assumed that the following ideas were not new to the children although some revision would be required.
(I)   Knowledge of the terms – diameter, radius, circumference, and that $d = 2r$, $r = \frac{1}{2}d$
(II)   Conservation of length.
(III)   Circumference seen as distance round but also measured linearly.
(IV)   The fact that the cross-section of a cylinder is a circle.
(V)   The ability to measure to nearest cm.
(VI)   Knowledge of coordinates and relationship graphs.
(VII)   Appreciation that $A = 3B$ implies $B = A/3$.

Lessons

(1)   Collection of circular objects of diameters 1, 2, 3, 4 dm. Measurement of the circumferences, each stated as n and 'a bit' diameters after estimation. Discussion of measurement of circumference by marking and rolling and also with a strip of paper stretched round a tin lid.
(2)   Emphasis on multiplicative relationship. Measuring circumference to nearest cm.
(3)   Teacher demonstrates that 3 strips each the length of the diameter will go round the cylinder and leave a small space. Children repeat this activity with all 12 cylinders.
(4)   Circle drawing and patterns (an ongoing activity).
(5)   Making graphs. Diameter on x axis. Length of ribbon which is the length of circumference parallel to y axis. Discussion of the pattern made by the ends of the ribbon, line of best fit drawn.
(6)   Graphs drawn of 3 and 4 times diameter.

Formalization lesson

The lesson in which π was defined and discussed came after four lessons in which the children had been measuring the diameters and circumferences of cylinders. The lesson was of nearly an hour's duration and contained a number of different aspects. The details as recorded and observed by the researcher are shown in Table 5.2

The teacher presented many facts in the formalization lesson and the importance of these to the children is illustrated below. The children were 'taught' the formula for the circumference of a circle on Friday and the (PostF) interviews were on the following Monday.

THE VALUE OF π

Each child was asked 'This sign, π, was on your blackboard. Can you tell me what it means?' The responses below indicate different interpretations of '3 and a bit' and how to use it, the practical work having suggested that the circumference was more than three diameters. The letter π was new to the children and the teacher spent some time explaining that the value of it had been investigated by mathematicians. Ellen said for π:

(I: Interviewer; E: Ellen)
E: It means Pi and it means if you have a number and there are several of them ... say 35 numbers all going along, if you had something like, say 3.000, no ... 3.5555, 35 times afterwards, then it would be π. Because it's a large number following afterwards.

Table 5.2: Formalization lesson – School 7, Class A

---

(1) Revision of circumference as three and a 'bit' diameters.

(2) Worksheets given out. They show a drawing of hexagon inscribed in a circle which in turn is inscribed in a square. The teacher reminds the class that the hexagon edge is the length of the radius. The children are asked for the length of the hexagon perimeter.

(3) After questioning five children, the hexagon perimeter is stated as three times a diameter. The circle perimeter must be a little more than three times the diameter.

(4) The teacher points out that the perimeter of the square is four times the diameter. The circumference of a circle is more than 3 diameters and less than 4 diameters.

(5) The second worksheet shows a circle circumscribed by a decagon and having a decagon inscribed in it. The children are asked to find the perimeters of the two decagons, then the circle is said to be half way between. Calculators are given out.

(6) The two decagon perimeters are measured as 10×4.1 and 10×4.3. The teacher says that the circle circumference is therefore 42 cm (half way between). The children are asked to find how many times the diameter this is, using calculators.

(7) A child asks 'Take away?' and a brief interchange with other children elicits that the calculation to be done is a division, $42 \div 13.4$.

(8) The teacher suggests that the calculator result be rounded to nearest 100th. The teacher takes 3.13 as the amount and says we are 'getting very close to this "little bit" we have been looking for'.

(9) The teacher explains the contents of the information sheet given to the children. This gives a brief history of π, seen first as $3\frac{1}{7}$, then 3.1416, then a 'number with 35 numbers after the decimal point' and finally 'computers have worked out its value to many thousands of decimal places'. For class use, π is taken to nearest hundredth, 3.14 or $3\frac{1}{7}$.

(10) The children *calculate* the circumference of all the cylinders previously used, writing the results in tabular form.

(11) Circumference written as πd ('they just put the two signs together like that and it means multiply').

(12) Circumference can be $\pi \times 2$ radii. In response to a child's question the teacher explains that the multiplication can be done in any order.

(13) Ellen (in sample) says circumference is double the diameter. The teacher reviews previous measuring experience with her and explains privately to her about 3.14.

(14) The children are asked to take measurements of circumference of cylinders found previously and divide by the diameter to find the closeness to 3.14. The teacher goes round class to offer help.

I: Is it a large number following anything, or does it always follow after 3?
E: No, I don't think it could follow any number.
I: Could you give me another value of π then? You say it's 3.5555.
E: No, it just means the number after the point goes on and on and on for about 35 times.
I: And that's called π? The number after the point? Or the fact that...
E: That's if it's a long number. You have to round it off.
I: Well, if I had 7.66666, could that be called π?
E: Yes.

Nigel thought that π was 'the bit' that needed to be added to the result of multiplying by three.

(I: Interviewer; N: Nigel)
N: Sorry, 3.14.
I: And you want to multiply 3 centimetres by that? 3 cm is the diameter is it?
N: It is, yes. Then you times 3 cm by 3 which gives you 9 cm, then you add the 3.14 which gives you 12.14.

[Later when asked for the circumference when the radius is 7 cm.]

N: Sorry, the radius is 7, so you need 2 radii to make a diameter 7 times 2 equals 14, then you times 14 by 3 which is 42.

I: Right.

N: Then you add the 3.14.

I: When you times it by 3, why do you do that?

I: Well, we did an experiment in science and made estimates. It wasn't twice as much as the diameter, it wasn't 3 times as much and it wasn't 4 times as much. It was in between 3 times and 4 times as much, and it was Pi.

On a closer analysis of the teacher's statements she had said (amongst a great many other things)

Therefore the circumference is approximately 3.13 times the diameter – that's what your calculator has just told you. Now that is getting very close to this 'little bit' we have been looking for, .13, 3.13, getting very close to this little bit we have been trying to get an accurate estimate of. In fact, so close, as close as I could get drawing pictures. This is the bit we mentioned yesterday briefly, what we have been calling pi.

Ann described π as below and drew a diagram to show three line graphs, through an origin and of different slopes.

(I: Interviewer; A: Ann)

A: It's called a pi and if we had...say 3 lines, the middle line would be called pi. I think something like that.

I: Show me.

A: If you had a graph, there's *[draws graph]* and the line went like that and then you had another line went like that and another line went like that and another line went like that. This one would be called the pi line. *[Points to 'one in the middle'.]*

I: Ah, how about those two? What would they be called?

A: Nothing really.

I: Nothing really, alright. What are they used for then?

A: Um...instead of writing a lot of numbers you write pi.

I: Any numbers?

A: I don't think so.

I: Does it have any sort of value?

A: Yes, I think so.

Ronald and Tracy stated that π was 3.14 and used it as a multiplier of the diameter to find the circumference. There was no record of Don's response (PostF). Three of the six children interviewed therefore, even though they had experienced the same lesson, had each selected a different point made in the lesson and interpreted that further.

Teaching outcomes

THE CIRCLE

The main objective of the series of lessons was the acquisition by the pupils of a formal method (using π) to find the circumference of a circle. The teacher had stated that a prerequisite of the teaching was the children's knowledge of the terms used to describe parts of a circle. On the first interview (I) all of them knew the meaning of circle, centre and circumference; Ann and Tracy were confused over radius and diameter but the others were not. At the second interview they were asked how they would describe a circle to a Martian. Four children said it was 'like a full moon' and went on to say they would provide an example such as a wheel. Ronald extended his reply to include a more abstract but fundamental idea not stated by the others.

(I: Interviewer; R: Ronald)

R: I'd say it was a round.

I: Ah, but he doesn't know what round means.

R: Oh yes...I'd say...if I had something, I'd show it to him, but...a circle is...a shape that...instead of having line for its sides...well it hasn't really got any sides. It just has one continuous line that joins in one place.

I: Alright, now my line...I think that gives me a clue, but my Martian says, oh, you mean...like that. [*Interviewer draws* ⬭ *, an oval.*]

R: No, the distance from each...the distance from each side...the diameter should be...

I: Well I can ask you what the diameter is...

R: Well the...if you had a centre point, in the centre of the circle, the diameter should be exactly the same...

THE CIRCUMFERENCE

At each interview the children were also asked to find the circumference firstly of a cylinder and then a drawn circle which on the last two interviews was shown with centre and radius ($r = 7$ cm). Table 5.3 includes a summary of the response data for the circumference of the cylinder for the children in each of the four interviews.

Table 5.3: School 7, Class A responses for circumference of a circle and circumference of a cylinder

Type of response	Cylinder				Circle			
	I	PreF	PostF	D	I	PreF	PostF	D
πd or 2πr			R	E R			D N R	D E N R T
diameter/radius used	A D* N R T	N	T	A N	A D E N R T	A	E T	A
string	A E N R T	A D E N R	A E N T	E N R T				E
rolling		A	A N R T					
other					A D R T	E R		
no attempt								

* Don, cylinder, data only reported for PreF interview.

Interviews

Key
A Ann
D Don
E Ellen
N Nigel
R Ronald
T Tracy

arranged

A D E
N R T

The responses are not intended to indicate any particular order, i.e. that one is better, or worse, than another, except that the formula is marked at the top, that being the aim of the lessons. 'Rolling' means that the child suggested the cylinder be rolled along a ruler, the starting and finishing points being marked. 'String' means that the child suggested winding a piece of string or tape around the cylinder, then measuring the length with a ruler. On occasion the child would want to use the diameter but be unable to find it, or suggest that one obtained the circumference, by multiplying the diameter by three; this is denoted by 'Diameter Used'. Note that on the final interview all the children had at least two available methods for finding the circumference of a cylinder.

Table 5.3 also includes the responses when the group was asked for the circumference of a drawn circle. After the formalization lesson three children used πd to find the circumference. The three girls were still using '3 and a bit'.

Ellen's use of three radii for finding the circumference was thus:

> E: And if you could take that out and measure it round and round and round 3 times, there should be a little gap there and you measure that and add it onto 3 times 7 equals 21, so adds the little gap onto 21.

Ann multiplied diameter by three and said 'estimated', Tracy multiplied by three when asked to find the circumference of the drawn circle but later in the same interview offered, 'If you times π by the diameter you get the circumference'. All but Ann could suggest the use of the formula at the final interview (D), when the circle with which they were presented was marked with centre and radius. Note that by (D) the favoured method was the formula and the practical methods had been discarded unlike attempts at the cylinder example.

NOTATION

During the formalization lesson when asking the children to draw up a table from their measurements of a cylinder the teacher had written πd and said, 'Because that is a very quick way of writing pi times the diameter and that is the way you will see it written in a lot of your maths books. They just put the two signs together like that and it means multiply.' She went on to remind them that they had met formulae before when dealing with the area of a floor. At (PostF) the sample was asked for the meaning of πd and $2\pi r$. Ann did not know the meaning of $2\pi r$ and suggested three times the diameter for πd. Ellen said $2\pi r$ meant '2 times π and the radius'; for πd she said 'the diameter is π . . . it's very very long'.

The conversation with Nigel concerning $2\pi r$ and πd went as follows:

> (I: Interviewer; N: Nigel)
> N: Um . . . 2 radius . . . I think, oh 2 pi radiuses.
> I: What does it mean, 2 pi radiuses. What would you do with the 2, what would you do with the pi? What would you do with the radiuses?
> N: Two radius equals the diameter and pi . . . I think you add it in.
> I: Does that say add it in then?
> N: No.
> I: What does that say then, if somebody asked you to translate.
> N: I've forgotten. We did this last Friday.
> I: So if you had that and I want you to translate that.
> N: That's pi plus the diameter.
> I: Alright.
> N: Pi plus the radius. Pi plus 2 of the radius.

Ron after further questions thought the operation being used was multiplication but initially stated '2 times 3.14 equals the radius'. The children's remembrance of the exact meaning of the algebraic notation varied considerably.

PERCEPTION OF THE MATERIALS

The children were asked on the final interview, whether they saw any connection between the activities involving the measurement of circles and the formula. Summary information for

School 7, Class A in Table 5.3 shows that they had two practical methods of finding the circumference of a cylinder still available three months after the teaching. Nigel referred to 'Well the class researched and did a load of work and that was the nearest we could get to it' when asked how he knew $\pi = 3.14$. When asked how he would advise a new boy on finding the circumference of a circle he said:

(I: Interviewer; N: Nigel)

N: Well, I'd tell him that... well I'd explain that the diameter of a circle is um... is... well, the diameter... there's two radius that make up the diameter.

N: And I'd tell him what pi was, which was 3.14. I'd tell him to find the circumference, you would times the diameter by 3.14. It doesn't matter whether it was a large circle or small circles.

I: So whatever the diameter was, you'd just multiply by pi.

N: Yes.

I: And what if he was a bit of a strange fellow and he said to you, just to be difficult, 'but why do I want to multiply it by this number', where does it come from, is it a magic trick ... what would you say to him.

N: I don't know.

I: Would you use the string at all or would you use the rolling out in any way?

N: Yes, I'd show him that and say...

I: And how would you connect the length with... the rolled out length, with the diameter?

N: ... I don't know.

Don and Ronald said that they would tell the new boy the formula and that would be sufficient. Ellen said she would rather use the string to find the circumference and would explain

(I: Interviewer; E: Ellen)

I: If a new girl came to your class, how would you explain what you were doing?

E: Just say that we were trying to find the circumference of a circle, and tell her what ... and I'd just say to her the ways that you can find the circumference by it.

I: And which way would you tell her?

E: Well, I'd show her both ways and see what one she preferred. But I prefer... well, doing it by string, but if you want more of an accurate answer you'd have to do it by timesing.

I: I see. And how would you describe pi to her? What would you tell her pi was?

E: Very, very large number that goes on... goes on and on and on, really.

I: And do you know where it came from?

E: Um... no, I think I've learnt it, but I can't remember.

Ann thought the measurement of cylinders was quite helpful but the 'new girl' would not need to use it. Tracy said she would instruct a new child to multiply π by a number, the length of the diameter. She might also explain the 'rolling method' but was unable to explain any connection between the two. Although some of the sample said they thought the measurement activities were helpful, the demonstration (through measuring cylinders) that the existence and value of π were reasonable was not mentioned.

Misconceptions

Prior to the sequence of lessons nobody mentioned π although Don did suggest that to find the circumference: 'If you times the radius by the diameter, that would be your answer.' 'Yes I learnt it in school.'

Two children thought a good method of finding the circumference was to use a pair of compasses, an interesting suggestion since these were used to draw the circle initially.

School 8, Class A (aged 11–12)

School 8 was a middle school and the class involved in the research contained 25 boys and girls aged 11–12 years who were taught as a class. The six children interviewed were chosen to represent a range of attainment within the streamed class which was considered to be 'top average'. They were called Laura, Sally, Bob, Raymond, Sam and Jane. There were four double lessons and a single lesson of about 35 minutes.

The scheme of work

The teaching scheme described in Table 5.4 was based on exercises from the textbook used in the school as well as the teacher's own ideas. Within the sequence of lessons on circumference, one period was devoted to computational practice. It was during this lesson that children were withdrawn for the (PreF) interview.

Table 5.4: Scheme of work – School 8, Class A

---

(1) Examples to elicit responses of terms perimeter and area. The terms circumference, radius and diameter introduced. Children given instructions on how to draw circles using a pair of compasses and then set to draw some with given radii.
(2) Children asked to measure diameters of drawn circles and give results in a table showing radius and diameter. The relationship $(2r = d, \frac{1}{2}d = r)$ written on board. Children asked to draw circles with given diameter.
(3) Method of finding the diameter of a cylinder by drawing a square to circumscribe the base, taught and practised.
(4) Circles drawn and folded, to introduce terms semi-circle, quadrant, sector, segment, chord. Discussion on difference between diameter and chord.
(5) Rolling and string methods for finding the circumference of cylinder introduced and used on cylinders by children.
(6) Formalization lesson.

Formalization lesson

The lesson in which π was defined and discussed came after four lessons dealing with the names of parts of circles, drawing circles and measuring the circumference of cylinders by two practical methods. The connection between the lengths of diameter and circumference was not discussed until the formalization lesson and so the multiplicative relationship was also introduced at this time. A summary of the researcher's observation and tape of the lesson(s) is given in Table 5.5.

Teaching outcomes

THE CIRCLE

The object of the series of lessons was the learning and use of the formula πd or $2\pi r$ for finding the circumference of a circle. Part of the teaching however was intended to make the children familiar with names for various parts of the circle. Before the teaching started, Jane, Bob and Raymond knew the meaning of 'circle, centre, radius, circumference' and that the radii were all the same length. Laura and Sally did not know 'radius' or 'circumference' and Sam called it the edge (he also called the centre, 'the vertex'). Asked (PreF) how they would describe a circle to a Martian, Raymond and Jane said they would describe the names of the parts of a circle. Jane said she would show him something round and Sam would have drawn a circle in the air to demonstrate, but on being shown a counter example, he added 'It's got an edge'...'um...equal all round from the centre'...'From the middle, it's all the same...'.

Table 5.5: Formalization lessons – School 8, Class A

---

(1) Worksheets given out and children told that they can use any materials they wish and any method of solution. The task was to measure the circumference and corresponding diameter of a range of cylinders (8) and to write the results in tabular form.

(2) The teacher went round class giving individual advice to members of the class. She reminded some children of how to find the diameter of a cylinder by drawing round it and then circumscribing a rectangle around the circle. She recommended others to find the circumference by using a strip of paper and a pin. She questioned measurements written as decimals or in millimetres.

(3) The teacher had a more general discussion on the meaning of 'relationship' since the worksheet asked (after the table), 'Can you see any relationship between the circumference and the diameter?' She said, 'That's what the relationship means, looking for a pattern between two sets of figures, two sets of numbers'.

(4) The class was asked to stop the activity and listen whilst the teacher gave some examples of relationships, e.g. $12 \times 2 = 24$ or $12 = \frac{1}{2}$ of 24. The children were then asked to look at the diameter and circumference to see if they could find a relationship.

(5) Various children proffered ideas, one pursued by the teacher involved multiplying the diameter by 3 and then adding on a certain amount to reach the circumference, e.g. $3d + 10$.

(6) The teacher referred to a Greek discovering that if one multiplied the diameter by a 'magic number' one could obtain the circumference. The magic number was called π, value $3\frac{1}{7}$ or 3.14. 'If you multiply the diameter by 3.14, you should come back to your circumference.'

(7) The children were set to multiply the first diameter in their table by 3.14 to see if they obtained the circumference. Many of the diameter measurements involved decimals and the results of multiplication were checked by the teacher.

(8) The teacher demonstrated 3×3.14, then instructed the children to copy 'π (pi) $= 3.14$ or $3\frac{1}{7}$' into their exercise books.

Follow-up lesson

(9) The teacher referred to Greek and magic way of finding the circumference. She then wrote a list of diameters 2, 5, 3, 9, 7 and asked for ideas on the size of the circumferences. Children suggested (a) 3 times, (b) 3.14 times.

(10) Teacher demonstrated the multiplication 9×3.14.

(11) The children were set multiplication examples with diameters which were whole numbers or 2.5, 3.5. These were followed by examples where the radius was given.

Bob explained, 'It's a line that's curved all the way round . . . it's a line that meets itself'. When the interviewer drew an oval he added, 'It's got a diameter which is its length all the way across, and it can go down . . . it can go every way . . . as long as it goes through the centre of it'. Raymond thought 'a radius helps you to build a circle' but that mention of it would not help to describe a circle. Sally said, 'It's got no sides on it . . . it's just a round thing . . . it's curved'.

THE CIRCUMFERENCE

The children were also asked at each interview to find the circumference of firstly a reel of tape and secondly of a drawn circle. During the teaching sequence this class was taught a method for finding the diameter of a cylinder unlike the class in School 7. Table 5.6 shows the responses for both the cylinder and circle tasks. 'String' means a response which indicates putting string or tape round the circle and then using a ruler to measure the tape. 'Rolling' involves rolling the shape along a ruler. Both of these methods were taught in the lesson before the 'formalization lesson'. 'Diameter/radius used' means that the child mentioned using one of these measurements.

Table 5.6: School 8, Class A responses for circumference of a circle and circumference of a cylinder

Type of response	Cylinder				Circle				Key
	I	PreF*	PostF	D	I	PreF*	PostF	D	
πd or 2πr			B J L / R S Sm	B / R S Sm			B J L / R S Sm	B J / R S Sm	B Bob
diameter/radius used	R S	S	L		S		J	L	J Jane
string	J L / R Sm	B J	B J / R	J		B J	Sm	B J	L Laura
rolling	B	J / R S	J L / R S Sm	J / R S Sm	J		Sm	J	R Raymond
other					J / R				S Sally
no attempt		Sm			B L / Sm	R S			Sm Sam

| | | | | | | | | | arranged |
| * No PreF interview data available for Laura. | I | PreF* | PostF | D | I | PreF* | PostF | D | B J L / R S Sm |

Interview

Table 5.6 shows clearly that all but Jane and Laura not only accepted the formula post-formalization but would still use it three months later. For finding the circumference of a cylinder five pupils had available an extra, more practical method, after the lessons. Raymond (PostF) summed up the differences in the three approaches.

(I: Interviewer; R: Raymond)

I: Now I was watching you yesterday, you were drawing round cylinders and cutting out strips of paper, and today you're doing sums, is there any connection between those two activities?

R: Well, no, 'cos you're just doing it, um ... a simpler way, just by timesing it, but you have to find the, um ... diameter.

I: If I wanted to find the circumference of a circle then are there a number of ways of doing this?

R: Well, yes, you could mark the cylinder on one point and then mark on a piece of paper the equivalent length, and then you just roll it until you come to the end, when the cylinder has done a complete turn, 180 degrees, then you mark it off where it stops, then you measure between the lines.

I: That's one way.

R: Yes, but it's not always accurate.

I: Oh.

R: The other way is if you take a strip of paper and you put it round the cylinder and then you tick off with a pencil, a complete turn, and then you stretch it out and measure it, and that's how you get the ...

I: And is this another way?

R: Yes.

I: I see, and is there any connection between all these ways?

R: Yes, they all add up to the same thing.

Jane, who (D) offered only practical methods for finding the circumference of the cylinder was asked:

(I: Interviewer; J: Jane)
I: Supposing we didn't have the circle there. All I told you was the diameter of the circle?
J: Then you'd do, um...radius times radius times pi...oh, no, that's...you'd have to ..um...I think you'd have to find out the diameter.
I: Mmm...
J: And then measure it by 3.14.

Sam mentioned (D) finding the diameter but then went on to say 'Find the centre point...but it hasn't got any middle'. Laura had remembered (D) the formula as πr so used that on both cylinder and drawn circle. Overall the class seemed to have accepted the formula and used it.

Jane was able to suggest three methods for finding the circumference of a drawn circle on the last interview. In this example the diameter could be obtained by folding or was given in the question. Raymond suggested (PostF) that the formula would work with whole numbers only but later changed his mind.

(I: Interviewer; R: Raymond)
I: I'll draw you an enormous circle. How would you find the circumference of that, you've told me how you'd find it of that.
R: You times it by...you measure the diameter, and then you times that by 3.14, because as long as the...the thing is a whole number, you can times it by...
I: As long as what's a whole number?
R: The diameter.
I: Ah, now this particular diameter is 7.7.
R: Mm...I suppose it still would go into it.

Unlike the pupils in School 7, only Laura (after the lessons) mentioned multiplying the diameter/radius by any number other than π – she suggested (D) using '3' but later in the same interview changed the value to 3.14.

PERCEPTION OF THE MATERIALS

At both the post formalization interviews, (PostF) and (D), the children were asked whether there was any connection between the activities involving the rolling and taping of cylinders and the multiplications of the diameter by π. All of those interviewed (PostF) said that the two activities amounted to different ways of doing the same thing, i.e. finding the circumference. Raymond said of the activities, 'It was...sort of like a build up to pi. I thought it helped me a lot.' None of the children thought they had discovered the value of π. Sam said they believed in its existence 'Because when we measured the cylinders, we got a diameter, we times it by 3.14 and then it came out. The circumference was right, because we measured them first with the tape'. Jane said, 'Well, because if 3 times is 15, it's sort of got to be more than that. Because if you measure it out on a ruler, it's a bit more.' Sally's response was similar, 'Because we first done the tape, the paper and then we times that and it worked out the same'. Bob thought there was no connection between the activities and π.

On the final interview, each child was again asked to state the connection between the two types of activity and then asked to explain to a 'new child' in the class how to obtain the circumference of a circle. Their explanations to the 'new child' were as follows:

Laura: Explain names and how to find radius. Then 'find diameter, half it, then times by 3.14'.
(Practical materials used only to find diameter and then formula used.)

Bob: (Explain names and how to find radius.) 'I'd teach him at first an easy one...in fact I
think I've got that one wrong...'
(He was then diverted by trying to remember the formula as π*r*.)
Sally: 'Tell her what the diameter was, then tell her to times it by π'. Interviewer: 'You
wouldn't teach her the rolling method?' Sally: 'Yes.'
(She thought there was no connection between the two methods however.)
Sam: (Thought he could not teach a 'new boy' about π.) 'Well...ask someone who knows
about it.'

Raymond:

(I: Interviewer; R: Raymond)
I: Right, I see. So in fact if you had to teach somebody who didn't know about it...about
pi.
R: You'd start off with the rolling method, then mark a point then you roll it till the point
comes straight and then you mark it...but that can't be always accurate so then you've
got to find out where the exact point is.
I: How long would you go on doing the rolling method, with somebody who didn't know
anything about it?
R: About 3 weeks, 4...and then you'd do some number practice sheets to get you into the
hang of multiplying and then you would multiply...you know...multiply the decimals,
sorry.
I: Yes, and what about them though, would you...look at how much they'd learnt? At
what point would you think that they were ready for this multiplying?
R: Um...well.
I: Or would you do it for 3 weeks and then reckon that was long enough.
R: Yes, well, if they...if the standard of work becomes good and all of the books, you
know it shows understanding of the work.
I: But how would you know that whoever it was had understood?
R: Well you'd study the person to see if they were working out on pieces of paper, you
know, trying to learn and gradually build up their knowledge.

Most of the group seemed to think that the practical build up to π was unnecessary for the
'new child'. The descriptions included the naming of parts which was of course in the series of
lessons. Raymond's decision to include practice at multiplying may have expressed a heart-felt
need!

Child methods and misconceptions

We have already mentioned that Laura mis-remembered the formula (D) but others vaguely
remembered a formula or method prior to the teaching. Bob thought the circumference of a
circle was the same as two diameters in length. Sally's answer was somewhat confused but
entailed finding the radius and, 'When you find the width, that to that. Then you put it on the
ruler to find the length, and then you do it round, on the other side and put it together.' Laura's
response seemed similar: she said one should take a piece of cotton and step it round the circle
to see how many times it fits. At (PreF) Raymond stated one and a half diameters would go
round a circle. Jane suggested the circumference was the same as the diameter.
Pairs of compasses seem to have been considered useful for finding the diameter of the
cylinder. The number of radii in a circle (pre-teaching) was limited according to some children.
Bob thought there were only two radii. Sally's decision was 12 radii in any circle and even after
the formalization lesson she considered there were four diameters in any circle.
Sally, at the final interview, measured the cylinder by rolling it along a ruler to obtain 29 cm,
she then incorrectly multiplied 3.14 by 3.7 to obtain 97.08 and considered that having two
different results was 'alright'. The multiplication of two decimals was very difficult for the

children and Laura for example considered modifying the question (D): 'I know what to do but...can I just round it off and have it as three?'

Conclusion

In neither school did the children use a formula for finding the circumference prior to the teaching. The existence of the value π was not mentioned by anybody. Ten of the 12 children interviewed had a workable method for finding the circumference of a cylinder (I). Incorrect methods such as adding two diameters or stepping off radii round the circumference were also apparent prior to the series of lessons.

The difference between the responses of children in the two schools is striking. Immediately after the formalization lesson in School 7, three children were very confused as to which essential points about π they should remember, whereas in School 8 they all quoted the value of π. The teacher of School 7, Class A had provided historical evidence on the value of π described by mathematicians at various times besides arriving at π in class by gradually refining the value found experimentally. It appears that a good part of the confusion of the children stemmed from their inability to identify which of all these were important aspects. Additionally the first remembrance of the formula by three children was incorrect. Few children in the School 7, Class A interview cohort adopted the formula for finding the circumference of a cylinder, which might have been caused by the difficulty of finding the diameter. The need to know the diameter was mentioned by a number of pupils in School 8, Class A (interview cohort) and they had been taught a method for finding it (see point 3 in Table 5.4). The response on the circumference of a drawn circle was very similar three months after the teaching, but immediately after the lesson more of the children interviewed in School 8, Class A had accepted the formula.

Asked to describe a circle to a Martian, many children omitted the crucial fact that the curve consists of points which are all the same distance from the centre and some instead listed all the names of parts of circles they knew. This suggests that children do not necessarily recognize the crucial elements in a topic, and as a result, many ideas of lesser importance are given equal weight.

There was a reluctance on the part of the pupils to insist that a 'new child' went through the measuring experiences prior to using the formula although Raymond suggested a lead-up to the formula which was concerned more with multiplication techniques rather than showing that the formula was reasonable.

Children in School 7 still mentioned multiplication by 3 rather than π even after π had been introduced. The methods children suggested one should use when dealing with an extra 'bit' when an approximation of π was stated to be 'three and a bit', varied. In order to accommodate the extra amount children multiplied whole amounts and then added 'a bit' or, added 'a bit' first then multiplied, e.g. (3 × radius) + b or (3 + b) × radius. The 'bit' was, of course, intended to be part of the multiplier – however the practical work introduced it as a gap in the circumference after three diameters had been measured round the object and hence this could quite easily be thought of as an amount which was added. The transition from addition to multiplication was difficult and the significance of the order of operations was not apparent to the group.

Unlike other topics reported in this book, the children retained more than one method of finding the circumference although there is some suggestion that to use the formula fully children do need to be taught how to find a diameter of a disc which cannot be folded.

Chapter 6
Area of a Rectangle
Linda Dickson

Introduction

This chapter is concerned with the topic 'Area' and in particular the 'Area of a Rectangle' and the teaching of this with reference to the formalization aspect of multiplying length by width. In any discussion concerning 'Area' it is important to draw the distinction between the general concept of area in terms of surface and the measurement of this in terms of finding how much surface. Williams and Shuard (1982) in their section on measuring area point out that 'At 8 or 9 years of age children often compare length and breadth or perimeter and show no awareness of the quantity of surface.' (p. 244)

In *Nuffield Maths 3 Teachers' Handbook* (Latham and Truelove, 1980) it is stated:

> The confusion between area (the amount of surface) and perimeter (distance round a region) is nearly always due to inadequate preparation in the early stages. In the past, most children responded to the word 'area' by saying 'length times breadth' irrespective of the shape being considered. The slick formula $A = L \times B$ is completely divorced from the idea of covering surface. (p. 140)

What are now often regarded as being the main considerations for any treatment of area are briefly outlined below and are based upon the Nuffield scheme of work for this topic:

- Fitting shapes together: 3-D and 2-D shapes.
- Covering surfaces (irregular and regular) with 3-D objects leading on to 2-D objects so there are no gaps.
- Developing conservational aspects of area through for example tangram activities.
- Comparing surfaces (irregular and regular) leading to notion of need for same sized unit to be used for covering surfaces.
- Recognizing the need for a standard unit of measure of surface and for this to be based on unit of length leading to introduction of square centimetre.
- Measuring area of irregular and regular shapes by counting squares.
- Using grids of squares for measuring area.

Alongside all of this, some work on multiplication and its commutative properties is directly relevant, as in drawing a distinction between rows and columns in rectangular arrays, e.g.

3 rows of 4 → 4 + 4 + 4
4 columns of 3 → 3 + 3 + 3 + 3

and interpreting this in terms of multiplication, i.e. 4×3 or 3×4.

Finally the aspects of area and multiplication are brought together in the step:

- Begin to calculate area of a rectangle on the basis of the number of squares in a row and the number of rows.

Nuffield Maths 4 Teachers' Handbook (Latham and Truelove, 1981) comments on such an approach to calculating the area of a rectangle by stating:

> ...the number of squares in a row and the number of rows. This has two great advantages, firstly, even when calculating, the children are thinking in *squares*, not in lengths, secondly it helps to avoid the glib answer that 'area is length times breadth'. (p. 88)

By *Nuffield Maths 5 Teachers' Handbook* (Hargreaves, 1982) (for approximately 9- to 10-year-olds) there is the recommendation for developing this method of calculating the area of a rectangle by multiplying the number of centimetre squares in a row by the number of rows, saying:

> Although this amounts to multiplying the number of centimetres in the length by the number of centimetres in the breadth, some children still need to be reminded that in doing so they are really working out the number of centimetre squares required to cover the rectangle. (p. 20)

Williams and Shuard (1982) note that as children 'get older' they:

> ...will usually have discovered by this time how easy it is to find the area of a rectangle when it contains a whole number of rows each consisting of a whole number of squares. No longer do squares need to be individually counted: 5 rows of 6 squares make 30 squares in all. The product of the number of units in the length and the number in the breadth recalls early work on making patterns with rods and strips to show what multiplication means. Now children realise that this product states the area in terms of a square unit. (p. 246–7)

This introduction to the teaching of area sets the scene for the rest of this chapter which is concerned with the monitoring of pupils' performance on items regarding aspects of area. In particular this relates to children's strategies for finding the area of a rectangle and whether they adopt a 'length times width' formalization within the context of the teaching programme they experience.

The sample

The sample consisted of three classes from three different schools, one junior school, pupils aged 7–11, and two middle schools, age range 9–13. The pupils in the three classes were all aged 9–10. The junior school class and one of the middle school classes were mixed ability, with class sizes of 17 and 25 respectively, while the other middle school class, with a class size of 17 pupils, was the top set (of three). The corresponding interview samples were six, six, and eight.

The mathematics curriculum for each of the classes would normally have included work concerning the area of a rectangle. Each teacher chose those pupils who reflected the spread of ability across their particular class and these six or eight children constituted the interview cohort for that class. The progress of these pupils was monitored before, during and after the implementation of their teacher's programme of work – i.e., each child was interviewed four times: before the teaching, interview (I); just prior to the formalization lesson(s) (PreF); immediately after the formalization lesson(s) (PostF); and three months after the teaching (D).

Analysis

The findings will be outlined in some detail for one of the classes and in brief for the others. Class (A) from School 13 has been chosen for the more detailed account of the analysis. This is because the teaching programme for this particular class displayed an approach to the work which closely reflected many of the aspects of the teaching of area which were mentioned in the introduction to this chapter. Furthermore, somewhat atypically, most of the pupils from the interview cohort seemed to make meaningful progress in developing an appropriate formalization of length times width for finding the area of a rectangle. The one pupil who did not, provided some very useful information of where difficulties may occur and an insight into the nature of these problems. These insights are further substantiated and expanded from the findings of the two classes in Schools 12 and 14. The data from the three groups is then collated into some concluding thoughts at the end of the chapter.

School 13, Class A (aged 9–10)

The programme of work which was devised for this class was more heavily weighted in terms of an introduction to area in general rather than being mainly concerned with finding the area of a rectangle in particular. However it was the transfer of this to the case of a rectangle which was the predominant feature of the interviews. The emphasis of the scheme of work was very much concerned with 'pre-formalization' aspects of area.

The programme was organized into eight sessions over a period of seven consecutive school days. Mainly these were of about an hour's duration with two of them being 20 minutes and 30 minutes long. A couple of similarly shorter periods were used for some further work on the two days following the end of the scheduled programme and immediate post-formalization interviews.

Prerequisite knowledge and skills

The prerequisite knowledge and skills as assumed by the teacher were as follows:

(i)   Knowledge of metric length: mm, cm, m.
(ii)   The ability to measure using ruler and tapes.
(iii) The ability to manipulate simple numbers – realize that multiplication is repeated addition.

The pre-teaching interview (I) responses

Table 6.1 shows a summary of the pre-teaching interview (I) responses. In terms of the prerequisites which had been assumed by the teacher it appeared that all pupils, in the main, were well versed in these aspects. In contrast to other pupils in this study the children from School 13 made frequent mention of appropriate units of linear measure, although on several occasions Nelson would utter 'inches' before immediately correcting himself to 'centimetres'. Sandy was already using a formal multiplicative approach to determining area. Cloë and Jason were using a formal approach, but to a lesser extent, and for Jason this was linked with some inappropriate ideas which are mentioned below in the section on 'non-multiplicative approaches'. Some brief discussion will follow concerning some of the categories of response outlined in Table 6.1.

LINEAR MEASUREMENT

On the whole all the pupils showed appropriate skills in determining the linear measurements of various rectangles either by measurement with a ruler or by using the information shown on the diagrams. There were a few instances of idiosyncratic or less sophisticated approaches.

Sheila used the marks on the ruler in the following way:

(I: Interviewer; S: Sheila)
I: And how did you get the 6 cms long?

Table 6.1: Summary table for interviews I and PreF – School 13, Class A

Items	Ann I	Ann PreF	Cloë I	Cloë PreF	Jason I	Jason PreF	Nelson I	Nelson PreF	Sandy I	Sandy PreF	Sheila I	Sheila PreF
Linear Measurement												
Sheet of paper, rectangles (a), (b), (c) (see below)	√?	×?	√	√	√?	√	√?	?	√	√	√?	√?
Conservation of Area Piece of paper cut into 2 and pieces rearranged (I) Two squares of tin with holes punched out. Do they have the same amount of tin left? (II)	√		√		√		√		√		√	√
The Concept – Area												
What does the word 'area' mean?	–	√	–	√	–	√	–	√	–	√	–	√?
Multiplication-based Strategies												
How would you find out how many dots?	–	√	√	√	√	√	–	√	√	√	–	–
How much paper in this shape (a)? (a) What is the area of (a)?	–	√	√	√	√?	√	–	×	√	√	–	–
How much paper in this shape (b)? (b) What is the area of (b)?	–	×	√	√	√?	√	–	–	√	√	–	–
How much paper in this shape (c)? (c) What is the area of (c)?	–	√	√	√	√?	√	–	–	√	√	–	–
Paper How much paper? What is the area?	–	–	–	–	–	√	–	√	√	√	–	–

Table 6.1 contd

Non-multiplicative Approaches

	C1	C2	C3	C4	C5	C6
[dots figure] How would you find out how many dots?	√	√	√	√	√	√
[grid figure] How much paper in this shape (a)?	×	–	×	×	√?	√?
(a) What is the area of (a)?	√	–	√?	–	√?	√?
[ruler figure] How much paper in this shape (b)?	×	–	×	×	√?	√?
(b) What is the area of (b)?	×	–	×	–	√?	×?
[square figure, 5] How much paper in this shape (c)?	×	–	×	–	√?	√?
(c) What is the area of (c)?	×	–	×	–	√?	×?
Paper How much paper?	×	×	×	×	√	√
What is the area?	√?	√?	√	×	√	√?
Appropriate use of shapes to cover sheet of paper	×	√?	√	√×	×	√?

Appropriate Units mentioned

	C1	C2	C3	C4	C5	C6
Linear measure 1-dimension	√	×(c)	√	√	√	√
Area measure 2-dimension	×	√	√×(c)	×(a)(b)	√?	×(a)

√   indicates use of sound strategy
?   some doubt or contra-indication
×   does not indicate use of sound strategy
–   not mentioned or asked

S: Because with these dots here, you add them up and there's five there and you always add one at the end, which is six, and you do the same with these . . . you always add one at the end.

(It transpired during the course of interview (D) that this method of determining length had emanated from her Geography lessons.)

Jason measured the sides of rectangle (b) by using the ___0___1___ section of the ruler and moving the ruler along to align this section with each gap between the marks.

Ann measured the width of the sheet of paper obtaining what she described as being 'ten and a half centimetres and one millimetre'. She was unable to express this in any other way.

THE USE OF MULTIPLICATION-BASED STRATEGIES

Sandy consistently used a multiplication-based strategy for determining 2-dimensional measure on the various interview items. In the main Cloë and Jason did as well but with the exception of the item concerning the sheet of paper. The other three pupils were not using a multiplicative approach at all and, in particular, not for finding the number of dots in the 4 by 6 array.

THE USE OF NON-MULTIPLICATIVE APPROACHES

This section deals with strategies not based on a clear '$l \times w$' formalization.

Ann, Nelson and Sheila were able to find the number of dots by counting in multiples of either 4 or 6. However on the other items neither Ann nor Nelson was generally able to offer appropriate strategies for finding the amount of paper in each of the rectangles. Ann seemed to want to take into account the sides of the unit square which would cover each rectangle. For instance rectangle (a)

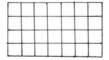

she said was 45 cms big which she arrived at through a one-by-one account of sides like this:

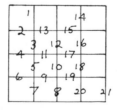

etc.

Nelson added the length and width together for each rectangle except (a) for which he counted squares one by one and then described it as just being 7 cms long and 4 cms wide in size. Sheila consistently used this method of stating the dimensions as a means of expressing the amount of paper in each rectangle. Jason's method for rectangles (a), (b) and (c) was the following. For rectangle (a) he measured the sides of one unit square and a diagonal like this

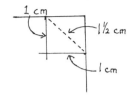

and then said 2½ centimetres.

The conversation continued:

(I: Interviewer; J: Jason)
I: ...how did you get 2½ from all that?
J: Well I just took one of the lines down there, 'cos they're all the same length and I just measured the distance in between and that gave 1½ cms. So I just put that 1 and that ½.
I: So did you add them together or something?
J: Yes.
I: So you took one of the sides and the diagonal and added those together.
J: Yes.

He then said there were 4 times 7 squares altogether and then he would do 2½ times 28 and the answer would be in centimetres and ½ centimetres. Jason adopted the same sort of approach for (b) and (c) saying he would draw in the squares and proceed as for (a).

As has been previously indicated one of the items involved finding the amount of paper in a sheet of paper. There was available a ruler, cm squared paper and a selection of plane shapes comprising squares, triangles and circles of various sizes and many of each type available. If a pupil did not utilize the shapes he or she was subsequently asked how any of them might be used. There was a wide variety of responses to this task with only Sandy choosing a fully appropriate strategy. Ann, Sheila and Nelson each decided to cover the sheet with a selection of different shapes, although they recognized that there should be no gaps or overlapping. Nelson started to position the shapes as follows:

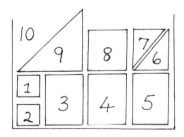

At this point the following conversation took place:

(I: Interviewer; N: Nelson)
I: Supposing you just covered that bit that you've done there, what would you say? How much was there? *(i.e. paper)*
N: 1, 2, 3, 4...10.
I: Ten, so you are imagining you've filled that in with a shape there, so that's all sort of filled in, so you did 1, 2...10...what sort of shape would you fill that bit in with, the ten?
N: Triangle.

I: Another triangle. So you would say the amount of paper there is...? (*see note*)
N: Um...11 cen...no...um...11 'p'.
I: What does the 'p' stand for?
N: Pence.
I: Pence? Why did you say that?
N: Because if you were wanting to buy a sheet of paper and you wanted it that big in length...
I: And 11 comes from what, the number of pieces?
N: Yes.
I: Well we said ten, didn't we, with that one?
N: Yes.
I: So what would it be?
N: Ten pence.
I: Ten pence. That's because ten shapes fit in is it?
N: Yes.

Note It is possible that Nelson may have been misled by the interviewer's use of the term 'amount' in making an association with money. (A pupil from School 12, Class A used 'p' for pence as a unit of measure for length.)

MENTIONING APPROPRIATE UNITS

All pupils made frequent use of appropriate units of linear measure. This was not the case for units of 2-dimensional measure which were usually described as being centimetres. Only Sandy used the term 'square centimetres' but this involved some confusion as can be seen from the following in response to the area of rectangle (a):

(I: Interviewer; S: Sandy)
S: ...28 cubic cen...28 square centimetres.
I: 28 square centimetres. You were going to say 'cubic' first, what are cubic...?
S: Um...it's...it's a cub...cube...and each surface is a square and it's...if you say cubic square centimetres...it means that each um...top is 1 cm and then its so many...to cover the surface.

SUMMARY

At the beginning of the teaching sequence, then, Sandy was already operating at the formalized level of determining area by means of multiplying '$l \times w$' as indeed were Cloë and Jason in a less complete way. Ann, Nelson and Sheila were not using multiplication at all. There were instances of some inappropriate ideas concerning 2-dimensional measurement and only Sandy indicated any knowledge of the units of such measure before the onset of teaching.

The pre-formalization work

The approach adopted by the teacher was of generating questions to elicit discussion, followed by tasks/exercises which culminated in further discussion. Approximately 5½ hours of class time spread over six lessons were devoted to the pre-formalization work. It concentrated on developing the notion of area initially by considering the size of a room and the arrangement of furniture within it. The idea of area as surface was further developed by focusing on the amount of colour covering irregular shapes bounded by curved and/or straight lines: the scope of interest was then narrowed down to rectangles. The measurement of area was considered in relation to covering surfaces with various units and finding those which would tessellate.

Interest was then directed towards determining the most appropriate unit to use for measuring area, i.e. the centimetre square. This led to the introduction of transparent centimetre square grids. Consideration was then given to the question of which shapes would not necessarily require these grids for finding their areas – namely rectangles. Thus the scene was set for developing an alternative method for determining the area of a rectangle which was to be the focus of the formalization work which followed.

The pre-formalization interview (PreF) responses

Table 6.1 gives a summary of the pupils' responses to the items asked on interview (PreF) which occurred following the pre-formalization work and just before the formalization lesson. The significant features in terms of a comparison with the pre-teaching performance on interview (I) include the observation that two more pupils, namely Nelson and Ann, were now offering multiplication-based strategies for some of the items. Sheila was the only pupil not using multiplication at all – not even for the dots item. There was a marked improvement in the mention of appropriate units of measure for specifying area but this was linked with the development of some inappropriate units being named for linear measurement. Further details of these points are discussed under the relevant headings.

LINEAR MEASUREMENT

There were no items specifically concerned with performing linear measurements but where this was incidental to other considerations there were few problems. Only Ann showed some inadequacy in this respect in terms of her treatment of rectangle (b)

which she determined to be 3 by 5 by virtue of just counting the marks on the length and width. For the following item rectangle (c)

she then interpreted the 5 and 7 as measuring lines at first saying the 7 meant 7 lines going across and the 5 meant 5 lines going down but then decided it was the other way round, i.e. 7 lines going down and 5 across, all a centimetre apart like a grid but inside the figure and not including the sides of the rectangle already drawn. Although she did not actually draw the lines it appeared from what she was saying that she actually meant this:

THE USE OF MULTIPLICATION-BASED STRATEGIES

All pupils with the exception of Sheila were now multiplying on the dots item. Jason was employing an appropriate multiplication strategy which was no longer linked to an inappropriate consideration of the sides of the unit squares as had been the case throughout interview (I). Ann used the unsound strategy of multiplying together the number of marks on the length and the width of rectangle (b), i.e. 3×5 rather than 4×6, and Nelson specifically stated there was no quicker way of determining the area of rectangle (a) other than counting the squares one by one.

THE USE OF NON-MULTIPLICATIVE APPROACHES

On rectangle (c), with dimensions 5 and 7, Nelson added the sides as he had done on interview (I), although this time it was two 7s and two 5s giving 24 (although he was not sure whether it was centimetres or square centimetres) whereas previously on interview (I) it had been just 5 + 7 giving 12. For rectangle (b) he seemed to count imaginary squares firstly inside the shape and then those around the edge, with a shift during the counting to focus on the marks on the sides rather than the interval, reaching a result of 20.

Sheila, for both rectangles (b) and (c) gave the area in terms of considering the dimensions in conjunction with addition-based strategies. Again pupils were asked how they could determine the area of a sheet of paper by making use of a selection of plane shapes as units of cover. All pupils recognized the need to fit shapes together without any gaps or overlapping and thus cover the sheet but Ann and Nelson were still offering inappropriate means of measuring the area by this method. Ann recognized that the size of the units of cover had to be taken into account. She chose squares of side 3 cms and said she would cover the sheet with them and count how many there were one by one. She would then measure the sides of each unit square and add all four sides together and then times this result by the number of squares. Nelson repeated his method from interview (I), saying he would cover the paper with different shapes and count them one by one. He maintained that this number of shapes, regardless of their size, would be the same as the number of squares on a cm square grid, which would be necessary to cover the sheet.

MENTIONING APPROPRIATE UNITS

Generally the mention of inappropriate units of measure for length involved the use of square centimetres. This was particularly evident in Cloë's case for rectangles (a) and (b) where the grid of squares and the marks on the perimeter seemed to attract this sort of response. However for rectangle (c) where there were no visible clues as to a square grid she used centimetres as units for both linear and area measurement as follows:

    (I: Interviewer; C: Cloë)
    I: Now how big is this shape here? (*interviewer points to (c), the 5 × 7 rectangle*) What's its area?
    C: 35 centimetres
      .

      .

    I: How did you get that?
    C: Times 7 by 5.
      .

      .

    I: How long is that shape?
    C: 7 centimetres.
    I: And how wide?
    C: 5 centimetres.
    I: Right, now you're using centimetres, before you were using square centimetres. Why have you changed now?
    C: Because there isn't squares on that piece of paper.
      .

I: Were there any squares on this one with the marks? (*Interviewer points to (b), the 4 by 6 rectangle with marks on the perimeter.*)

C: No, but I knew it was, because you'd drawn little lines on it.

I: So they would show you...

C: Yes.

I: What?

C: The squares.

SUMMARY

Following the pre-formalization work the pupils all seemed to have a grasp of area as surface and could conserve area within the limits of the interview material. However not all pupils were consistent in the appropriateness of the methods they used for determining the amount of area, as was evident on occasions with Sheila and Nelson and to a lesser extent, with Ann. Probably the most significant feature of the (PreF) interviews was the fact that all the pupils, with the sole exception of Sheila, were using appropriate multiplication-based strategies on some, if not all, of the items. This was occurring before the onset of the formalization stage of the teaching, which was to be aimed at developing this 'length times width' approach to finding the area of a rectangle. This is outlined in the next section.

The formalization work

The work aimed at developing the formalization of multiplying length by width for finding the area of a rectangle was conducted in a lesson of about an hour's duration. The format was mainly in terms of question and answer with discussion. There was some blackboard work accompanied by exposition to consolidate points arising from the earlier exchanges between pupils and teacher.

The lesson began with a recap of the notion of area as surface and the use of a square centimetre grid for measuring the amount of surface. It then moved on to discussing a way of finding the area of a rectangle without using a grid. One pupil suggested using the measurements marked on the shapes, i.e. the length and the width. Another pupil suggested multiplying them. The teacher asked 'why multiply' them and recounted that in a previous lesson when grids were used he had noticed some pupils finding quicker ways of obtaining the number of squares and one of these was to multiply. One pupil said, with reference to this

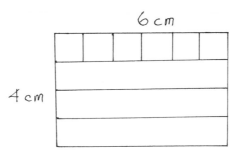

on the worksheet, that because there were six square centimetres in the first row and there were four rows, then it was 6 + 6 + 6 + 6 and that was why you multiplied.

This idea was reinforced through the example of a 3 cm by 5 cm rectangle where the length indicated the number of square centimetres in a row and the width indicated the number of rows. On the board the teacher wrote the following:

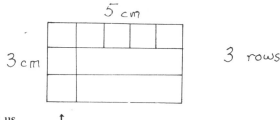

This tells us   ↑
how many rows:

Area of rectangle = Number of squares in first row × number of rows
                  = 5 square centimetres × 3
                  = 15 square centimetres

The class did further examples together and then started a worksheet.

The pupils did not have to use the teacher's method if they could find an easier one of their own. They could draw the diagrams straight into their books or on to squared paper first. The teacher moved around the class and the example below illustrates the conversations, which took place between teacher and pupils:

(T: Teacher; P: Pupil) (working with the diagram of a rectangle, 4 cm by 11 cm, in an oblique position)

P: Do you write 4 times 11 as your calculations?
T: Yes and I would like you to say why you are multiplying both ... start off by saying first, well that's a rectangle you're trying to find the area of, so write that, area of the rectangle equals ... length multiplied by the width, because the length of it will tell you how many square centimetres will fit along the first row and the width of it will tell you how many rows you're going to have. That'll be four rows with eleven square centimetres in each row giving you a total number of ... then you can work it out ...

The post-formalization interview, (PostF) and (D), responses

Table 6.2 summarizes the responses of the pupils during the two sets of post-formalization interviews (PostF) immediately after the formalization lesson and (D) three months later. Several features are apparent. There is the overall similarity of the nature of the responses on each aspect for each pupil between interviews (PostF) and (D). For items which were the same as those on (PreF) there again appears to be widespread consistency in terms of the nature of the responses given by each pupil. These consistencies over interviews (PreF), (PostF) and (D) are particularly evident from the diagrams of pupil profiles which are shown in Table 6.3. Again a selection of pupil responses are discussed under subheadings from Table 6.2.

LINEAR MEASUREMENT

Most of the children displayed a grasp of linear measurement during their discussion of the various items. Ann, however, on both post-formalization interviews continued to count the intermediary marks on the adjacent dimensions of rectangle (b) thus multiplying 3 by 5 for the area as she had done previously. Sheila also retained her method of counting the marks and adding one for each dimension resulting in obtaining the correct length and width as was outlined above for interview (I).

THE CONCEPT – AREA

All the pupils understood 'area' as surface when asked what 'area' meant and whether the leaf had an area. Initially (PostF) Sheila said she would determine the area of the leaf by placing

Table 6.2: Summary table for interviews PostF and D – School 13 Class A

Items	Ann PostF	Ann D	Cloe PostF	Cloe D	Jason PostF	Jason D	Nelson PostF	Nelson D	Sandy PostF	Sandy D	Sheila PostF	Sheila D
Linear Measurement												
Sheet of paper, rectangles (a), (b) etc.	×(b)	√×(b)	√	√	√	√	√	–	√	√	?(b)	√
Conservation of Area												
Two grass fields with houses in. Do they have the same amount of grass left as each other?	–	√	–	√	–	√	–	√	–	√	–	√
The Concept – Area												
What does 'area' mean?	√	√	√	√	√	?	√	√	√	√	√	√
Does this leaf have an area?	√	–	√	√	√	√	√	√	√	√	?	√
Draw a shape with an area of 12 sq. cms.	×	×	√	√	√	√	×	×√	√	√	√	×√
Multiplication-based Strategies												
How would you find out how many dots?	√	√	√	√	√	√	?	?	√	√	–	–
What is the area of (a)?	√	√	√	√	√	√	√	?	√	√	–	–
What is the area of (b)?	×	×	√	√	√	√	√	–	√	√	?	–
What is the area of (c)?	√	√	√	√	√	√	√	√	√	√	?	–
What is the area of (A)?	√	√	√	√	√	√	√	√	√	√	?	–
What is the area of (B)?	×	×	×	×	√	–	×	×	√	√	–	–
Sheet of paper	–	–	√	√	√	√	√	–	√	√	–	?
Non-multiplicative Approaches used												
How would you find out how many dots?	–	–	–	–	–	–	√	√	–	–	√	√
What is the area of (a)?	–	–	–	–	–	–	√	√	–	–	√	√
What is the area of (b)?	–	–	–	–	–	–	√	√	–	–	×	×
What is the area of (c)?	–	–	–	–	–	–	?	–	–	–	×√	×
What is the area of (A)?	–	–	–	–	–	–	–	–	–	–	?	×
What is the area of (B)?	–	–	–	–	√	–	–	–	–	–	×	×
Sheet of paper	×√	×	–	–	–	–	–	–	–	–	√	√
Appropriate units Mentioned												
Linear measure: 1-dimension	√×	√×	√×	√×	√	√×	√×	√×	√	√	√	√
Area measure: 2-dimensions	√	√	√×	√	√	√	√	√	√	√	√×	√×
Connections												
Number of squares in each row and	A √	√	√	√	√	√	√	√	√	√	√	×
Number of rows from *l* and *w*	(c) √	?	√	√	√	√	√	√	√	√	√	×
Connection between using grid and *l* × *w*		?	–	?	?	–	?	–	?	–	√	– ×

√ indicates sound strategy × indicates unsound strategy – not mentioned or asked ? indicates some doubt or contra-indication

Table 6.3: Responses to interview items – School 13, Class A

Item — **No. of dots** (I and PreF):
```
• • • • • •
• • • • • •
• • • • • •
```
PostF and D:
```
• • •
• • •
• • •
```

Response type	C J / S	A C J / N S	A C J / N S	A C J / N S
Multiplies	*(C J S)*	*(A C J N S)*	*(A C J N S)*	*(A C J N S)*
Counts in multiples of one dimension (e.g., 4, 8, 12, etc.)	A Sh	Sh	Sh	Sh
Counts in multiples of one dimension by ones (e.g., 1, 2, 3, *four*, 5…)	N			
Counts in ones	A Sh	N Sh	N Sh	N Sh

Area of (a) *(grid rectangle)*

Response type	C J / S	A C J / S	A C J / N S	A C J / N S
Multiplies $l \times w$	*(C J S)*	*(A C J S)*	*(A C J N S)*	*(A C J N S)*
Counts squares one by one	N	N Sh	N Sh	N Sh
Gives l and w dimensions	N Sh			
Inappropriate use of sides and/or diagonals of unit squares	A J	Sh		

Area of (b) *(dashed rectangle outline)*

Response type	C J / S	C J / S	C J / N S	C J / S
Multiplies $l \times w$	*(C J S)*	*(C J S)*	*(C J N S)*	*(C J S)*
Counts imaginary squares one by one		A N	N	N
Gives l and w dimensions		Sh		
Counts marks on perimeter and multiplies		A	A	A
Inappropriate use of sides and/or diagonals of unit squares	A J			
Adds l and w dimensions	N	Sh	Sh	Sh

Area of (c) *(box, width 7, height 5)*

Response type	C J / S	A C J / S	A C J / N S Sh	A C J / N S
Multiplies $l \times w$	*(C J S)*	*(A C J S)*	*(A C J N S Sh)*	*(A C J N S)*
Counts squares one by one				
Gives l and w dimensions		Sh		
Inappropriate use of sides and/or diagonals of unit squares	J			
Adds l and w dimensions	A N	N Sh	Sh	Sh

I ↔ PreF ↔ PostF ↔ D   Interview
7 days   same   84 days
or next
day

Key

A	Ann
C	Cloë
J	Jason
N	Nelson
S	Sandy
Sh	Sheila

arranged

```
A C J
N S Sh
```

Interviews

S ⎫
J ⎬ consistently able to determine the number of dots by multiplying together the number of dots on
C ⎭ each dimension.

A   On (I) counted one by one but then in multiples of six, i.e. 6–12–18–24. On all subsequent interviews she multiplied together the number of dots on each dimension.

N   On (I) he counted in multiples of four but saying the intervening numbers under his breath, e.g. one, two, three, FOUR, five, six, seven, EIGHT, etc. On all subsequent interviews he initially counts one by one but then multiplies. He says he prefers counting one by one.

Sh   On each interview counts in ones then in multiples of one dimension.

S ⎫
C ⎭ Consistently multiply length and width throughout.

J   On (I) measures sides and diagonal unit square but finds number of unit squares by multiplying *l* and *w*. On subsequent interviews just multiplies *l* and *w*.

A   On (I) counts sides of unit squares. On subsequent interviews multiplies *l* and *w*.

N   On all interviews prefers counting squares one by one but on (PostF) and (D) says can multiply *l* and *w*, but on (D) gets different answer from that for counting one by one so doesn't think 'timesing' works here.

Sh   On (I) just states dimensions. On all subsequent interviews counts squares one by one. On (PreF) also counts sides of unit squares as a way of expressing amount of paper in rectangle but says this does not give the area.

S ⎫
C ⎭ They both multiply *l* and *w* appropriately throughout.

J   Throughout multiples *l* and *w* appropriately but on (I) this is in conjunction with the measurements of side and diagonal of unit square.

N   On (I) focuses on perimeter. On (PreF) tries inappropriately counting imaginary squares one by one. On (PostF) and (D) counts imaginary squares appropriately one by one. On (PostF) with prompting he suggests 'timesing' 6 × 4.

A   Throughout all interviews she counts intermediary marks on perimeter. On (I) counts 16 and doubles to 'get other piece of each square in'. On subsequent interviews she multiplied 3 × 5. On (PreF) she also counted imaginary squares one by one to 24.

Sh   On (I) amount of paper in rectangle given by stating *l* and *w*. On remaining interviews gives area in terms of adding dimensions although on (PostF) with prompting makes uncertain reference to multiplying *l* by *w*.

S ⎫
C ⎭ Multiplied length by width appropriately throughout.

J   Multiplied *l* by *w* appropriately throughout but on (I) this was again in conjunction with the side and diagonal measurements of the unit square.

A   On (I) she added *l* and *w* and doubled the answer. On all subsequent interviews she multiplied *l* by *w* appropriately.

N   On (I) and (PreF) he added dimensions. On (PostF) and (D) he multiplied *l* and *w* appropriately although on (D) he initially suggested adding but immediately corrected himself.

Sh   On (I) she just stated the *l* and *w*. On all subsequent interviews she added dimensions. On (PostF) and (D) she also made reference to counting squares but it was not clear whether she meant all squares or just those around the perimeter. On (PostF) she made reference to there being 35 squares found by 'adding five sevens'.

---

string round the perimeter and measuring its length. However she indicated that really area meant the 'middle' and that she would measure this by means of a grid of squares. All pupils, on both post-formalization interviews, were asked to draw a shape with an area of 12 square centimetres. This in fact had been on the task sheet for the formalization lesson. The shapes drawn by each child are reproduced in Table 6.4

THE USE OF MULTIPLICATION-BASED STRATEGIES

Tables 6.3 and 6.5 provide details of the children's use of multiplication-based strategies for most of the interview items. On the whole all the pupils, except Sheila, were employing basically sound multiplicative strategies for finding the areas of rectangles. Sheila, although making an occasional mention of 'timesing' as a result of some prompting, was not displaying much grasp of this aspect.

The item which caused most difficulty was (B) prompting unsound multiplication strategies from Ann, Cloë and Nelson on both sets of interviews. Ann consistently multiplied all the dimensions together while Nelson and Cloë, on both interviews, multiplied pairs of dimensions together and added the resulting three products.

(B)

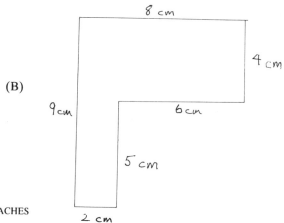

THE USE OF NON-MULTIPLICATIVE APPROACHES

On (PostF) and (D) interviews Sheila again employed inappropriate non-multiplication-based strategies for finding the areas of rectangles. As on the (PreF) interview she initially used methods involving the addition of dimensions for all the items except the dots and rectangle (a); where each individual unit was readily visible and countable.

The following extract from interview (D), rectangle (A), illustrates some of her difficulties:

(A)
(Drawn accurately at an angle on plain paper
with dimensions shown)

5 cm   12 cm

Table 6.4: Pupils' responses to 'Draw a shape with an area of 12 sq cm' – School 13, Class A

Pupil	Interview (PostF)	Interview (D)
Ann	Uses lined paper and ruler. Each line 4 cm long.	Uses ruler to draw square of side 3 cm on lined paper – not very accurately.
Cloë	Rectangle 6 cm by 2 cm drawn accurately on cm sq paper.	Drawn accurately on cm sq paper.
Jason	Rectangle 2 cm by 6 cm drawn accurately on plain paper with ruler.	Drawn accurately on cm sq paper.
Nelson	Draws square of side 12 cm on cm sq paper.	Uses ruler to draw sq of side 12 cm on lined paper. Then uses ruler to draw rectangle 1 cm by 12 cm on lined paper. He realized square did not have area of 12 sq cm.
Sandy	Drawn accurately on cm sq paper.	Drawn accurately on cm sq paper. Has hole in the middle.
Sheila	Uses ruler and lined paper to draw 2 cm by 6 cm rectangle. Draws in squares.	Draws square of side 3 cm on cm sq paper and then a 3 by 4 rectangle on cm sq paper.

(I: Interviewer; S: Sheila)
I: Can you tell me what the area of this shape is here (A)?
S: I'd add the two 5s at each end and the two 12s on each side of it together.
I: Mmm...any other way you could do it?
S: Cover it with squared paper

   .

   .

   ...put it on there and then draw round it and count how many squares there is in it.

The interviewer showed her such a rectangle already drawn accurately on centimetre squared paper but without the dimensions marked. (It was displayed in an upright position on the reverse of the card showing (A) on plain paper so direct comparison was not possible.)

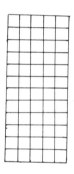

I: Now is that the same size as that one (A)?
S: Mmm...
I: How could you tell?
S: ...It looks the same, as big as this one.
I: Mmm...so what's the area of that then?
S: 32 square centimetres.
I: How did you get that?
S: By counting the two 12s together on either side and counting the two 5s together.
I: So you've gone back to the plain one...and that's how many squares there are in this one on the squared paper, is it?
S: Mmm...
I: Okay? Yes. Do you want to count them? You do.

Sheila counts in ones and is stopped by the interviewer when she reaches 39.

I: Right, now what's happened?
S: ...there are more.
I: So how's that worked out then?
S: This one is bigger than that one.
I: This one on the squared paper is bigger than the one...
S: Mmm...

So in order to resolve the conflict yet justify the validity of the two strategies, i.e. adding dimensions and counting squares one by one, Sheila could only conclude that one rectangle was larger than the other.

From Table 6.5 it can be seen that for the sheet of paper item, Ann, on both post-formalization interviews, used an inappropriate non-multiplicative approach to finding its area.

Table 6.5: Performance on finding the area (amount of paper) of a sheet of paper School 13, Class A

Type of Response	I	PreF (J)	PostF (C J)	D (C J)	Key
Measure length and width and multiply	S	N Ⓢ	N S	S Sh	A Ann
Use square grid and count squares 1 by 1	J	A C Sh	A Sh	Sh	C Cloë J Jason
Covers surface with shapes and can proceed no further				N	N Nelson S Sandy
Measures length and width and states these dimensions	A Sh				Sh Sheila
Covers surface with shapes and proceeds inappropriately	Ⓙ		A	A	arranged
Measures length and width and adds	C N				A C J N S Sh

Ⓞ around name indicates questionable interpretation

I ↔ PreF ↔ PostF ↔ D   Interview
7 days   same   84 days
or next
day

Summary

S   Throughout uses *l* × *w*. On (PreF) folds paper 3 times (i.e. into 1/8s), places it on cm sq grid to find *l* and *w* and multiplies. Then multiplies result by 3 as he made 3 folds. Later realizes he should multiply by 2, then by 2 again and by 2 again.

J   On (I) says he'll draw lines to form 2 cm sq grid then each square is 4 cm so should count squares 1 by 1 in fours, 4 and 4, etc. The 4 cm seems to come from adding rather than multiplying sides (since for 3 cm squares he says they are 3 + 3 or 6 cm). On subsequent interviews he measures *l* and *w* and multiplies.

C   On (I) adds *l* and *w*. On PreF would use cm sq grid and count squares 1 by 1. On (PostF) and (D) measures *l* and *w* and multiplies.

Sh   On (I) measures *l* and *w* and states these dimensions. On subsequent interviews would place on cm sq grid and count squares 1 by 1. On (D) she is asked to measure *l* and *w*; she then suggests 'you could times them'.

N   On (I) adds *l* and *w*. On (PreF) and (PostF) uses cm sq paper, counts squares along *l* and *w* and multiplies. On (D) he covers sheet with shapes – squares and triangles and can proceed no further.

A   On (I) measures *l* and *w* and states these dimensions. On (PreF) and (PostF) says would use a grid. Also on PostF and (D) uses 3 cm square from shapes saying she would count them 1 by 1 and multiply the number by the length of the side, i.e. 3, but then decides to multiply by 4, as 4 squares can be drawn in the 3 cm square. See p.108.

When determining the area of the sheet of paper by using shapes to cover it, Ann made repeated sitings of the largest square shape available (side 3 cm) chosen because 'it tessellates'. She performed a one by one count of the number required to cover the paper but realized she must take into account the size of the square. On interview (PreF) she measured the perimeter, 12 cm, and described the area in terms of the number of squares times 12. On (D) she took into account the length of just one side of the square and gave the area as the number of squares times 3. However she did not appear to be very sure about this and then continued to explain that she felt a quarter of the square was a square centimetre and thus the number of squares should be multiplied by 4. The conversation continued.

(I: Interviewer; A: Ann)

I: So you're saying that a quarter of that orange square is a square centimetre. Why do you say a quarter of it?

A: Because if you put a line down there and a line down there...(*indicating*

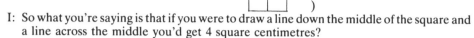

)

I: So what you're saying is that if you were to draw a line down the middle of the square and a line across the middle you'd get 4 square centimetres?

A: Yes.

I: And how long was the side of that square?

A: Three centimetres.

I: Is that alright?

A: Yes.

It is interesting to note Ann's failure to make the connection between the linear dimensions of this square and the number of square centimetres making up its area. It is an appreciation of this relationship which is fundamental to understanding the formalization, 'area of a rectangle equals length times width'. The following section looks further at this aspect.

CONNECTIONS

On some of the items, particularly those rectangles without squares drawn or marks on the perimeter, the children were asked whether they could ascertain how many square centimetres would fit across the top row of the rectangle and how many rows there would be. On the whole the pupils responded appropriately to these questions but Sheila's performance gives further insight into the difficulties which can be experienced. On interview (PostF) for rectangle (c) she had said correctly that 7 squares would fit across the top row and there would be 5 rows. However three months later for the same item the conversation was as follows:

(I: Interviewer; S: Sheila)

I: ...what do the numbers stand for that are on there?

S: It tells you how long and how wide it is.

I: So how long is it?

S: 7 centimetres long and 5 centimetres wide.

I: Mmm...if you were to draw squares in on that shape, how many squares would there be in each row?...(*pause*)...do you know what the rows are?

S: Four.

.

.

I: And where would they be? Show me, show me a row.

S: Down here...(*indicating*)

I: And there would be 4 squares in like that?

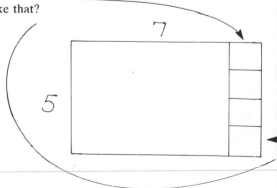

S: Mmm.
I: Why do you think there would be 4?
S: Well if you look at these, these give you a width and if you put them down there...
I: So you are comparing it with the bit of squared paper you've got there... just looking at that and then looking at this; you're not actually putting them together at all?
S: No.

.
.

I: ...how many of those rows going down would you have then, to cover all of that?
S: Four...five.
I: Five...why do you say that?
S: Well, like the width of that one, try and compare it with another row, and another row and another row...
I: So you're just sort of imagining it and putting your finger there and you think altogether you're going to have 5 rows of those squares...going down?
S: Yes.

On the basis of her indications the interviewer drew

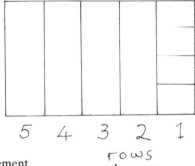

and Sheila nodded in agreement.

I: And you've just done that just by sort of looking at it and trying to judge what it would be; yes. And how wide apart would each of these rows be?
S: One centimetre.

.
.

I: And how wide apart would these squares be going down the side?
S: One centimetre.

Sheila's judgements were based on an intuitive, approximate visual comparison of the accurately drawn rectangle (c) on plain paper with a piece of centimetre squared paper on the table. She made no attempt to perform any more accurate comparison or measurement with the ruler. Furthermore she seemed to be oblivious to the fact that she had made incompatible statements in terms of her recognition that the '7' and '5' represented the length and width in centimetres and then her judgement that 4 squares each one centimetre would fit in the rows, five in all, again each one centimetre.

Even when Sheila *did* make suitable connections between the length and width and the number of squares in each row and the number of rows she was not able to ascertain, with any degree of certainty, the number of squares which would cover the surface of the rectangle.

On interview (D) the pupils were asked whether there was any connection between using a centimetre square grid for determining area and multiplying length times width. Nelson and Ann indicated that they thought there was some connection but they did not know what it was. Cloë thought there was a connection for shapes with corners. She then tested this for the shape she had created with an area of 12 sq cm, writing the dimensions shown:

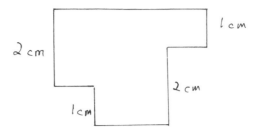

She said:

(I: Interviewer; C: Cloë)

C: ...times them together.
I: And what would you times?
C: Two by one and then one by two?
I: And would that give you the area?
C: Yes...two times one is...two...then one times two is two...so you'd get...hang on.
I: Would that give you the area?
C: No...no. I don't think you can do length and width on that.

Cloë then said she thought you could only do length times width on rectangles and squares. Jason thought there was a 'bit of a connection', giving the following example:

(I: Interviewer; J: Jason)

J: You could times...say there's an oblong what's 5 cms wide and 7 long. You just times five 7s and you get how many squared centimetres in the middle.
I: So is there a connection?
J: A bit of one.

Sheila's remark was very much in line with the fact that she had experienced certain difficulties:

(I: Interviewer; S: Sheila)

I: Now some time ago in class you were using transparent see-through grids for measuring area, weren't you?
S: Mmm...
I: And another time when I was in your lesson you were using area equals length times width, do you remember?
S: Mmm...I think so.
I: Vaguely? What's the connection between using the grids and using length times width?
S: What's the length times width?
I: You don't remember the length times width bit?
S: No.
I: You don't remember that? You just remember the grids.
S: Yes.

Sandy indicated that he had a good general grasp of area and its measurement. Throughout all four interviews he had shown a working knowledge of the 'length times width' formalization and had been adept at subdividing the L-shape in (B) into rectangles to enable him to apply the formalization. His response to the question on 'connections' was as follows:

(I: Interviewer; S: Sandy)

I: ...is there a connection between using transparent grids and using length times width to find area?

S: Um...I don't think so.
I: Is there any way that they could be connected at all?
S: They could be if the shape is...say...it's a square or an oblong.
I: So only if it's a square or an oblong?
S: Yes, or a shape that can be covered exactly with square centimetres without leaving any gaps and without cutting off any squares into bits.

Sandy was indicating a grasp of the limitations of the applicability of the 'length times width' formalization but at the same time was perhaps not entertaining or realizing the possibility of its suitability for finding the area of a rectangle where the dimensions may involve some fractional quantity.

MENTIONING APPROPRIATE UNITS

The most significant feature in terms of the mention of units of measure was the increased occurrence of the inappropriate mention of square centimetres instead of centimetres for linear measurement by Ann, Cloë and Nelson in particular. This was especially evident for rectangle (a) where the grid prompted the length and width to be measured in terms of counting squares. On the occasions where these three pupils made appropriate mention of centimetres as the unit of measure for length, this was usually for the items where no cues pertaining to the covering of square units were visible, e.g. the sheet of paper, rectangles (c) and (A).

It would appear that the use of centimetre square grids had some bearing on a misuse of square centimetres as a unit for linear measurement. There was also some evidence indicating that when such a grid was not visible then all measurements, linear and area, would be given in centimetres.

Summary

In summary then it can be stated that all pupils from this group had a reasonable general grasp of area as surface; although for some this was incomplete as shown in Table 6.4 which displays their responses to drawing a shape of 12 sq cms. However from the point of view of 'covering' they all recognized that any such technique for measuring the amount of surface should involve no gaps between units of cover and no overlapping. Even so, at the pre-formalization stage some pupils did not realize the necessity of taking into account the size of the unit of cover (nor indeed whether or not all were of the same size).

The employment of appropriate multiplication strategies for determining the area of a rectangle, based on the formalization 'length times width' is summarized in Table 6.6.

Although three children were using such a strategy with varying degrees of completeness during the pre-teaching interviews, by the end of the pre-formalization work five out of the six pupils were doing so. On the post-formalization (PostF) these same five children employed the formalization in a more complete and consistent way than before for simple rectangles (i.e. not the more complex shape given in (B)) and this situation continued through the delayed post-formalization interviews (D) three months later, although Nelson was not using '$l \times w$' to quite the same extent. The only pupil not to indicate any real grasp of the 'length times width' formalization was Sheila. She made some mention of 'timesing' following some prompting immediately after the formalization lesson but basically this was not a strategy she used when left to her own devices. Significantly, at no time did she employ a multiplication strategy for determining the number of dots in the rectangular array and it would seem reasonable to presume that she would benefit from more work on the nature of multiplication and its application.

After the formalization lesson five children could determine from the linear dimensions how many centimetre squares would fit across the top row of a rectangle and how many rows there would be. They could then proceed to use this information to establish the total number of

Table 6.6: Table summarizing the general use of the multiplication-based formalization '*l* × *w*' for finding the area of a rectangle for each pupil at each interview – School 13, Class A

Interviews			Pupils			
	A	C	J	N	S	Sh
I	–	√	√	–	√	–
PreF	√̲	√	√	√̄	√	–
PostF	√̲	√	√	√	√	–
D	√̲	√	√	√–	√	–

Key (names)   *Key (entries)*: '*l* × *w*'

A Ann   –   not used on any item*   √– used on half the items
C Cloë
J Jason   √   used on all items*   * perhaps occasional exception
N Nelson   √̄   used on just under half the items
S Sandy
Sh Sheila   √̲   used on just over half the items

Summary: 3 out of 6 using '*l* × *w*' on every interview
2 out of 6 developed use of '*l* × *w*' from PreF onwards
1 out of 6 did not use '*l* × *w*' throughout.

centimetre squares of area by appropriately multiplying. Again the exception was Sheila who seemingly could not visualize nor ascertain the number of squares required to cover a rectangular region unless they were all drawn in. On the delayed post-formalization interview Sheila had regressed somewhat in terms of not now being able to repeat her earlier facility for accurately determining the number of rows from the linear dimensions of a rectangle. Also at this time Ann was displaying an incomplete grasp of this connection (as noted earlier) when deciding that the 3 cm square she was using as a unit of cover for the sheet of paper was 4 sq cms in area.

There now follows a brief summary of the results from each of the other two groups, School 12, Class A and School 14, Class A.

School 12, Class A (aged 9–10)

Six pupils from School 12, Class A provided the interview cohort for the purposes of the investigation. A summary of their performance on each of the four interviews is shown in Tables 6.7 and 6.8.

The pre-teaching interview (I) responses

Before the onset of the teaching programme the pre-teaching interviews (see Table 6.7) indicated that Orton already had a working knowledge of the '*l* × *w*' formalization and Judy was well on the way to this. The other four pupils did not display an adequate grasp of certain aspects such as the appropriateness of a multiplication strategy for finding the number of dots in a rectangular array. For instance Ada indicated that the dots in the 4 by 6 array could be counted in fours but categorically stated that this had nothing to do with 'timesing'. Also there was a lack of competence in linear measurement and the understanding of the units of measure as for example Linda, who measured the length of her table which was three 30 cm ruler lengths and an 'extra bit' of 24 cms which she recorded as 90.24 saying that the 90 and the 24 were different and the 24 was millimetres really as it was not the full length of 30.

Table 6.7: Summary table for interview I and PreF – School 12, Class A

Items	Ada I	Ada PreF	David I	David PreF	Judy I	Judy PreF	Linda I	Linda PreF	Martin I	Martin PreF	Orton I	Orton PreF
Linear Measurement												
Measuring length of desk:	√?	–	×	–	√	abs	×	–	√	–	√?	–
Other occasions involving it, e.g. (b) (see below)	–	–	–	–	×	abs	–	×	–	–	√	√×
Conservation of Area												
Two squares of tin with holes punched out. Do they have the same amount of tin left as each other?	–	√	–	√	–	abs	–	√	–	√	–	√
Multiplication Used												
How many dots in [array] or [array]	×	–	–	–	√	abs	–	√	?	√	√	√
How much space in [grid] (a)	–	–	–	–	–	abs	–	√?	–	–	–	√?
How much space in [marked rectangle] (b)	can't do					abs		√?				√?
How much space in 5 [rectangle] (c)	–	–	–	–	√	abs	–	√	–	–	√	√
How much space in this sheet of paper/table top?	–	–	–	–	√?	abs	–	√	–	–	√	√
Non-multiplication Approaches Used												
How many dots in [array] or [array]	√	√	√	√	–	abs	√	√	√	–	–	–
How much space in [grid] (a)	–	×	–	√	–	abs	–	√	–	√	–	√
How much space in [marked rectangle] (b)	–	can't do	–	√	–	abs	–	×?	–	√	–	–
How much space in [rectangle] 5 (c)	–	can't do	×	can't do	–	abs	×	–	×	√	–	–
How much space in this sheet of paper/table top?	×	√?	×	√	–	abs	×	√	×	√?	–	√
Appropriate Units Mentioned												
Linear Measure 1-dimension	×	–	×√	–	√	abs	√×	–	√	√	√	√
Area Measure 2-dimension	–	–	√	–	×	abs	–	–	–	–	√	–

Key
√ Response indicates appropriate grasp
× Response indicates inappropriate grasp
? Some uncertainty or contra-indication
– No response given with respect to this aspect as not mentioned and not asked
abs Absent

Actual answers given may be either right or wrong in any category

The pre-formalization work

The scheme of work at the pre-formalization stage involved activities aimed at gaining a working knowledge of area as surface covering. There were some tangram activities but mainly the emphasis was on using the surfaces of 3-dimensional objects such as covering the faces of boxes with paper and also using boxes, tins, etc., to cover surfaces. The work progressed to developing the realization of the need for standard units of measure and cubes were used for covering and then transparent square grids.

The pre-formalization interview (PreF) responses

The second set of interviews following this pre-formalization work and immediately before the formalization lesson indicated that the pupils were now beginning to take more into consideration the 2-dimensional aspect of surface in terms of covering with shapes. All pupils readily conserved area within the context of the item involving two squares of tin, see Table 6.7 (but for David this was temporary as in a parallel item on (D) he did not conserve). Also on (PreF) Linda was implementing the formalization 'length times width' for finding the area of some of the items. Ada, David and Martin were not employing multiplication-based strategies at all and in particular not for the 'dots' item. One of the most significant features of this set of interview data was the lack of mention of appropriate units of measure. Only Martin and Orton made isolated references to units of linear measure. No pupil stated any units for 2-dimensional measurements. It was also noticeable during the ensuing formalization lesson that the teacher in fact often made numerical statements concerning linear and area measurements *without* mentioning units.

The formalization work

The approach chosen by the teacher for this class to progress towards the formalization of 'length times width' for finding the area of a rectangle was essentially based on recognizing numerical relationships from a tabular recording of measurements which were practically obtained. The pupils were required to measure the length and width of a rectangular face of a box and record these under the appropriate column headings in a table. They were then to use transparent square grids to determine the area of the rectangular face by counting squares and to record this. The task was to be repeated for several rectangles and the results collated in a table:

Length	Width	Area

The teacher pointed out that by multiplying together the numbers from the length and width columns the answer in the area column could be obtained.

The teacher asked the children to: '...do as many rectangles as you can. Measure the length, measure the width, see if the answer is area....' It was noticed that some children were using the centimetre square grids to measure the length and width of the rectangles by counting squares along these dimensions.

The post-formalization interviews, (PostF) and (D), responses

Again, as with School 13, Class A most of the responses across the two post-formalization interviews (PostF) and (D) (three months apart) were similar for each child in the sense that both either reflected an appropriate or inappropriate grasp of the aspect in question. The main exception was Linda who used a multiplication-based strategy for some of the items on (PostF) but for none on (D) (see Table 6.8).

Table 6.8: Summary table for interviews PostF and D – School 12, Class A

Items (NB Some items not asked on both interviews)	Ada PostF	Ada D	David PostF	David D	Judy PostF	Judy D	Linda PostF	Linda D	Martin PostF	Martin D	Orton PostF	Orton D
Linear Measurement Appropriate measurement of linear dimensions, e.g.	–	×	–	×	abs	×	–	×	–	√	–	√
Conservation of Area Two grass fields with houses in. More, less or same amount of grass	–	√?	–	×	abs	√	–	√	–	√	–	√
The Concept – 'Area' What does word 'area' mean?	×	–	√	–	abs	–	√	×	×?	–	√	–
Does this leaf have an area?	×	×	√	√	abs	√	×	×?	√	√	√	√
Multiplication Used How many dots in this array	–	×	–	–	abs	√	–	–	√	√	√	√
Find area of rectangle (a) (4 × 7)	–	–	–	–	abs	–	–	–	–	–	–	√
Find area of rectangle (A) (12 × 5)	–	–	–	–	abs	√	√	–	√	√	√	√
What is area of (B) (42 cm²)	–	×	–	–	abs	√	×	–	×	×	√	√
What is area of (b)	–	–	–	–	abs	×	–	–	–	√	–	√
What is area of (c)	can't do		–	–	abs	√?	–	–	–	√	–	√
What is area of this sheet of paper?	–	–	–	–	abs	–	√	–	√	–	√	–
Non-multiplication Approaches Used How many dots in this array	–	√	–	√	abs	–	–	√	–	–	–	–
Find area of rectangle (a) (4 × 7)	–	×	–	√	abs	√	–	√	–	√	–	–
Find area of rectangle (A) (12 × 5)	×	×	√	√	abs	–	√	√×	√	√	–	–
What is area of (B) (42 cm²)	×	×?	√	√	abs	–	√	×	√?	√	–	–
What is area of (b)	–	×	–	√	abs	√	–	√×	–	–	–	–
What is area of (c)	can't do		–	×	abs	–	–	×	–	–	–	–
What is area of this sheet of paper?	√?	–	√?	–	abs	–	–	–	√?	–	–	–
Appropriate Units Mentioned Linear measure 1-dimension	–		√		–		√		–		–	
Area measure 2-dimension	×		×?		–		–		–		–	

Key
√   Response indicates appropriate grasp
×   Response indicates inappropriate grasp
?   Some uncertainty or contra-indication
–   No response given with respect to this aspect as not mentioned and not asked
abs   Absent

} Actual answers given may be either right or wrong in any category.

A significant feature was the development of misconceived notions of area by Ada and Linda which were apparent on (PostF) and further entrenched by (D). Linda measured the sides of the rectangles with a ruler and calculated the perimeter for area. Ada was interpreting 'area as the space inside' as meaning the space inside a boundary of squares around the perimeter but inside the figure: so for instance she calculated the area of rectangle (a)

as being 10, i.e. 2 by 5, counting the squares one by one.

Neither Ada nor David used the taught method at all for finding the area of rectangles in post-formalization interviews. On the other hand, Orton did so consistently with every item as he had done all along. Martin was the only pupil whose use of multiplication seemed directly to 'match' the progress of the teaching.

Summary

There were many instances when pupils displayed an inadequate grasp of linear measurement and unit of measure. There was in fact very infrequent mention of units in either linear or area measurement.

Some pupils, particularly those developing misconceived notions of area, had a tentative grasp of area as surface and two pupils were suspect in their ability to conserve area within the limits of the interview questions. Two of the six pupils were already using the '$l \times w$' formalization before the onset of the teaching. Another two developed its use during the course of the teaching programme although one of them did not retain its use on interview (D) (three months later), while the remaining two pupils did not use it at all throughout.

School 14, Class A (aged 9–10)

The work concerning the area of a rectangle for this top ability set was organized into a total of eight lessons each about one hour long and spread over a period of approximately three school weeks. There was an intervening week for half-term holiday, which occurred between the end of the two taped formalization lessons and the further consolidation work of four lessons which were then followed by the (PostF) interviews.

The interview cohort comprised eight pupils reflecting a spread of ability within the class, albeit already setted according to mathematical ability. Tables 6.9 and 6.10 relate to the pupils' performance on the four sets of interviews.

The pre-teaching interview (I) responses

The responses of the eight pupils to the pre-teaching interviews are summarized in Table 6.9. As can be seen several pupils were already using a '$l \times w$' approach to finding area – asked in terms of finding the amount of paper in the shape – especially for rectangle (a). Emma and Mark did not use a multiplication-based approach at all, and in particular not for the 'dots'. Sadi used multiplication only for the 'dots' and for the rest of the items she used inappropriate non-multiplicative approaches based mainly on finding the perimeter, as did Moh.

When asked how much paper there was in the sheet of paper no pupil gave a fully adequate response. Only Mark and Moh attempted any measurement with a ruler, Mark stating the length and width in centimetres and Moh calculating the perimeter in centimetres. Ric gave an estimate of just the length saying the amount of paper was: 'one sheet...about one foot two inches length'.

When using the selection of plane shapes to help determine the amount of paper Moh chose one of the largest triangles and measured its perimeter and could proceed no further. Sadi chose the largest size squares and used these to form a border and then counted them. Ric set about covering the sheet as though doing a jigsaw (his description), choosing a triangle for each corner and then putting the border in using squares like this:

but then admitted to not knowing how to determine the amount of paper. The children mentioned appropriate units of linear measure and for 2-dimensional measurement Emma and Sue described the units as 'squares' and in Mark's case 'blocks'. Inappropriate units of area measurement were mainly instances of just centimetres being given.

The pre-formalization work

The teacher assumed that the children had no previous experience of work on area. He considered them to have a very sound knowledge of the four rules of number. Two lessons were devoted to the pre-formalization work.

Lesson 1: Group work based on determining the size of various rectangular shapes, e.g. carpet, tablecloth and envelopes using non-standard measuring equipment, e.g. plastic coins, Ladybird books and sheets of lined paper. This was aimed at developing a recognition of the need for greater accuracy by means of standard measures.

Lesson 2: The use of plane shapes and transparent grids to find how many squares covered each of a variety of shapes including triangles and circles. The children then drew round templates on to centimetre squared paper and thus measured area by using cm squares as units (cm^2 introduced).

The teacher noticed that for finding the areas of rectangles about half the class were counting the squares one by one including Emma (somewhat to the surprise of her teacher who regarded her as being one of the more able), Mark, Ric and Sadi, while the rest, including Moh, Nina, Ray and Sue, were multiplying together the number of squares in each dimension.

The pre-formalization interview (PreF) responses

A summary of the responses for the second set of interviews appears in Table 6.9. There was slightly more frequent use of the '$l \times w$' formalization (not yet taught) particularly for rectangles (b) and (c) and the sheet of paper. Some pupils used the shapes on this latter item and multiplied together the number of squares fitting across and down the sheet in order to determine the total number required to cover the sheet. For example, Ric had reflected upon his earlier efforts (interview (I)) of covering the sheet of paper, in the same way as he would do a jigsaw, and decided it was better to use just the 'red' squares (these were of side 3 cm) placing them like this:

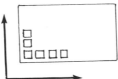

He determined that 7 squares would fit going down and 9¾ squares across. The conversation continued:

Table 6.9: Summary table for interviews I and PreF – School 14, Class A

Items	Emma I	Emma PreF	Mark I	Mark PreF	Moh I	Moh PreF	Nina I	Nina PreF	Ray I	Ray PreF	Ric I	Ric PreF	Sadi I	Sadi PreF	Sue I	Sue PreF
Linear Measurement Sheet of paper, rectangles, etc. Edge of box	✓	–	✓?	✓	✓	✓	✓	✓	✓	✓	✓	✓	?	–	✓	✓
Conservation of Area Sheet of paper cut into two. Pieces rearranged. (I). Two squares of tin with holes punched out. Do they have the same amount of tin left as each other? (PreF)	✓	✓	✓	✓	✓?	✓	✓	✓	✓	✓	✓	×	✓	×	✓	✓
									×(a)							
Multiplication-based Strategies How would you find out how many dots?	–		–		✓		✓		✓		✓		✓		✓	
How much paper in (a)?	–		–		✓		✓		✓		✓		✓		✓	
How much paper in (b)?	–		–		✓		✓		✓		✓		–		✓	
How much paper in (c)?	–		–		–		–		–		–		–		✓	
How much paper in this sheet of paper?	–		✓		–		✓		✓		✓		–		✓	
	?														–	

Items	Emma		Mark		Moh		Nina		Ray		Ric		Sadi		Sue	
								Pupils								
	I	PreF	I	PreF	I	PreF	I	PreF	I	PreF	I	PreF	I	PreF	I	PreF
Non-multiplicative Approaches																
How would you find out how many dots?	✓	✓	✓	✓	–	–	–	–	–	–	–	–	–	–	–	–
How much paper in (a)?	✓	✓	✓	✓	–	–	–	–	–	–	–	–	×	–	–	–
How much paper in (b)?	×	×	✓	✓	×	×	–	×	–	✓	can't do	✓?	×	–	–	–
How much paper in (c)?	×	×	✓	–	–	×	×	–	–	–	can't do	–	×	×	–	–
How much paper in this sheet of paper?	–	✓?	✓?	–?	×	–	–	✓?	–	✓?	×?	–	–	–	–	✓?
Appropriate use of shapes to cover paper.	✓?	✓	✓?	✓	×	✓?	✓?	✓?	✓?	✓	×	✓	×	×	✓	✓
Appropriate Units mentioned																
Linear 1-dimension	✓		–		–		–		–		–		–		✓	
Area 2-dimension	✓ ×(b)		– ×(a)		–		–		–		–		×(b) –		✓	

Key   ✓   Response indicates appropriate grasp
       ×   Response indicates inappropriate grasp
       ?   Some uncertainty or contra-indication
       –   No response given with respect to this aspect as not mentioned and not asked

(I: Interviewer; R: Ric)
I: So how can you use that to tell you how much paper there is in that sheet of paper?
R: Um ... Ive got an idea. I'll just do it seven 9s ... and then seven ¾s. ... it might turn up to 6½.
I: I think it's a bit nearer to five, just a bit over 5.
R: Yes, I thought it would be ... um ... 63 ... 68¼ ... 68¼ red squares.

Neither Emma nor Mark were multiplying when determining the number of dots in the rectangular array although Mark did use this approach for rectangle (c) and the sheet of paper.

There were now occasions when Mark and Ray interpreted the numbers on rectangle (c) as measuring 'blocks' and 'squares' respectively rather than centimetres. The inappropriate units mentioned for measuring area were centimetres.

The formalization work

The children worked individually from workcards. The first set of five cards involved drawing rectangles on to centimetre squared paper either accurately or to an appropriate scale and finding the areas.

The dimensions for each rectangle were both given in millimetres or centimetres or metres. Area cards 6 to 10 each had 'AREA = LENGTH × WIDTH' written at the bottom. The pupils had their work checked individually throughout the lessons. If they were not employing the 'length times width' formalization they were advised to do so because of it being quicker and easier. In the words of the teacher:

> But there's an even easier way than counting the squares; to find out what the area is, you find out how long it is, find out how wide it is, and multiply the length and width together. The number of rows and the number of columns and you'll find the answer a lot quicker ...

Certain confusions were apparent during the second formalization lesson, e.g. giving lengths in 'centimetre squares', finding perimeter for area particularly on the questions involving squares. The teacher addressed the class on these points and they were set the task of drawing six different shapes each with an area of 12 cm² but with varying perimeters. Following the half-term break there were four more lessons when pupils completed the workcards and consolidated the work on perimeter and area from textbook exercises.

The post-formalization interviews (PostF) and (D) responses

A summary of the post-formalization interview responses is given in Table 6.10, page 122. On the immediate post-formalization interview (PostF), it was apparent that Emma was not using her ruler correctly since she was measuring from the '1' mark rather than from '0'. However three months later following some recent work on linear measurement she was aligning the ruler correctly. This work on length also involved the use of the term 'diameter' which several of the pupils subsequently confused with the term 'perimeter' on interview (D).

All the pupils seemed somewhat tentative in their expression of area as amount of surface. For instance, Moh, on (PostF) when trying to explain what area meant said: 'The area's inside it ... like in centimetres, it's just the edges ... round the edges, the area is inside it.' In fact on (D) he added the lengths of the sides for all items except the 'dots' and shape (B) whereas three months previously he had multiplied appropriately on all items except the sheet of paper.

On (PostF) Nina was asked if the leaf had an area:

(I: Interviewer; N: Nina)

N: No.
I: No, not at all?
N: It could do, going up along the middle.

On the (PostF) interviews there was a greater incidence of using the '$l \times w$' approach although Emma and Mark were still the exceptions.

One of the items on both sets of post-formalization interviews was taken from one of the workcards used in class. The question asked, 'Find the area of the following rectangle: 12 mm long, 7 mm wide'. Frequently the children made an accurate drawing of the rectangle although on (PostF) Emma drew hers 11 cm by 6 cm and labelled the sides 12 mm and 7 mm. On (D) she drew it accurately on centimetre squared paper and by a visual estimation said its area was ½ cm sq or a bit over, about ⅔. On (PostF) Ray drew the rectangle accurately but decided to add the dimensions because: 'I was thinking of timesing them but it was 84, but I thought it were a bit too big for this.'

This item prompted the greatest incidence of inappropriate units of measure being mentioned, i.e. millimetres for area. On other rectangles length was often given in centimetre squares particularly where the unit squares were visible as in rectangle (a).

On interview (D) no pupil was able to give an adequate account of any connection between covering surfaces with squares, etc. and using the '$l \times w$' formalization.

Summary

The children from this group did not have a very sound grasp of area as surface. The teaching scheme had been mainly concerned with the measurement of area and in particular the area of rectangular shapes.

It was interesting to note that, although this class was a top ability set, two out of the eight members of the interview cohort did not on the whole use the '$l \times w$' approach for finding the area of a rectangle, nor did they ever do so for finding the number of dots in a rectangular array. Three pupils, Sue, Ray and Nina, predominantly employed this multiplicative approach throughout, even before the onset of the teaching programme. The remaining three pupils, Moh, Ric and Sadi, progressed in their 'take up' of the '$l \times w$' approach in accord with the teaching, although for Moh this was not maintained following the three-month period after the teaching. It is perhaps worth mentioning that Ric who was judged to be one of the slowest workers in class gave some of the most thoughtful and meaningful responses during the interviews and was the only pupil to always give the correct units of measure whether they be linear or 2-dimensional.

Conclusions

A pattern which emerges from an analysis of the data from the three classes (groups) is the apparent division into three subgroups which reflect the progress achieved. First are the pupils who already have a working knowledge of the formalization '$l \times w$' from the outset and use it predominantly if not exclusively. Secondly are those who appear to learn it during the course of the teaching, and finally the third group is typified by those who do not use it at all or very seldom throughout the duration of the study. The breakdown of pupils falling into each group from each school appears in Table 6.11.

It is interesting to note that out of a total of 20 children seven developed the use of the '$l \times w$' formalization during the course of the teaching. Of these seven children, six began making predominant use of '$l \times w$' on interview (PreF), that is, following the pre-formalization work and before the actual teaching of the formalization. Only one child from the whole study, namely Martin from School 12, Class A, began using the '$l \times w$' formalization for the first time following the lesson in which it was taught. This probably indicates the relative importance of having a sound grasp of prerequisite aspects such as the nature and applicability of the multiplication process and an understanding of a general concept of area, as readiness factors which would then naturally lead to the development of a '$l \times w$' approach emerging before being specifically taught.

Turning now to the question of retention of such an approach it can be seen from the previous discussion that altogether four pupils – namely Linda (School 12), Nelson (School 13)

Table 6.10: Summary table for interviews PostF and D – School 14, Class A

Items	Emma PostF	Emma D	Mark PostF	Mark D	Moh PostF	Moh D	Nina PostF	Nina D	Ray PostF	Ray D	Ric PostF	Ric D	Sadi PostF	Sadi D	Sue PostF	Sue D
Linear Measurement Sheet of paper, rectangles, etc.	×	✓	✓	✓	✓	✓	✓	✓	✓	✓	✓	✓	–	✓	✓	✓
Conservation of Area Two grass fields with houses built in. Do they have same amount of grass left as each other?	✓	✓	✓	–	✓	–	✓	–	✓	–	✓	–	✓	–	✓	–
The Concept – 'Area' What does the word 'area' mean?	✓?	✓?	?	?×	×?	?	✓?	×?	?	✓?	✓?	?	✓?	✓?	✓?	?
Does this leaf have an area?	✓?	✓?	?×	✓	?	✓	✓	×✓	?	✓	✓?	✓	✓?	✓?	✓?	✓
Multiplication-based Strategies How would you find out how many dots?	–	–	–	–	✓	✓	✓	✓	✓	✓	✓	✓	✓	✓	✓	✓
How would you find the area of (a)?	–		–		✓	–	✓	✓	✓	✓	✓	✓	✓	✓	✓	✓
How would you find the area of A?	–		?–		–		✓	✓	✓	✓	✓	✓	✓	✓	✓	✓
How would you find the area of B?	–		–		✓		×	✓	–		✓	✓	✓	✓	✓	✓
How would you find the area of (b)?	–		–		✓	–	✓	✓	✓	–	✓	✓	✓	✓	✓	✓
How would you find the area of (c)?	–		✓?		✓	–	–	–	✓	–	✓	✓	–		✓	✓

What is the area of a rectangle 12 mm by 7 mm?
What is the area of this sheet of paper?

Non-multiplicative approaches
How would you find out how many dots?

(a)

How would you find the area of (a)?

How would you find the area of A?   (A)

How would you find the area of B?   (B) (42 cm^2)

How would you find the area of (b)?   (b)

How would you find the area of (c)?   (c) 5

What is the area of a rectangle 12 mm by 7 mm?
What is the area of this sheet of paper?

Appropriate Units Mentioned
Linear 1-dimension
Area 2-dimension

Connections
Is there a connection between covering surfaces with squares, etc. and using $l \times w$ for finding area? What is the connection?

Key

✓   Response indicates appropriate grasp

×   Response indicates inappropriate grasp

?   Some uncertainty or contra-indication

–   No response given with respect to this aspect as not mentioned and not asked

Table 6.11: 'Take-up' of the formalization '*l* × *w*' for each cohort from each school

School/ class	No. in cohort	No. using '*l* × *w*' predominantly from outset	No. learning to use '*l* × *w*' during teaching	No. not using '*l* × *w*'
12/A	6	2	2	2
13/A	6	3	2	1
14/A	8	3	3	2
Total	20	8	7	5

and Moh and Nina (School 14) – regressed in the three months between the two sets of post-formalization interviews. In the main this was as a result of calculating perimeter instead of area on interview (D). Only Nelson from School 13 showed signs of regressing in terms of sometimes adopting a counting rather than a multiplication strategy. This counting approach was one with which he had always felt more comfortable, even when employing '*l* × *w*'. One or two pupils needed to 'see' all the unit squares of cover for a rectangular surface in order to have any confidence in the validity of the total they had found.

The pupils from School 13, Class A had been specifically directed towards determining the connection between the length and width dimensions of a rectangle with the number of centimetre squares in a row and the number of rows. By and large, they could grasp this although for one or two pupils it did not readily transfer to the situation where squares of side 3 cms were being used as units of cover for the sheet of paper. It may be that children need to actually draw in the squares as accurately as possible by going through the whole process of measuring the sides and marking off along these dimensions in preparation for constructing a grid. Such an approach may have helped Ray (School 14, Class A) on the 12 mm by 7 mm rectangle where he had discarded his first idea of multiplying the 12 and 7 together as the resulting 84 was 'too big'. In fact for this item another pupil, Ric, drew the rectangle accurately and then proceeded to mark the millimetres along one side before giving 84 mm^2 for the area. None of the teaching schemes involved any work of this nature, although that of School 13, Class A did include drawing the squares in the top row and down one side but these were not required to be based upon accurate measurement.

Another advantage from such an approach could be to draw attention to using linear units of measure for length in moving towards determining 2-dimensional square units of measure for area. In practice a reverse situation inadvertently occurred in all three classes where the availability of ready-made grids (transparent or centimetre squared paper or squares already drawn on the shape) led to situations where pupils were using these to measure length and often giving such linear measurements inappropriately in terms of units of square centimetres since they had in fact counted the number of squares along the dimension. There may be thus an argument for limiting the use of such ready made grids and placing more emphasis on the pupils constructing them as appropriate on each region in question if necessary.

Finally it is perhaps helpful to identify the interview items which elicited some very useful information. The rectangular arrays of dots were particularly valuable for identifying the child's propensity for recognizing the suitability of a multiplicative approach to this kind of situation. The responses also indicated a high incidence of an intermediate strategy between the less sophisticated counting in ones and the more formalized multiplying of dimensions, namely the counting in multiples of one dimension. It also appeared to serve as a possible indicator to the readiness of pupils for developing a '*l* × *w*' approach to determining the area of a rectangle. This is because, in the main, when pupils did not multiply for the 'dots' item during an interview then they did not use a '*l* × *w*' approach for any item on that interview.

Another useful item was rectangle (b).

Not only did this help ascertain pupils' facility for linear measurement but also whether they could make connections between the marks on the perimeter and how they could relate this to determining the area.

The last item of particular value to be mentioned is the sheet of plain paper especially when pupils used the selection of plane shapes as units of cover for determining its area. This task was useful for investigating various basic notions associated with area and its measurement. These include covering techniques in terms of overlapping or leaving gaps: choice of units, whether they are the same and whether size is taken into account: actual approaches to covering in terms of say a 'jigsaw' strategy, a haphazard method, a spiral method, e.g.

or rows and columns, etc. and then how this is used to give some measure of area.

These three items then, the 'dots', rectangle (b), and the sheet of paper with shapes are suggested as being particularly helpful in eliciting an insight into children's understanding of area and its measurement.

Chapter 7
Volume of a Cuboid
Kathleen Hart

Introduction

The formula for finding the volume of a cuboid is taught in British primary schools, usually after earlier experiences of finding the capacity of containers by filling them with sand, water or solid objects. Piaget distinguished between 'interior volume' where the space is confined within boundaries (e.g. the volume of space inside a box) and 'occupied volume' where the volume is viewed in relation to other objects (e.g. the volume occupied by a solid block). Both these aspects are included in the measuring experiences suggested by Williams and Shuard (1982) in their chapter on Volume. They suggest children build different shapes using the same number of small cubes. Later they advise the finding of the number of cubes contained in a cuboid box (probably by counting). They suggest that children will readily accept the multiplication of the numbers of units in the three dimensions having already been introduced to the product of two numbers to find the area of a rectangle. The evidence obtained in the CSMS measurement research suggests that children continue (well into the secondary school) to count and not multiply for area and volume. The CSMS interviews produced examples of 14- to 15-year-olds who avoided using multiplication for finding the volume by counting how many cubes there were in a layer and then adding that number to itself for each layer. This is difficult to achieve if one of the dimensions contains a fraction.

The CMF investigation of the volume of a cuboid which forms the subject of this chapter focused on the acquisition of the formula $V = l \times b \times h$. This is probably the second formula introduced in primary school mathematics, the first being $A = l \times w$. The transition is from counting cubes one by one when they are used to fill a block, to an orderly repetition of layers and then a multiplication of numbers needing no cubes or even the box but simply the dimensions.

The sample

The classes which formed the sample for this topic (see Table 7.1) were varied in nature. Two final year (11-year-old) junior classes in London were considered to form the core of the investigation. Of these School 5, Class B was the first class to take part in the CMF research and every lesson on volume taught by the teacher was attended by one of the researchers. The second group, from School 9, Class A, was taught on a one-to-one basis by the teacher who had no responsibility for the rest of the class. The other two schools' results are included here in an abbreviated form. The interviewing of children from these classes was carried out by mathematics educators from Manchester, using the same methodology and questions as the main CMF team.

Analysis

All the classes were assumed by their teachers to have already been given a variety of experience which involved filling containers with sand or water. The questions asked the

Table 7.1: Sample for volume of a cuboid

	Age	Class size	Sample interviewed
School 5, Class B	10–11	31	7
School 9, Class A	10–11	6	6
School 10, Class A	10–11	20+	6
School 11, Class A	12	20+	4

children during the four interviews included:

(1) How to find how much a box held
(2) Use of the terms 'volume', 'how much space'
(3) Conservation of volume (the skyscraper question – shown as Figure 7.1)
(4) Volume of a cuboid when it was a block which could be held
(5) Volume of a cuboid represented by a two-dimensional picture, (i) drawn to show the faces of cubes and (ii) with dimensions labelled
(6) Volume of a container or object which was not a cuboid
(7) Multiplication of three numbers
(8) Meaning of abbreviations such as cm^2, cm^3.

School 5, Class B (aged 10–11)

The class in primary school 5 was taught the formula for finding the volume of a cuboid in the Spring term of the final year. There were 31 boys and girls in the class, which was taught as a whole although for the purpose of using the worksheets, children sat in groups at tables and they could work at different rates. There were seven lessons, over four weeks, leading up to the rule. The researchers attended every lesson including the two 'formalization lessons'. The seven children interviewed were chosen by their teacher to represent a range of ability; their names were Ian, Lisa, Frank, Peter, Larry, Sarah and Gerald.

The scheme of work

The worksheets written by the teacher were designed after reading textbooks and resource material other than that normally used in the school. There was a collection of boxes in the class together with small wooden cubes, cuisenaire rods and centimetre cubes.
    It can be seen from Table 7.2 that the final worksheets were designed to encourage the children to tabulate their results under length, breadth, height and volume headings as well as numbers of layers. The final sheet used diagrams; the children had met this format before.

Formalization lessons

The formalization lesson took place six days after the last lesson with the worksheets (described in Table 7.2). A summary of the lesson(s), prepared by the researcher from the tape recording and observation, is given in Table 7.3. During the lessons the teacher at no time showed the children an actual cuboid; the diagrams for cuboids were the basis for the statements leading up to the volume formula. The introductory work for the formula involved finding the number of cubes in a layer and multiplying by the number of layers but the emphasis then changed to the three dimensions and the name given to each. The final formula was $V = l \times b \times h$ and it was this which was practised. The multiplication of the three numbers was done orally with the teacher asking for products of pairs. The computation was not written on the blackboard. The second lesson was used to reinforce the formula and its use was illustrated with numbers which were multiples of ten. An example in which the volume was

Table 7.2: Scheme of work – School 5, Class B

Prerequisites:
Revision of area of a rectangle as ($a \times b$).
Some filling of receptacles with water, sand, marbles at the beginning of teaching sequence.

Lessons
Built around worksheets involving:

(1) Using matchboxes to fill a box and cubes to fill the matchbox
(2) Finding how many centimetre cubes fill a box
(3) Building a tower the same size as a box
(4) Using 20 cubes to build a shape. The volume is...
  Drawing the shape
(5) Using 36 cm³ (new notation). Building a cuboid and finding how many layers and how many in a layer
(6) Finding the volume of Cuisenaire rods in cm³
(7) Filling a box with Cuisenaire rods and then converting so that volume of box is found in cm³
(8) Comparing the volume of two boxes
(9) Finding volume shown a 2-D picture and asked to build the cuboid it represents
(10) Making a cuboid and recording the number of cubes in a layer, number of layers, in table form
(11) Given pictures of various cuboids making a table showing the number of cubes in length, breadth, layer, height, volume

---

given together with two dimensions, the third being sought, was referred to as 'how many layers?' Thus new ideas were introduced into the second lesson.

Teaching outcomes

The main outcome sought by the teacher was that the children would have an effective general method for finding the volume of a cube or cuboid. This was taught in the form $V = l \times b \times h$ but another useful method mentioned (as a previous step) was to use the number of cubes in a layer times the number of layers. The teacher emphasized that the formula was not universally applicable but only for cuboids and cubes.

The formula

The initial interview prior to teaching (I) was quite brief and the children were asked how they would find the amount of space in, or how much could be held by two boxes, one open and the other closed. Rulers, centicubes and Unifix were on the table for the children to use if they wished.

Sarah, Ian and Larry were not asked for the volume of the open box. Peter and Frank placed cubes on the base of the open box and then suggested computations could be made although they did not carry these out. For the closed box Peter guessed 400 and Frank eventually measured the length and width with a ruler and then added two lengths, two widths and the total of columns of cubes placed along one edge.

Gerald suggested that the method he used for an open box, i.e. finding the number of cubes in the width and length and multiplying these two numbers to find a layer then repeating the layer, would suffice for the closed box. The difference being that cubes would need to be put on the outside of the box or the edges measured with a ruler. Ian, having found the height of the closed box to be three cubes, intended to build similar columns all over the lid. Lisa measured the three dimensions of the open box with cubes and multiplied to find a layer and then multiplied again to find the total. She measured the closed box with a ruler (inaccurately) and although saying she would multiply the three numbers, in fact multiplied only two of them. Sarah measured accurately and multiplied all three numbers.

On subsequent interviews the children were shown closed boxes and asked for the volume/ space occupied (the word volume appeared to cause no trouble). Table 7.4 shows the methods

Table 7.3: Formalization lessons (2) – School 5, Class B

(1) The children were reminded that they have been working on worksheets concerned with the volume of cubes and cuboids.

(2) Diagram of cube (squares shown) drawn on board. Children asked what has been used to find the volume – 'cubic centimetres' or 'centimetre cube' accepted.

(3) Layer of nine cubes (3 × 3) drawn on board and children asked how many cubes in a layer; how many in length; how many in breadth; how many altogether. 'You could just say three threes.'

(4) Looking at diagram to see how many layers of nine there are. Teacher says this is the 'height'.

(5) How many altogether is explained as found from 9 (a layer) × 5 (the height). Then, this is said as 'length times breadth times height'.

(6) Teacher asks whether it matters which line is labelled 'length'. New diagram labelled

with numbers, squares on faces not drawn.
Children asked how many in one layer, prompted by how many in length, breadth. Volume answer written 4 × 2 × 10.

(7) Individual children in class asked for (4 × 2) and (8 × 10)
Children asked to come to board to mark length, breadth, height on diagram.

(8) New diagram drawn, squares not shown. Children asked to suggest dimensions (8, 3, 5). Class asked 'what sum' has to be done to find volume, and (8 × 3 × 5 cm³ = Volume) written on board.

(9) Example (same diagram as 8) in which length is 7 cm, breadth is 2 cm and volume is required. Children say a third measurement is needed.

(10) Child asked to suggest height of block 'anything you like'. Class multiplies 7 × 2 × 5; (7 × 2) and then (14 × 5).

(11) Formula stated with warning that it works for cubes and cuboids but not other shapes, $l \times b \times h = V$ written and letters described. Children repeat in chorus.

(12) Worksheets given out. They involve the distinguishing of l, b, h, from dimensions on a diagram, then finding the volume.

Second lesson (next day)
(1) Teacher writes $V = l \times b \times h$ on board and asks for its meaning. The fact that it works for cube or cuboid only, is stressed.

(2) Teacher draws cuboid on board and labels dimensions 30 cm, 20 cm, 40 cm. She asks child to say what 'sum' must be done to find the volume.

(3) Discussion on best way to multiply 20, 30, 40 with correction of 'add noughts'. 30 × 20 done first.

(4) Example (cuboid drawn) in which volume is known and two dimensions but not third. Height referred to as the 'number of layers', and question interpreted as how much in each layer.

(5) Worksheet containing questions designed to use the formula are given out and the children work at them.

Table 7.4: School 5, Class B and School 9, Class A: responses for volume of a box

Type of response	School 5, Class B			School 9, Class A		
l×b×h			G			
layer × number of layers	S	Li G I L S	S			
finds layer by multiplication and then repeats number	G	P	P	E K	E	E S
counts for layer then repeats number				S		
builds same size with blocks (or suggests this)	I					
finds dimensions, but no multiplication				R	L K	R
finds dimensions, multiplies only two	Li	F				
finds dimensions, adds		Li	I L			
fills with bricks and counts					L T	K T
forms skin with cubes		F				
other wrong	F P					
data unavailable		L		T	R S	
	I	PreF	D	I	PreF	D

Interview

Key

School 5	School 9
F Frank	E Elaine
G Gerald	K Ken
I Ian	L Lynn
L Larry	R Ruth
Li Lisa	S Sheila
P Peter	T Tina
S Sarah	

arranged   arranged

```
F  G  I L        E K L
Li P S           R S T
```

used by the children on the initial interview (I), immediately prior to the formalization lessons (PreF) and three months after the teaching (D). The question was not asked at the interview which followed the formalization lessons (PostF). The 'types of response' shown do not demonstrate a hierarchy but the correct use of the formula is regarded as the most sophisticated method since its acquisition was the object of the teaching. A distinction has been made between counting and multiplication for finding a layer.

Peter (PreF) needed to build a layer with bricks whereas on interview (D) he found the dimensions of a layer and multiplied immediately. The seemingly poor final performance of Lisa, Larry and Ian is accounted for by the fact that each measured the dimensions of the box but *added* the results. This was later corrected by Lisa in other questions. On the final interview Ian was shown an *open* box and to find the volume filled it with cubes which he counted one by one; his strategies at (PreF) interview were inconsistent since at one stage he multiplied the number of bricks needed to cover a face by the number needed for another face. Frank's (PreF) method with the closed box entailed covering it with a skin of cubes and counting these; the open box he filled with cubes. At (D) he measured (with a ruler) only two dimensions of the box, multiplied them and said 'area' was the same as 'volume'.

Other cuboids were shown the children: (i) a solid made of centimetre cubes which could be dismantled if absolutely necessary, (ii) a two-dimensional picture which had faces marked in squares to suggest faces of small cubes, and (iii) a two-dimensional picture with measurements shown (sometimes extra sides were labelled and in one case one dimension was 2 and ¼). The performance of the children on these three different questions is shown in Table 7.5. At (PostF) and (D) all but Frank could explain what $V = l \times b \times h$ meant; on the final interview Frank said that he had forgotten.

The formula '$V = l \times b \times h$ was used very infrequently by the children; they appeared to much prefer the use of a layer times the number of layers. The layer taken was not always the base layer, it could be the front face, particularly if the other dimension was two centimetres. The computation for the layer could be counting or multiplication and the layer repeated (addition) or multiplied by the number of layers. Counting followed by addition does not immediately suggest $V = l \times b \times h$.

Frank, (PreF), was the only child who used the small cubes to find the volume; he counted all those he could see when given a block made of them, allowed for some in the centre but lost his place and so counted incorrectly. He also tried to cover the sides of the diagram with cubes until asked whether he assumed the figure was accurate. Frank, on interview (D), was also led astray by redundant figures on the diagram, multiplying every figure in sight. Lisa started to measure the dimensions of the diagram with bricks but then realized that the lengths were already marked. Peter's errors were very often computational and Larry's were concerned with multiplying three numbers. Both these cases are considered later, under 'Basic skills'.

DECOMPOSITION OF A BLOCK

The skyscraper question (see Figure 7.1) asked on the interviews (PreF) and (D) was one of those used in the CSMS Research (Chelsea Diagnostic Tests – Measurement (1985)) which in turn was adapted from an item used in clinical interview by Piaget.

The responses could be split into those who saw it as a visual problem, (making up three layers of the new shape by rearranging one of the old) or a simple computation involving 36 and 4. The children's responses were as follows:

Gerald: (PreF) Starts to physically construct tower with blocks as far as 7 storeys. Does 7 × 4 and counts on from 28 to 36 to obtain 2 more layers.

            (D) Talks in terms of two columns three storeys high built on base of four and a 'thin' four, three storeys high which can be split and balanced on top of the column six storeys high.

Table 7.5: Volume of a cuboid School 5, Class B

		P	F	L	Li	I	S	G
Solid cuboid made of small cubes	PreF	r layer	counts cubes	n layer	n layer	r layer	n layer	n layer
	PostF	n layer	r layer	n layer	n layer	n layer	n layer	n layer
Diagram cross hatched	PreF	~~~	~~~	n layer (layer by counting)	l × b × h	n layer	n layer	n layer
	PostF	n layer (×)	n layer (×)	n layer (layer by counting)	n layer	l × b × h	n layer	n layer
	D	r layer	n layer (×)	Adds dimensions first. Then, n layer	n layer	~~~	n layer	n layer
Diagrams with dimensions	PreF	n layer (×)	Puts cubes over diagram (×)	l×b×h	Starts to measure sides with cubes then l×b×h	r layer	n layer	n layer
	PostF (A)	n layer (×)	Multiplies all numbers	wants to do l × b × h but cannot	l × b × h	l × b × h	l×b×h	n layer
	D (A)	n layer	Multiplies all numbers	Adds dimensions	Adds dimensions Corrects for A	l × b × h	n layer	~~~
	(B)	–	Tries 2¼×3(×)	Adds dimensions	but not for B	~~~	n layer	Takes 2 layers of 12 then ¼ of 12

Key

P Peter
F Frank
L Larry

Li Lisa
I Ian
S Sarah

G Gerald

× wrong
n layers – layer × number of layers
r layers – layer repeated

~~~ not asked
– not attempted

Figure 7.1: The skyscraper question

This block is made by putting some small cubes together

How many cubes make this block 'C' if there are no gaps inside? ....

All the cubes from *block 'C'* are put into a pile:

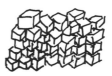

I am now going to use *all* these cubes from block 'C' to build a 'sky-scraper' so that the bottom floor is 4 cubes

How many cubes high would this 'sky-scraper' be from the ground? ....

Frank:	(PreF) Talks of building up bases of 4 but says there are only 3½ of them. Does not find original volume.
	(D) Finds two bases on each layer ('You'd take it to bits and have two on each'). He insists the tower will be 6 cm high 'Because that will go on top of that, it will be three...six centimetres'.
Peter:	(PreF) Sees three ⊞ configurations in each layer, 'this is four, four and four, so it's 3'. 'Yes...three times it – sounds a bit like a table'. 'And all come up to 12 high.' Does not find original volume.
	(D) 'Four there, so there's going to be 1, 2, 3, 4...the same, 6, 7, and there's another 4 there...8, 9, 10.' (He has missed 5 in counting.)
	Peter is still visualizing the question but is now more accurate.
Larry:	(PreF) Cannot attempt the problem.
	(D) 'Would it be 8 high?' 'You see how many fours go into 36.'
Ian:	(PreF) 'Well, three floors up, that's one floor here (*indicating base*), two and three (*indicates building up*), because three 4s are 12.' '3 floors make 12, then another 3 floors, then another 3 floors...9.'
	(D) Not asked.

Sarah and Lisa treated the question as one concerned with multiplication and division of numbers on both occasions whereas the others talked of the physical model.

VOLUME OF A TRIANGULAR PRISM

One of the teacher's repeated statements during the formalization lesson was that the formula applied only to cubes and cuboids. A cardboard triangular prism with its cross section a 3, 4, 5 triangle was shown to each child on three occasions (PreF), (PostF) and (D). On all three occasions Sarah found the volume of a cuboid and halved the result. Lisa at (PreF) fitted cubes on the triangular end (8½) and suggested multiplying by the length but could not compute 8½ by 15. On the latter two interviews she found the volume of a cuboid but did not halve, although on interview (D) she so intended. Peter carefully built up the triangular face and took a length to correspond to each cube in the triangle providing an adequate method for finding the approximate volume each time. Gerald used this method (PreF), then took a base layer and repeated it (inaccurately) on the last two occasions. Larry and Ian multiplied or added the numbers from the dimensions on all occasions. Frank covered all faces with a cuboid (PreF) and counted the number used, even though it was not a cubic centimetre. (PostF) he did the same but then halved his answer and at (D) he multiplied just two dimensions.

BASIC SKILLS

The formula involves multiplication and therefore the ability to recall number bonds was often called into play. Peter seldom gave the correct result to a multiplication; he had a variety of ways of getting to an answer from a fact he thought he knew, but too often that fact was incorrect. He could often see that his answer contradicted other numbers in the question and he would try again to establish the answer. This is illustrated with the interview (PostF) on the question 'The volume is 42 cm^3. How long is the side marked with a question mark' (a diagram is presented with base dimensions 3 and 2 and height shown as '?'). Peter firstly suggested '3' since the sides in the diagram looked equal and then tried:

(I: Interviewer; P: Peter)

P: I think that would be 5 and 3 so, um,... three fives are fifteen.
I: True.
P: And two fifteen's, um...make 30 so that wouldn't be really the answer.
I: Why wouldn't it be the answer?
P: Because that's 42 centimetres, it should make up to 42.
I: Oh I see, so what are you going to do?
P: Oh, I'll just, you see these 2 make 30 so I'm trying to get higher than that, so...um I think that's 11.
I: Well, why don't you try that?
  ⋮
P: Well it can't be 11 because if you had two 32s makes 64, so it can't be the answer, could it?
I: 32...where did 32 come in?
P: Well, um...I got 11 and three 11s.
I: Ah, three 11s are...
P: 32.
I: I see, and two of them, you said...
P: Makes 64, I think.
I: Yes.
P: And well, I don't think that could be the answer.
I: Why not?
P: Because it's 42 centimetres.
I: I see, well it's somewhere then in between which numbers?
P: So it must be about six.

This question was expressed as 'six times something gives 42' by at least three children (PostF). Sarah and Gary divided the volume by 2 and then said, '3 times something gives 21'. Lisa and Larry wrote $6\sqrt{42}$. An important aspect of the use of the formula is that the child must multiply three numbers. In the formalization lesson the teacher dealt with this orally by asking individuals in the class to give her the product of two numbers, in each case dissecting the problem into two pairs. (PreF) each child was asked (verbally) to multiply 5 by 2 by 7 or ($3 \times 2 \times 7$). Peter wrote 3 2 7 and could go no further. Ian tackled the question correctly but failed to give the right answer for ($5 \times 7 \times 2$) '5 times 7 times 2? I know it's 35, times... times 2? Right 35 times 2...2 fives are 10. 3 fives are 15 and one 16, so 160.' Gerald's conversation with the interviewer went as follows:

(I: Interviewer; G: Gerald)

G: 5 by 7 by 2. Dunno! Can I put it like that, and put 5 by 7 and then by 2?
I: Put it any way you think.
G: (*Writes*   57) ...like that
           $\times$ 2
I: What have you written here?
G: 57.
I: Is that what I said?
G: 5 by 7. Oh! I know...5 times 7 (*writes* 5 × 7)...oh, 35. 35 times 2 (*writes*   35)...70
I: And how did you get the 35? $\times$ 2
G: I did the 7 times table, in my head, once 7 is 7, two 7s are 14...like that.

Larry never discovered how to multiply three numbers. For a problem with dimensions 5 × 4 × 2 he wrote   5 correctly, but guessed it might be 25. On the final interview Larry added
            $\times$ 4
            $\underline{\quad 2\quad}$
the dimensions until faced with a $3 \times 3 \times 4$ cuboid (see Figure 7.1). His conversation with the interviewer when faced with this diagram is given below.

(I: Interviewer; L: Larry)

L: Three add four add, um...three, I don't think it would be, um...
I: Oh, three add four add three, you're doing.
L: And I don't think it would be seven, because that's 1, 2, 3, 4, 5, 6, 7, 8, 9, 10, 11, 12 on its own.
I: Oh...oh dear me, so what's gone wrong?
L: Oh, it's twenty...twenty-one, because it's, um...three across and seven on each one, so three seven's are 21.
I: Are there seven on each one?
L: No...there's 12...thirty...thirty-six.
I: Okay. I see. Now when you did it the other way by saying the four and the three and the three, it didn't work, did it?
L: No, I think you're meant to times them.
I: Oh I see. Would you like to check that? How would you check it?
L: Three times four times three.
I: And what's that?
L: Um...Three times four times three...it's what you said.
I: Can you do three times four? Here, do you want a pencil? (*Long pause*)...is the difficulty you don't know what to do with these three numbers?
L: Well yes, because I always forget how to times three numbers, I can do two but...

Sarah and Lisa appeared to be able to multiply three numbers at (PreF) and (PostF) interviews. Frank was not asked the question on (PreF) and his attempts at using the formula at (PostF) resulted in him multiplying all figures in the picture so he multiplied five numbers (inaccurately but confidently).

In some descriptions of the child's performance it will have been noticed that the measurement by ruler is considered to be important. This is because it occurred relatively rarely – the children generally either counted squares to find the length or lined centimetre cubes along the edge.

PERCEPTION OF THE MATERIALS

In previous sections it has been shown that children used cubes on the final interview in order to find a volume. When asked at interview (D) however to explain why $V = l \times b \times h$ was true, the responses neither linked to the 'layer × height' method (which was in general use) nor to the tables formed from results obtained from building cuboids.

Ian said, 'I've no idea...somebody invented it for us'. Larry said he did not know when to use it although he could repeat length, breadth, height. Peter thought the formula could be used on any shape with straight edges and said of his teacher, 'I can't remember Miss saying anything about that, she just told me that length times breadth times height equals volume'. Lisa explained that the formula worked because, 'If it was all in cubes, all centimetre cubes, you'd be able to say how many little cubes you could get inside'. Gerald reckoned, 'Because you could get the answer and if you don't believe that...you could take the cubes out and count them'. Sarah said:

> It's a quicker way than counting all these squares, making up the cuboid and taking it to bits... and you say the breadth is 3 times 4, you say it's three columns, four each would be 12 and you've got to find how many layers for the height, how many layers is that, three, it would be 12 times 3 would be 36.

Frank said:

> (I: Interviewer; F: Frank) $l \times b \times h = V$
>
> I: Right, let's look at this one. '1' – can you tell me what that means?
> F: Um...1, q, t, s. That's...is that one or...
> I: No, it's an '1'.
> F: Well, a, b, c, d, e, f, g, h, i, j, k, l – 1, 2, 3, 4, 5, 6, 7, 8, 9, 10, 11, 12. That'll be 12 times 2 and...
> I: Can you tell me how you know that?
> F: Well, l is...um...the tenth letter of the alphabet.
> I: Yes.
> F: So, 10.
> I: Ah...who told you that?
> F: ...(*long pause*)...
> I: Did you just make it up?
> F: Think so, yes.
> I: Okay, and 'b' will be? And 'h'?
> F: H...um...eh 4...a, b, c, d, e, f, g, h...1, 2, 3, 4, 5, 6, 7, 8, 9, 10 two's is twenty...eight, twenty eights will be one hundred and...one hundred and...eight ...oh, two hundred and, oh, one hundred and forty.
> I: Alright, and then it says equals V.
> F: Equals V? 140.
> I: How do you know that that's not right, shaking your head?
> F: V isn't the 120th letter of the alphabet...(*laughs*)...

Discussion

The most popular method used by the children to find the volume of a cuboid was 'layer times number of layers' and not $V = l \times b \times h$. The pupils did not link the two nor did they refer to the area formula $l \times b$ to find the number of cubes in a layer (but neither did the teacher use the area formula).

Three months after the teaching when given pictures of a cuboid at interview (D) five of the children used layers (see Table 7.5) and they had been using the same strategy just before the formalization lessons. The diagram questions were not asked on initial interview (I), but two of these five children had cumbersome or deficient methods for finding the volume of a closed box on that occasion (see Table 7.4). However, Sarah and Gerald used layers even then. Larry had difficulty with multiplication of three numbers and at (D) added dimensions. Peter and Frank started (I) with wrong methods for the closed box and although by (D) Peter could correctly solve diagram problems he was likely to have an incorrect answer because of his poor grasp of number facts. Frank on (D) used both the layers method and multiplication but with both strategies he obtained wrong answers. He multiplied all numbers on a diagram, not just the three dimensions.

On the (D) interview none of the children remembered the tabular link which gave $V = l \times b \times h$ as a generalization obtained from a record of practical experiences.

School 9, Class A   (aged 10–11)

The teacher of the six children in School 9 was a Masters degree student who had taught at the school the previous year but was no longer employed there. She was offered the chance to teach a small group of pupils for the purposes of the research. The children were called Elaine, Ken, Ruth, Tina, Lynn and Sheila.

The scheme of work

The notable feature of the children in School 9 was that they seldom came together as a class. Individuals worked with a teacher on a subject area and were then set to carry out a task. The six children in the sample were seldom all in the same room; the teacher taught them by talking to one child or a pair and then setting them the next piece of work before moving on to find another pair in the sample who needed work on volume. The teaching took place during five one-hour lessons, with the main focus of each session as follows:

(1) Children given containers and asked which contained the most and how this could be found out – leading to discussion on the most suitable materials for finding the space inside the container.

(2) Volume of cuboids by filling with materials, comparison and making of other cuboids containing same amount of material. Discussion guided towards the need for a standardized unit.

(3) Given a number of cubes, children are asked to make different shaped cuboids and record results.

(4) Looking at their recordings the children are asked to suggest a quick way of finding the volume.

(5) Formalization lesson.

Formalization lesson

Both the scheme of work and formalization lesson (as summarized by the researcher – see Table 7.6) indicate an emphasis on accommodating the material taught to what appeared to be the needs of the child.

Table 7.6: Formalization lesson (1 hour) – School 9, Class A

(After the introduction the teacher did not bring all six children in the sample together but spoke to two groups).

(1) Teacher reminds children all together that the previous week they had obtained how many cubes there were in a layer by multiplying the length and the width. Three children are sent away to practise some multiplication questions, e.g. 4 cubes wide, 6 cubes long. How many in layer?, while she talks to three. Each child has a multiplication square for number facts.

(2) Teacher corrects child who is using bricks to find the size of a layer and says that a quicker way should be used.

(3) Teacher requires a child who answers 4 times 6 to rephrase it as length multiplied by (times) width to give how many in a layer.

(4) Teacher explains the task as finding a quick way of discovering how many cubes there are in a cuboid rather than a layer.

(5) Child finds the number of cubes in a layer and then adds layers to find the total. The teacher asks him if there is any other part of the cuboid which could be measured and eventually they settle on 'height'.

(6) Child gives the height as the number of layers but with encouragement he states it in terms of 'cubes high' although initially stating that there is no connection between the number of layers and the height.

(7) New (solid) examples are shown the children and they are encouraged to say how many 'cubes high' each is and then to find the size of a layer by multiplying length by width.

(8) Children are told to write the sentence explaining one multiplies length by width and then by height. The teacher volunteers to write the statement in a 'quick mathematical way'. She puts brackets round $(l \times w)$ to show that it should be done first.

(9) Teacher works in a very similar way with the second group of three children. Starting with how many in a layer. Children firstly count and then state that one should add the length to the width. The teacher perseveres until they say 'multiply' or 'times'.

(10) There is a break for playtime and then the teacher returns to finding
    (i)   how many in a layer;
    (ii)   how many layers;
    (iii) the number of layers is the same as the number of cubes in the height;
    (iv) writing the volume as length × width × height.

Teaching outcomes

The concern of the teacher was that the six children in the sample should acquire and subsequently use the formula for the volume of a cuboid. She approached the formula through finding the number of cubes in a layer. In the planning of the scheme of work she used a number of resource books on primary mathematics.

THE FORMULA

The first interview was similar to that used in other schools and entailed the child making a decision on which of two boxes would hold the most and then giving a reason for the choice. Two subsequent interviews also included questions on the volume of boxes and the results for the three interviews, (I), (PreF) and (D), are shown in Table 7.4, page 130 (this question was not used in (PostF) interviews). The questioning usually started with a closed box, which was later opened if the child wished. Some children tried to cover the closed box with bricks prior to opening it, when they put cubes inside.

Children appeared to use at least two methods one after the other when faced with the box. This was particularly true of the children who found the dimensions, either with a ruler or by measuring with cubes and then either did nothing with the two/three numbers or multiplied just two of them. They then began to fill the box with cubes.

Ruth's incorrect methods were not consistent and were idiosyncratic. On the initial interview she measured two dimensions of the box with a ruler and then multiplied 18 and ½ by 13 ($l \times w$). On the final interview (D) Ruth multiplied two dimensions, 'That's going to be the answer of how big the top bit is' but then filled the box with cubes, the number of which she proposed to halve.

Table 7.7 shows the type of response given on three interviews to questions in which the children were asked for the volume of (i) a cuboid made of actual cubes (so easily countable), (ii) a diagram of a cuboid showing squares on the faces and (iii) a diagram on which the dimensions were marked in cm and redundant information was given. A second diagram, (b), on which one of the dimensions was 2 and ¼ cms caused considerable difficulty.

The solid cuboid had only two layers and every child before and after the formalization lesson, found the number of cubes in a layer and then repeated that number. For the diagram in which the square faces of cubes were shown Tina simply counted the squares she could see (on all three interviews) although she had found the volume of the solid correctly. There was greater success on this question than when the diagram was simply labelled with numbers for the dimensions. Only Ruth on interview (D) used $l \times b \times h$ and although at this time two other children (Elaine and Ken) could obtain an answer from using layers when the dimensions were integers, they could not apply this method when one dimension was 2 and ¼ cm. Ken stated that it was impossible to use this method when one of the dimensions was 2 and ¼, e.g. 'I done the base, but on that one it's got quarters'.

The formula itself was never stated (unprompted) by a child in the group. On the interview immediately after the formalization lesson (PostF), the children were asked to complete the statement, 'The volume of a cuboid is the length times the width...'. Four of them supplied 'times the height' and one thought there was no extra statement to be made. At the delayed interview, (D), each child was asked for the meaning of $V = l \times b \times h$ and none could give a meaning; four said they had never seen it before. Similarly all but Elaine said they had never before seen cm[3]; she said it meant 'three centimetres'.

Finding the volume of a triangular prism was asked in every class in order to test whether the formula was used indiscriminately. In School 9, Class A we have already noted that the total formula was very seldom used even on cuboids. Given the triangular prism (D), Ruth tried to multiply length and width after measuring each with a ruler but her stated measurements were 75 and 30 millimetres which she said, '... if you times that together that'll come to about 300 and ... that's well ... I'd say too much to go into this box'. It transpired that she thought a millimetre cube was half the size of a centimetre cube which she could see. She had previously (PostF) said '... if I had it on this side that is ... I'd get the length and the width ... the length then width and then do the height ... And then I'd time it all together and find out.' She did not actually carry out this intention however. Tina (PostF) could not find the volume and on the delayed interview (D) said that it did not have a volume 'Cos it's a triangle'. Sheila (PostF) multiplied three measurements of sides but later thought the height might be from the middle of the base of the triangle. At (D) she multiplied together all three sides of the triangle and then multiplied this result by the length. Ken (D) could not find the volume having started by lining up cubes, 'Cos it's going to be in all halves and that'. Elaine (PostF) covered a triangular

Table 7.7: Volume of a cuboid School 9, Class A

		E	K	R	T	L	S
Solid Cuboid made of cubes (only 2 layers)	PreF	Correct answer, states no method	4 lots of 3 (slices). Correct	–	Top counted, then answer added to itself. Correct	Adds two layers Correct	–
	PostF	Counts top layer "Then do it twice"	l × w for layer Counts layers	layer taken twice	Top counted, then answer added to itself. Correct	–	Finds layer and takes twice although finds l,w,h
Diagram showing cubes	PreF	~	r layer	~	Counts squares seen	Top layer times h	–
	Post F	Front layer x 3	r layer	n layer	Counts squares seen	–	Layer x height but states 3 dimensions
	D	Six faces of 12 = 72	r layer	n layer	Counts and then gives up	Correct but no method stated	12 on each face 6 faces (5×12)+12
Diagrams with measurements	PreF (a)	~	Adds all shown dimensions	~	Adds all dimensions	Adds dimensions	~
	PostF (b)	Slice of 6 (counted) multiplied by 5	n layer	l×w to find base and then left	Adds all dimensions (counts on)	~	Layer (l×b) Volume (l×b×h)
	D (a) and (b)	r layer ("It would not work for fractions")	n layer (Cannot do question with fractions)	l × b × h Fractions also done l × b × h	Adds all dimensions and multiplies total by height. Fractions – (adds dimensions)	Adds l,b,h Fractions – Adds dimensions	Takes one dimension twice for each face

Key   E Elaine T Tina
       K Ken   L Lyan
       R Ruth   S Sheila

~ not asked
– not attempted
x wrong

n layer – layer × number of layers
r layer – layer repeated

end with bricks and also put them all along the longest side. Three months later she measured the base of the triangle and the length of the box with a ruler and suggested she might multiply the two dimensions.

COMPUTATIONAL SKILLS

In School 5, Class B Larry had considerable difficulty in multiplying three numbers. To test whether the inability to deal with three numbers was widespread we asked children in School 9, 'Can you multiply 3 times 2 times 7 for me?' and wrote the three numbers. In (PreF) interviews, Elaine and Ken did $(3 \times 2) + (2 \times 7)$; Tina said, 'I can't do times' and Lynn tried $(3 \times 2) \times 7$ but gave the wrong answer. Generally there was little immediate recall of multiplication bonds but the children made attempts to build up the answer, some of these examples are illustrated below:

Tina (I) '3 lots of 7. 2 times 7 is 15, no 14, add another 7; 14, 15, 16, 17, 18, 19, 20, 21,' (*Counting on fingers*)

(PostF) she counted in fours to find the height of the 'skyscraper' with a base of four and volume 36 but ran out of fingers to tally the fours: '1, 2, 3, 4, 5, 6, 7, 8...9, 10, 11, 12...13, 14, 15, 16...17, 18, 19, 20, oh, I can't do it'.

Ken (I) '7 nines...2 nines is 18.
If you do it the other way 3 times 7 is 21.
3 times...4 times 7 is 28.
35, next one.
So this is five times 7...is 35.
Then 42.
5 times 7 is 42.
6 times 7 are...are 49.
7 times 7 is, um...56.
8 times 7 is, um...63. 9 times 7 is 70'.

Between each number statement, there was a pause long enough for the interviewer to either provide an encouraging statement or to repeat the statement just made. The work entailed to produce '9 × 7' was considerable and track had to be kept of each step.

Sheila (I) could add 24 three times in her head and obtain the correct answer, however on interview (D) she found the number of cubes in six layers by multiplying by 5 and then adding the original layer.

Elaine (PostF) asked to find the height of the skyscraper said: 'I'm doing it in two's till it gets to 36.' She was told again that the floor has four cubes but continued counting 15, 16, 17...and then said, 'Oh I don't know'.

(D) She said for the same question, '13...I counted up in my mind'.

Ruth (I) was prepared to try quite hard multiplications, e.g. 18 × 13 for which the computation was written

$$
\begin{array}{r}
18 \\
\times\ 13 \\
\hline
22 \\
30 \\
30 \\
\hline
82 \\
\hline
\end{array}
$$

'Well I was... timing three... three times 8, and then 3 times 10, and 3 times ten again, then getting the answers and then writing it down like that'.

MISCONCEPTIONS

At each interview a number of empty boxes were used; these were usually familiar containers which showed the nature and quantity of the previous contents. Lynn (I) when asked about the amount of space said:

(I: Interviewer; L: Lynn)

I: Which of these two boxes do you think holds the most?
L: This one.
I: You think this tall one?
L: Yes, 'cos it would have forty in it, wouldn't it?
I: It says 40 tea bags on it, doesn't it?

Elaine made a similar response (I) when faced with an empty tissue box.

(I: Interviewer; E: Elaine)

I: And I'm asking how could we find how much it holds, and you don't know. If I opened it, would it help?
E: It would just depend how thick the tissues are.

In each case the interviewer interpreted 'how much does it hold' in a way different to that of the child. Tina (PreF) filled the larger box with big bricks and the small box with centicubes since they fitted better but was unable to suggest how she might compare the two amounts. Tina (D) also appeared to think the diagrams presented to her were accurate so that given that the volume of a cuboid was 42 cm^3 and shown that two of the line segments were 2 cm and 3 cm she said:

(I: Interviewer; T: Tina)

T: Two.
I: Can you tell me what you did?
T: Looked at that one.
.
.
.
I: Why did you choose 2 then, why not 3?
T: Because 3 is longer.
I: Three is longer than that line there?
T: Yes.

Lynn, when asked about the volume of a pencil said:

(I: Interviewer; L: Lynn)

I: If I wanted you to find the volume of that pencil for me, have you any bright ideas what you would do?
L: No.
I: Does it have a volume?
L: It isn't empty, is it?
I: No, it isn't empty.
L: So I don't think it has.
I: I see, so can you tell me what volume is then – what does the word 'volume' mean?
L: The space inside.

Discussion

School 9, Class A (the six children) was of particular interest because each child was taught separately or as one of a pair. The formula $V = l \times b \times h$ was never stated by children in the sample and three months after the teaching only Ruth used this form of the generalization whilst Elaine and Ken preferred 'a layer times the number of layers' approach. The number skills of the children were very limited and computations required considerable work on the part of the child. They often measured the dimensions of a cuboid with a ruler or cubes but did not multiply all three numbers, instead they turned to the more practical method of lining up cubes to fill a box, thus using two methods for solution. There was evidence at (PreF) that three of the children did not know how to multiply three numbers and a fourth used the correct method but obtained an incorrect result.

Table 7.7 shows that different strategies were attempted, depending on which diagram was presented to the child. At the three-month interview (D) only two of the six children consistently succeeded.

School 10, Class A (aged 10–11)

The scheme of work

School 10, Class A was a set of 28 third-year juniors (aged 10–11) with whom the teacher spent six lessons of 20 minutes each, with some opportunity for individual children to build with blocks during free time, leading up to the formalization $V = l \times b \times h$. The teacher's scheme of work is summarized below.

(1) Revision of formula for area (done the year before).
(2) Handling of cuboids and the building of robots, etc., with them.
(3) Discussion and building of cubes, number of faces, etc.
(4) Building of cuboid using 27 cubes.
(5) Pattern of $2^3, 3^3, 4^3$, etc., built up. It was initiated from the number of cubes in cuboids built by the class.
(6) Building different shapes with a constant number of cubes.
(7) Filling a box with centimetre cubes dealt with very briefly.
(8) Revision of how to multiply three numbers together.

(Lunchtime activity of building an enormous cube.)

Formalization lesson

A novel experience not mentioned in the teaching ideas of others was the task of building an enormous cube during the lunch hour, the exercise eventually being abandoned because 'we did not have enough time'. In the formalization lesson the teacher alluded to this attempt and led towards the finding of a rule as a way of obtaining the volume if the dimensions were very large. A summary of the lesson, prepared by the researcher/observer, is given in Table 7.8

The introduction of the formula was not a result of identifying a relationship from a table of results obtained from building cuboids. The children were asked for a quicker way of finding the volume and a number of them volunteered that one should find the area of a layer and multiply by the height.

The results of the investigation with children from School 10 are discussed here briefly and used to amplify the information already obtained from the two groups previously discussed.

Table 7.8: Formalization lesson – School 10, Class A

---

(1)   Each child was asked to make a cuboid and to hold it up for the class to see. Individuals were asked for the volume of the cuboid made.

(2)   Children were asked to think of a method of finding the volume of an enormous cuboid, without counting centimetre cubes. A child almost immediately said, 'length by the...breadth and the height, all together'.

(3)   The teacher continued asking other children and one pupil suggested 'length by width' to find the area and then 'area by height'. This suggestion was also made by others and encouraged by the teacher. The version 'area × height' was tried with numbers by the teacher who stressed the units being used at each stage. Alternative multiplication pairs were mentioned.

(4)   Children were asked how they could write a short form of the way of finding volume and the teacher pursued $V = l \, w \, h$ enquiring for the missing multiplication signs. Children copied the formula into their books.

(5)   One example of substitution of numbers into the formula was done by teacher and children, using an example on a written sheet.

(6)   The children were set more exercises to practise the formula with numbers. The second set of examples had no diagrams.

Teaching outcomes

THE USE OF THE FORMULA

All six of those interviewed could state the meaning of the formula $V = l \times b \times h$ (PostF). All five children available for interview three months later, (D), could give the meaning. The incidence of the use of the formula varied slightly according to the item given. This is demonstrated in Table 7.9.

The responses on the delayed interview, (D), to the two diagrams were different with two children using 'layer × height' for the example which showed squares. When only the dimensions were given, four of the five children interviewed correctly used $V = l \times b \times h$. The fifth child, Edna, multiplied all the numbers on the diagram, i.e. even the extra height.

DECOMPOSITION OF A BLOCK

In the skyscraper question (see Figure 7.1) the children were shown a diagram of a cuboid with dimensions 3, 4, 3 and firstly asked its volume and then the height of a tower built from the cuboid but on a base of four cubes. Adam (PostF) answered '10', 'Because there is 4 in a line and there's three 4s in each and I counted the 4s on each line'. Kate (PreF) was given the cuboid rather than shown the diagram and she used its layout rather than compute:

(I: Interviewer; K: Kate)

K: There's 4 there, and then you could put that like that, be another 4, and there'd be 2 four's there, and 2 four's there...5 and 7.
 I: And how is it going to tell you how high the skyscraper would be from the ground?
K: 9 centimetres.
 I: 9 centimetres high from the ground, and can you just tell me again how you did that?
K: I got them into fours.
 I: Yes...
K: And I counted the fours up.

These two children made use of the layout of the shape they were given rather than seeing the problem as one of division.

Table 7.9: Use of the volume formula School 10, Class A

SOLID		E	K	I	L	B	A
	PreF	$l \times b$	Layers added	$l \times b \times h$	Edge × height	Layer × height	Layer × height
	PostF	$(l \times b)$ doubled	Counts in chunks to find layer then repeats	$l \times b \times h$	Method unknown	$l \times b \times h$	Layer × height
Shown with squares	PreF	Counts 6 faces on a solid block	Counts bottom layer and adds another 3 layers given block	~	Counts (×) but given cuboid not diagram	'Layers × height' Not asked in diagram form	'Layers × height' Not asked in diagram form
	PostF	Multiplies numbers from areas of 2 faces	Layer × height	$l \times b \times h$	Counts faces	$l \times b \times h$	Layer × height
	D	Counts what can be seen	Layer × height	Correct. No reason given	Absent	Faces, but correct	Layer × height
Diagram showing dimensions only some redundant	PreF	Multiplies all numbers	$l \times b \times h$	$l \times b \times h$	$l \times b$	$l \times b \times h$	Layer × height
	PostF	Multiplies 4 lengths and adds fifth	Layer × height	$l \times b$ forgets height	$l \times b \times h$	$l \times b \times h$	Layer × height
	D	Multiplies all numbers	$l \times b \times h$	$l \times b \times h$	Absent	$l \times b \times h$	$l \times b \times h$

Key

E Edna	L Linda	B Bob	A Adam
K Kate	I Ian		

n layer – layer × number of layers
r layer – layer repeated
~ not asked
– not attempted
× wrong

VOLUMES OF OTHER SHAPES

The children were asked to find the volume of a triangular prism on three occasions (PreF, PostF and D). They all noticed that the shape was different. Two children multiplied the length by either the height or side of the triangular base at all three interviews. Kate and Linda measured the base but could proceed no further. Ian and Bob however both found the volume of the related cuboid and halved even though on both (PostF) and (D) interviews Bob's first attempt was wrong:

(I: Interview; B: Bob)

B: That's 10 cm, the width is...5 cm and the height is...4 cm and then you double it.
I: You double it?
B: Because...it's half of a cuboid.
I: You double it because it's half of a cuboid?
B: Yes, that's only half of your...measurement.

On the three month interview, (D), the children were further asked if they could find the volume of a cup using $V = l \times b \times h$. Bob said, 'No, because it's not got square edges'. Ian said, 'No, because the teacup hasn't got straight sides'. Adam said, 'No, because it's not got length, breadth and height, properly'. Kate rejected the idea of using the formula to find the volume of a pen 'because it's a circle'. Edna however was undaunted:

(I: Interviewer; E: Edna)

I: We've got a teacup here, how would you find the volume of that teacup?
E: You could, that's the length and that's the width...
 .
 .
 .
E: That's the length.
I: So the...right round the rim of the cup...
E: That's all the length, that's the height...
I: Right.
E: And I don't know what the height is...
I: You said that's the height.
E: No...that's the length...the brim.
I: Right.
E: And...um...down the side of the cup is the width.

COMPUTATIONAL SKILLS

The formula $V = l \times b \times h$ requires the child to multiply three numbers. On interview (PreF) the children were asked to multiply together 3, 7, 2. Edna, Ian and Bob, could do this but Linda when asked 'can you multiply 3 by 2 by 7 for me?', wrote '32 × 7' which she evaluated as 224. Adam said:

(I: Interviewer; A: Adam)

A: 20.
I: Yes, and how did you get that, Adam?
A: I put the numbers in a row, first I timesed 2 by 3 which is 6 then I timesed 2 by 7 which is 14, then I added them both up.

At (PostF) and (D) interviews the children were asked to provide one dimension of a box when the volume (42 cm³) and the two other lengths (3, 2) were given. The question was illustrated with a diagram having a '?' for the height. Kate (Post-F) said:

(I: Interviewer; K: Kate)

K: 7 centimetres...because that times that is 6 and 6 times 7 is 42.
I: I see. So what were you doing in fact – you knew the volume was 42, and...
K: I was seeing how many 6s would go into 42.

On the final interview (D) however, Kate said the length was 14 cm, obtained from '3 times 14 is 42'.

Ian: (PostF) said, 'Because 2 times 3 which is 6 and you have got to find out what you times 6 by to get 42'. Three months later he had changed the statement of operation to 'Then you have to divide 6 into 42 which is 7'.

Edna: (PostF) said '2 by 3 by... I think it's 8' but at (D) she said the missing length was 36 and proceeded to demonstrate why, by saying '36 and 3 is 39 and 2 is 42'.

Bob: Said he needed to know how many 6s were in 42, on each occasion (PostF) and (D).

Adam: First (PostF) answer was 'I don't know' but at (D) he said he was working out how many 6s in 42, although this took him a little time.

Linda: (PostF) assessed the length required to be 3 cm since it looked almost the same length as the line labelled 3 cm.

USE OF UNITS

The group was asked for the meaning of cm^3 and particularly the significance of the '3'.

Bob: Said (PreF) 'It means you times 3 numbers to get the answer'. (D) 'To get the centimetres cubed, you times the height, the length and the breadth'.

Adam: Said (PreF) 'Centimetre cubed' and that the '3' meant 'cubed' but when questioned further he said this meant 'square centimetres'. At (D) he alternated between the index 3 meaning one should multiply by 3 and 'multiplying three numbers together'.

Kate: Said (D) that the '3' meant 'three times something' but then added 'Cubes... 3 stands for cubes' and insisted these two statements were the same. At (D) she intimated that 'Centimetre 3', 'Centimetre Cubed' and 'cm^2' were the same.

Linda: (PreF) did not know the meaning of the notation, but at (PostF) she said it stood for 'cubes'.

Ian: (PreF) said 'It's centimetre cubed', 'That you time the three sides together'. At (D) he said 'Centimetre cubed'... 'If it's squared it means just one surface of say, a cube, but if it's centimetres cubed, it means the whole area of it'.

The confusion between units of measure is demonstrated again in the skyscraper question when one asks for the height of the tower on a base of 4 cubes. On the delayed interview (D): Edna said '9 centimetre cubed' having already given the height as a number of blocks; Ian said '9 cubes high' and amended it only when the interviewer said 'And if each cube is 1 cm it would be...'; Adam said simply '9'; and Kate said '9 cm high' but she referred to the base of a box as '12 centimetre cubes' because she saw the problem as one of filling with cubes. Bob also referred to the height as '9 centimetres'. If the child measures the length or an area with cubes it would seem eminently sensible to state the measurement in terms of cubes. Whereas we expect an abstraction from the cubes to units in one (cm) or two (cm^2) dimensions.

Discussion

The interviews with School 10, Class A have been described briefly. Three months after the teaching the five children interviewed could give the meaning of $V = l \times b \times h$ and all but one used it correctly for the volume of a cuboid shown in a diagram marked with the dimensions. The 'layer × number of layers method' was alternatively used by two pupils when the diagram showed a squared face. The formula was used indiscriminately for other shapes by only one child although two tried to multiply two dimensions for a triangular prism. The problem of multiplying three numbers was presented (PreF) and two children could not obtain an answer. The group interviewed had considerable difficulty in interpreting 'cm³' and often gave linear measurements in terms of cubes since they had indeed found the length of an edge by using cubes.

School 11, Class A (aged 12)

School 11, Class A is included in the description of the formalization of the volume of a cuboid because it provides an example of secondary-aged children being taught the relationship. The teacher normally taught science. An outline of her scheme of work is given below.

(1) Use of ruler to measure length
(2) Familiarization with units of length
(3) Measurement of irregular area by covering with squares
(4) Area of a rectangle and meaning of cm^2
(5) Filling box with centimetre cubes
   Formula $V = l \times b \times h$

In the event, it seems that the box filling activities were crowded into the same lesson as the formalization and this joint aspect took one double lesson for completion. Dean, James, Neil, Philip and Stan were selected for interviews. However Neil was not present for all the interviews. Dean and Neil said they had met the idea of volume and the use of cubes in their primary school but they did not recall seeing the formula. James and Stan could remember using the cubes and the formula whilst Philip, although from the same primary class, could remember neither. It was the case that (for the four boys present for all the interviews) the formula was more likely to be used when a line diagram with the sides marked was provided. When the cubes were clearly shown on the block or displayed by cross hatching on a diagram (see the items for School 10, Class A in Table 7.9, page 145), Philip was inclined to count squares before and after the lesson. Dean never used the formula and his *ad hoc* methods never produced the correct answer. Stan did not use the formula before the lesson but used it consistently afterwards and James used it on all the cuboid questions. Although Stan and James appeared to have accepted the formula and were prepared to use it, they also applied it to the triangular prism.

Conclusions

The transfer from using blocks to build a cuboid or to fill a box, to the view that the same volume can be found from the multiplication of three numbers encompasses the acceptance of diagrams to represent solids, numbers to represent lengths and letters to represent words and corresponding lengths. The aim of each of the teachers reported in this chapter was that their pupils would be able to employ $V = l \times b \times h$ appropriately and with understanding.

The formula

The stage before the statement $V = l \times b \times h$ was usually that of finding the volume of a layer and either repeating or multiplying by the height to obtain the total volume. It was this method that was remembered and used by many of the children (see Table 7.10).

The advantage of using the cross section multiplied by the length is not only that the method can be used for any solid shape but also that the universally used skill of counting can be employed at each step. Although the formula for area $A = l \times b$ had probably been taught to all the children in the sample prior to the teaching sequence leading up to the volume formula, only one child employed it.

Table 7.10: Use of formula for volume (given diagrams), Delayed interview (D)

School/class	Number interviewed	Number using predominantly $l \times b \times h$	Number using both layer × height and $l \times b \times h$	Number using predominantly layer × height	Number using neither method
5B	7	1	1	3	2
9A	6	0	1	1	4
10A	5	1	3	0	1
11A	4	2	0	0	2
Total	22	4	5	4	9

It was not the case that the children having been taught a generalized form necessarily abandoned the blocks. The pupils in School 9, Class A on the final interview employed a method which involved multiplying at least two dimensions but then they would start filling containers as well. Peter and Ian in School 5 liked handling the cubes and so even on interview (D) spent a long while filling containers rather than calculating a result.

Representation in two dimensions

In the interviews the children were asked to find the volume of cuboids which were open boxes, solid blocks or shown by diagrams. They seemed to have no difficulty in seeing that a specific diagram represented a specific block. In fact in the skyscraper question children often referred to the physical removal of groups of four cubes and dealt with the problem by simulating the movement of blocks. In School 5, Class B, Frank at one stage covered the diagram with cubes to find the volume. Others compared lengths by measuring the drawn lines with cubes or judged one line longer than another on the basis of the diagram. It seems likely that for the child a diagram has much more significance and is seen to possess more attributes than is the intention of the person who provides it.

Prerequisite skills

The formula for volume involves the operation of multiplication and in order that it can be used quickly and effectively the multiplication number bonds need to be known. If multiplication usually results in error (see Peter in School 5, Class B), then the child will resort to counting which in turn is limited to small numbers if it is to be successful. Most of the children interviewed for Volume did not have an immediate recall of multiplication facts.

Of considerable importance is the lack of knowledge of the way to multiply three numbers (see Table 7.11). Larry in School 5, Class B never learned how to multiply three numbers and by the delayed interview, he was adding them because this was his only available operation. The children in School 10, Class A also had other methods for producing an answer for 3 × 2 × 7. It seems clear that the multiplication of three numbers must be taught (or revised) as a necessary prerequisite to using the volume formula.

Measuring

When the children were filling boxes in a systematic fashion prior to finding the formula in terms of dimensions they used rows of blocks to find the length, height, etc. The dimensions were found not with a ruler in centimetres but with centimetre cubes. The teachers all referred to cm lengths but the children did not. In School 5, Class B the children very seldom took a

Table 7.11: Multiplication of three numbers

School/class				Children			
	P	G	L	I	F	S	Li
5B [5×2×7]	527	57×2 initially	5 ×2 7	(5×2)×7 incorrect	–	√	√
	E	K	T	L	R	S	
9A [3×2×7]	(3×2)+(2×7)	(3×2)+(2×7)	I can't do times	(3×2)×7 incorrect	–	–	
	L	A	E	I	B	K	
10A [3×2×7]	32×7	(2×3)+(2×7)	√	√	√	–	

√ correct   – not asked

ruler to find a length, they nearly always used small cubes. In this exercise the child had been expected to use one form of measurement (the blocks) but to realize that the only part of the block which is relevant, is the edge. The children in School 11, Class A had great difficulty in describing the meaning of cm^3 and it would seem that greater attention needs to be paid to the unit of measurement used in Volume exercises. This is not trivial since in all the classes, whilst leading to $V = l \times b \times h$ the children had been expected to deal with length (edges) measured with cubes, layers (which are solid) and then volume. At each stage the counting of cubes was used to obtain an answer.

Chapter 8
Equations

Linda Dickson

Introduction

The two research projects, CSMS and SESM, have provided a very valuable insight into children's understanding of the use of letters for numbers in expressions involving arithmetic rules and operations, i.e. algebra. In the CSMS work Küchemann (1981) identified various categories of letter usage with the items asked of 14-year-olds. These included instances when pupils regarded letters as taking on numerical values, perhaps one specific value or several values or as a variable which can take on any value from a given set (e.g. the integers). Other categories involved cases where letters were ignored, or seen as having no meaning, or interpreted as shorthand notation for words or objects.

Booth (1984) extended this work with 13- to 15-year-olds. She identified three main areas of difficulty (the numbers in brackets indicate the percentages of children in the SESM Phase One interview sample who demonstrated that particular difficulty):

(i) The meaning children attached to letters: there was confusion between a letter representing a number and with it representing an object (48 per cent); different letters were seen as having to represent different numbers, thus $x + y + z \neq x + p + z$ (74 per cent); letters had to represent whole numbers (75 per cent); or they ignored the meaning of the letters, e.g. $2x + 8y + 3x$ would be added to give $13xy$ (58 per cent).

(ii) Operating with letters: an inappropriate method was transposed from arithmetic to algebra – the specific operational model was not available in arithmetic and so generalization was unlikely (56 per cent); children were unwilling to record an algebraic statement assuming that a specific numerical answer was required (46 per cent); even when children used a formal method and symbolized it correctly they did not necessarily recognize that this was an appropriate thing to do.

(iii) Notation and convention: equating $x + y$ with xy or $2 + k$ with $2k$ (49 per cent); misinterpreting the meaning of, say, $4m$ or xy by

(a) not recognizing that $4m$ is $4 \times m$ (49 per cent)
(b) stating that if 2 lots of x is $2x$ then 2 lots of 7 is 27 (31 per cent)
(c) for xy, if $x = 3$, $y = 2$, then xy is 32 (29 per cent);

not recognizing the equivalence of $m + m + m$ and $3m$ (32 per cent); failing to appreciate the need for brackets (88 per cent) and so carrying out the first written operation first, or failing to record brackets when they were necessary.

This summary provides the context for the present investigation with younger children as they learn to solve equations. Many of the aspects listed were monitored as well as other issues relating to equations and their solution. The formalization aspect of each teaching programme was the development of a formal procedure for solving equations. Each teacher placed an individual interpretation on what constituted the pre-formalization activities and the subsequent formalization (lessons) in their programme of work.

The sample

Classes from four different schools participated in the investigation (see Table 8.1). Teachers from three of the schools (3, 16 and 17) selected pupils who reflected the spread of ability within their particular classes. The six pupils from School 15 were chosen on an age basis. They were amongst some of the youngest in the school, being 13 years old for the duration of the study, and reflected the range of ability in roughly the more able half of the top ability set.

Table 8.1: Equations sample

School/ class	Type	Group	Size	Age	Number interviewed
3/B	Middle	Middle Band	24	12	6
15/A	Upper 13+	Top half of top ability set	26	13	6
16/A	Middle 9–13	Set 3 of 4	25	11–12	5
17/A	Middle 9–13	Set 1 of 3	22	11–12	6

School 16, Class A (aged 11–12)

As shown in Table 8.1, this was a class (n = 25) of third-year middle school pupils of average to below average ability (third set out of four). The programme of work was implemented in seven 70 minute lessons over a period of three weeks. In the teacher's words it was aimed at developing an 'understanding of the solving of equations and the realization that the equation is a statement of fact and should be treated as such'. The scheme was aimed at working towards the solution of linear equations of the type: $x + 5 = 13$, $7 = p - 10$, $14 = a + 8$ and the formalization was a generalizable method for their solution.

Assumed knowledge

The teacher assumed that the pupils had an understanding of the four arithmetic operations on number and that there existed varying levels of understanding of basic algebraic ideas. Relevant work which had previously been taught involved 'containers', e.g. $\square + 4 = 6$, so $\square = 2$.

The pre-teaching interview (I) responses

Five children were interviewed, answering questions aimed at identifying the nature of their understanding of certain numerical relationships and their symbolization, both of which might provide a foundation for algebraic operations (see Table 8.2).

THE INTERPRETATION OF THE '=' SIGN

The pupils were presented with a selection of small cards each displaying a symbol; the digits 0 to 9, the four 'rule' signs, and the '=' sign. The interviewer used cards to form

$$\boxed{1}\ \boxed{0}\ \boxed{+}\ \boxed{6}\ \boxed{=}$$

asking each pupil to read it out then select appropriate cards to complete it. All pupils placed $\boxed{1}\ \boxed{6}$ to the right of the $\boxed{=}$ sign. The interviewer then removed the $\boxed{+}\ \boxed{6}$, leaving

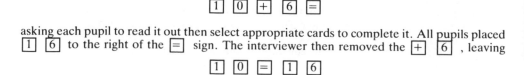

$$\boxed{1}\ \boxed{0}\ \boxed{=}\ \boxed{1}\ \boxed{6}$$

and asked the pupil to choose cards on the right hand side (RHS indicated) of the $\boxed{=}$ sign so that it was equal to the left hand side (LHS).

All pupils eventually formed $10 = 16 - 6$. However Ann also placed a second '=' sign thus, $10 = 16 - 6 =$ while Steve put $10 = 16 - 6 \quad 10$. Both read it aloud as 'sixteen take away six equals ten'. Steve indicated that he wanted the '10' on the LHS to be placed on the right. The conversation ran:

(I: Interviewer; S: Steve)

I: You want to put the '10' the other side do you?
S: Yes.
I: Why is that?
S: To make the sum more correct.

With the arrangement $10 + 6 = 16$, the interviewer then explained that she was going to multiply everything on the LHS by 3 and that she would use brackets to show this. The cards were now arranged $3 \times (10 + 6) = 16$. The pupils were asked to choose and place cards on the RHS (indicated) to make it equal to the LHS. Once again, one pupil, Ben, put in a second '=' sign giving: $3 \times (10 + 6) = 16 \times 3 =$.

The pupils were specifically asked what 'equals' meant and, without exception, explained it in terms of an answer to be found rather than of 'sameness' or 'equality of value'. As Booth (1984) has shown, this interpretation can lead to difficulties. In the present research it was also the case that this interpretation persisted throughout with the teaching.

OPERATING IDENTICALLY TO BOTH SIDES OF AN EQUATION TO MAINTAIN EQUALITY

This aspect was studied as described above; pupils placing cards on the RHS of $3 \times (10 + 6) = 16$ to restore equality. Only Ben showed an appreciation of the notion of operating identically to both sides of an equation without first calculating the LHS (see Table 8.3).

INVERSE OPERATIONS/OPERATORS

Another aspect to be investigated was the pupils' grasp of the general principle of inverse operations. The following item was asked, once again using cards and incorporating a symbol $\boxed{?}$ which was explained as representing a hidden number. The interviewer then said that 3 was to be added to this hidden number, selecting cards $\boxed{?}\ \boxed{+}\ \boxed{3}$.

Each child was asked what they would do next to bring it back to just the hidden number, so; $\boxed{?}\ \boxed{+}\ \boxed{3}\ \wedge\ \rightarrow\ \boxed{?}$. This procedure was repeated for such operations as

$$\boxed{?}\ \boxed{\times}\ \boxed{6}\ \wedge\ \rightarrow\ \boxed{?}$$
$$\boxed{?}\ \boxed{-}\ \boxed{7}\ \wedge\ \rightarrow\ \boxed{?}$$
$$\boxed{?}\ \boxed{\div}\ \boxed{4}\ \wedge\ \rightarrow\ \boxed{?}$$

Three of the pupils could not give answers to these. Sally felt it necessary to think of specific values for the hidden number which led her to give inappropriate inverse operations for $\times$ and $\div$ e.g. adding or subtracting a specific number to correct the particular result. Ben gave correct responses to all four operations but was unsure with his replies for the '$\times$' and '$\div$':

(I: Interviewer; B: Ben)

B: Think so.
I: Why do you only think?
B: Because I don't know with these two signs, because they're my hardest kind of ... I can do subtraction and addition, they're easy, but I don't know with division and multiplication.

With the exception of Ben, it seemed that these pupils had not grasped the central principle of inverse operators (see 'Appreciation of inverse operations' in Table 8.2).

Table 8.2: Summary of responses for School 16, Class A

Items	Ann				Ben				Dee				Sally				Steve			
	I	PreF	PostF	D	I	PreF	PostF	D	I	PreF	PostF	D	I	PreF	PostF	D	I	PreF	PostF	D
Interpretation of '=' sign What does '=' equals mean? (Response indicating notion of equality or 'sameness')	×	×	×	×	×	×	×	×	×	×	×	×	×	×	×	×	×	×	×	×
Operating identically to both sides of an equation 3 × (10 + 6) = 16. What must you do to the right han side so that it equals the left hand side? Response × by 3) (I); 3 × (11 + 4) = 15 (PreF): 4 × (6 + 3) = 9 (PostF & D):	DK	✓	✓	✓?	✓	✓	✓	✓	×	DK	×	?	×		✓	✓	DK	DK	✓	✓
Appreciation of inverse operations egs. [?] + 3 ∧ → [?]	DK	DK	×✓	✓	✓	✓	✓	✓	DK	DK	×	✓	?	✓	✓	✓	DK	DK	✓	✓
I have a hidden number. I add 3, [?] − 4 ∧ → [?]	–	×	×	✓	✓	✓	✓	✓	DK	DK	–	✓	×	✓	✓	✓	–	DK	✓	✓
what must I do next to get [?] × 6 ∧ → [?]	DK	DK	–	DK	✓	✓	✓	✓	–	–	–	DK	×	×	?	×	DK	DK	✓	✓
back to the hidden number? [?] ÷ 7 ∧ → [?]	–	DK	–	DK	✓	✓	✓	✓	DK	–	–	DK	×	?	?	✓	–	DK	✓	✓
Translating situations into mathematics (i) I think of a number, I add 17 and the answer is 31. How can you find out what the number is? (Appropriate generalizable strategy) (I); I add 14 and the answer is 32. (PreF); I add 19 and answer is 41 (PostF & D).	×	×	×	×	×	×	✓	×✓	×	×	×	×	×	×	×	??	✓	✓	✓	✓
Can you write it down in some way? (Recorded as an equation)	×	✓	✓	✓	×	✓	✓	✓	DK	DK	×	×	×	×	×	×	×	✓	✓	✓
(ii) I have a long piece of liquorice 6 m long and I'm going to cut it into 2 pieces. How long might the pieces be? (I) (Appropriate numerical values).	✓	✓	✓	✓	✓	✓	✓	✓	??	??	??	??	✓	✓	✓	✓	✓	✓	✓	✓
I have a length of string which is 8 m long to tie up two parcels (PreF): (6 m long)(PostF & D): Can you write it down in some way? (Recorded as an equation).	–	DK	×	DK	×	×	×	×	×	–	DK	–	×	?	×	×	DK	DK	DK	DK

Table 8.2 contd

Towards the notion of a variable and its symbolic representation

One unknown
(i) a) $\square + 3 = 5$; $\square$ interpreted numerically (I).
 b) $x + 5 = 8$; x interpreted numerically (I); $18 + a = 47$ (PreF); $x + 5 = 11$ (PostF and D).

Two unknowns
(ii) a) $\square + \triangle = 8$; $\square$ and $\triangle$ interpreted in conventional way (I)
 b) $\square + \square = 8$; $\square = 4$ only
 a) $x + y = 10$
 b) $x + x = 10$ $x = 5$ only   } (PreF)
 a) $p + q = 9$
 b) $p + p = 9$ $p = 4\frac{1}{2}$ only
  or $p + p = 10$ $p = 5$ only   } (PostF and D)
(iii) What does 5m (5x) mean?   (Response indicating appropriate interpretation)
 I and PreF
 {If m = 3 find 5m (PreF)}
 What does 4x mean   } (PostF and D)
 If x = 6 find 4x

Solving equations (Interviews PostF & D)
(i) $x + 5 = 11$ a) intuitively/informally
 b) balance drawing
 c) taught written method
(ii) $b - 8 = 3$ a) intuitively/informally
 b) balance drawing
 c) taught written method
(iii) $5 = y + 1$ a) intuitively/informally
 b) balance drawing
 c) taught written method

Connecting balance with written method
Is there any connection between drawing balance and writing the lines down? (What is it?)

Key

Symbol	Meaning
✓	indicates appropriate generalizable approach or interpretation
✗	indicates inappropriate or non-generalizable approach or interpretation
–	indicates not asked
DK	indicates don't know
G	pupil acknowledges response is a guess
?	indicates some doubt or contra-indication

Table 8.3: School 16, Class A pupil responses to the question: (given) 10 + 6 = 16

'If I multiply the left hand side of this 10 + 6 like this 3 × (10 + 6)… what must I do to the right hand side so that it equals the left hand side?'

(PreF: 11 + 4 = 15, multiply by 3)

(PostF and D: 6 + 3 = 9, multiply by 4)

Type of response

Type of response	I	PreF	PostF	D
Multiplies RHS appropriately without recourse to calculating LHS			B, S, St	A, B, D, S, St
Multiplies RHS appropriately having first calculated LHS		B	A	
Does not multiply RHS but uses some other operation to obtain equality having first calculated LHS	S	S		
Calculates LHS and wishes to put this answer on RHS – cannot operate with existing amount on RHS	A, D		D	
Does not know what to do to RHS	St	D, St		

I ↔ PreF ↔ PostF ↔ D   interview
20 days   7 days   91 days

Examples of responses:

S (I):   Adds 10 + 6 getting 16. Times 16 by 3 getting 48, on RHS puts '16 + 32'.

D (I):   Times 3 by 10 getting 30. Adds 6 to get 36 and puts '3 × (10 + 6) = 16   36'.

Ann (I): Calculates LHS by 3 × 10 added to 3 × 6 getting 48. Wants to remove 16 and put '3 × (10 + 6) = 48'.

Key

A   Ann
B   Ben
D   Dee
S   Sally
St   Steve

Arranged

A B
S St

TRANSLATING SITUATIONS INTO MATHEMATICS

Two questions were asked, requiring translation into mathematical language and a description of strategies for solution. The first involved one unknown, as follows: 'I think of a number, I add 17 and the answer is 31. How can you find out what the number is and can you write down the problem in some way?' Only one pupil, Steve, used an approach involving the subtraction of 17 from 31. Ann, Ben and Dee used a strategy of counting on from 17 to 31 by various means and Sally adopted a trial and error approach by trying different numbers. Profiles of their strategies across the four interviews are given in Table 8.4.

No pupil at interview (I), the pre-teaching stage, recorded the situation in the form of an equation. Ann, Ben, Sally and Steve all wrote an arithmetical calculation in line with their strategy, e.g.

$$\begin{array}{r} 17 \\ +14 \\ \hline 31 \end{array} \qquad \begin{array}{r} 31 \\ -17 \\ \hline 14 \end{array}$$

while Dee was unable to record it in any way.

The other question involved two unknowns and was the following:

I have a long piece of liquorice which is 6 m long and I want to cut it into two pieces to give one piece to Annie and the other piece to Jim. How long can the two pieces be? Supposing Annie likes liquorice more than Jim, how long might the two pieces be now? Can you write down the problem in some way?

All pupils were able to give integral values for the lengths and with a little prompting (e.g. 'Do they have to be whole numbers of metres long?') fractional quantities (halves). Dee had difficulty with fractional quantities in that they did not total 6 m and she also confused units, e.g. she gave 4½ cm and 2½ cm as two possible lengths.

No pupil could devise a way of recording the problem to cater for every possible combination of lengths. Ben and Sally could only offer separate statements for each possibility, e.g. 4 m and 2 m, 5 m and 1 m, while Dee wrote

$$\begin{array}{r} 6 \text{ m} \\ \times 2 \\ \hline \end{array}$$

A more detailed summary of the pupils' responses to this item across the four interviews is given in Part A of Table 8.5.

It seemed then that at interview (I), the pre-teaching stage, all five pupils were unable to translate situations into the appropriate symbolic format. They were able to solve the problems at an informal level but the unsophisticated nature of their strategies (e.g. counting on) would perhaps not be adequate preparation for a more structured approach demanded by the formalization for solving equations.

TOWARDS THE NOTION OF A VARIABLE AND ITS SYMBOLIC REPRESENTATION

Some further items were asked which involved the appearance of symbols representing variables. These were $\square + 3 = 5$; $x + 5 = 8$; $\square + \triangle = 8$; $\square + \square = 8$. All pupils recognized the $\square$ in $\square + 3 = 5$ as representing a numerical value, namely 2. However when they were shown

Table 8.4: School 16, Class A
Pupil profiles for strategies and written recordings for Question 1: I think of a number. I add 17 and the answer is 31. What was the number I thought of?
(The numbers for 'add' and 'answer' were 14, 13 and 19, 41 on some occasions.)

Strategies

	I	PreF	PostF	D
Formalization, e.g., $a + 19 = 41$; $a = 41 - 19$; $a = 22$			St	
Take given number from total, e.g., Takes 17 from 31	St	St	B	B / S St
Counting on from given number to total by various methods	A B D	A B D	A D	A B D
Trial and error – trying different methods	S	S	S	

Written recordings

	I	PreF	PostF	D
Appropriate generalizable form: letters, e.g., $a + 19 = 41$ symbols, e.g., $\Box + 19 = 41$ other, e.g., $14 + = 32$		A	A B / St	A / St
Written in the form of a calculation To match the strategy shown above e.g., $31 - 17$, $17 + 14 = 31$	A B / S St	B / S St	D / S	B / S
Inappropriate algebraic expression, e.g., $19A + 41C$				D
Unable to express in written form	D	D		

I ↔ PreF ↔ PostF ↔ D   interview
20 days   7 days   91 days

Key
A   Ann
B   Ben
D   Dee
S   Sally
St   Steve

Arranged

A B D
S St

$x + 5 = 8$, Ann and Steve did not know what x symbolized whereas Ben and Sally interpreted it numerically. For example Sally said:

> Sally: 'It's a number like...I don't know what...it's like a number; well a letter but it's sort of worth a number, like a number.'

A summary of pupils' responses to similar items across the four interviews is given in Table 8.2, 'Notion of a Variable'.

For the item involving two unknowns, $\Box + \triangle = 8$, various aspects were investigated. These are listed here:

(i)   Whether $\Box = \triangle$ is possible
(ii)   Whether $\Box \neq \triangle$ is possible (including possibility of representing fractional as well as integral values)
(iii)   Whether $\Box = 0$ is possible
(iv)   Whether $\Box = 10$ is possible
(v)   What can be said about $\Box + \Box = 8$.

A summary of the responses to these aspects for each of the four sets of interviews is given in Part B of Table 8.5. Mostly the five pupils gave appropriate interpretations of $\Box$ and $\triangle$ within the context of $\Box + \triangle = 8$, the one consistent difficulty being with the possibility of $\Box$ being 10. This was deemed not possible as it would bring the answer to more than 8. (Note that pupils had encountered negative numbers in earlier work.) For $\Box + \Box = 8$, Sally interpreted it in the same way as $\Box + \triangle = 8$, i.e. each term taking on different value without being restricted to the same values for each box and the 'solution' $\Box = 4$.

Table 8.5: Pupils' responses to items concerning the understanding and symbolization of situations involving two variables – School 6, Class A

	Ann				Ben				Dee				Sally				Steve			
	I	PreF	PostF	D	I	PreF	PostF	D	I	PreF	PostF	D	I	PreF	PostF	D	I	PreF	PostF	D
Part A																				
Liquorice/string cut in two																				
What can lengths be?																				
Both lengths equal	√	√	√	√	√	√	√	√	√	√	√	√	√	√	√	√	√	√	√	√
Different { positive integers	√	√	√	√	√	√	√	√	√?	√?	√?	√?	√	√	√	√	√	√	√	√
{ fractions	√	√	√	√	√	√	√	√	√?	√?	√?	√?	–	√	√	√	√	√	√	√
How would you write down the problem?																				
Numerical calculation for one possibility, e.g. 2)‾6	–	DK	√	DK		√	√	√	×	–	DK	–		√	√	√	DK	DK	DK	DK
Series of statements – one for each possibility	–	DK	√	DK				√		–	DK	–		√	√	√	DK	DK	DK	DK
Single generalized statement for all possibilities	–	DK	√	DK	√			√		–	DK	–		?	√	√	DK	DK	DK	DK
Part B																				
□ + △ = 8 (I) x + y = 10 (PreF)																				
p + q = 9 (PostF and D)																				
Both equal	√	√	×	×	√	×	×	×	√	LETTERS		×	√	√	√	×	×	√	√	×
Different { positive integers	√	√	√	√	√	√	√	√	√	NOT		√	√	√	√	√	√	√	√	√
{ fractions	√?	√?	–	√	×	×	√	√	?	INTERPRETED		√	√	√	√	√	–	√	√	–
One variable = 0	√	√	√	√	–	×	×	×	√	AS		√	√	√	√	√	√	√	√	√
One variable > sum, e.g. can x be 25?	×	×	×	×	√	√	√	√	×	VARIABLES:		×	×	×	×	×	×	×	×	×
For □ + □ = 8, (x + x = 10),		√	×	×	√	√	√	√	–	SEEN AS		–	×	√	√	√	–	√	√	√
(p + p = 9, '□ = □').										OBJECTS										
For □ + □: □s can't be different	–	?	?√	×	√	√	√	√	–			–	×	√	×	√	–	√	√	√

Key

√   Appropriate responses
×   Inappropriate responses
–   Not asked
DK   Don't know

SUMMARY

The pre-teaching set of interviews indicated that pupils could interpret problems intuitively and employ informal strategies for solving them. They had difficulty in formulating these situations symbolically, particularly in the format of an equation. On the whole they could interpret 'container' symbols, i.e. $\square$ and $\triangle$, as numerical variables but not letters, e.g. x, to the same extent.

Their interpretation of the '=' sign as indicating the answer was already giving problems particularly with respect to the idea of operating identically to both sides of an equation. In the main, with the exception of Ben, they showed an inadequate grasp of the notion of inverse operations and operators as well as showing a need to operate on specific quantities rather than being able to generalize with unknown quantities. These aspects may be regarded as fundamental to the learning of any formal generalizable method for solving equations.

The pre-formalization work

The pre-formalization work took place in five lessons, each 70 minutes long, and spread over a period of two weeks. This work is only described very briefly and may be regarded as the teacher's way of providing a general introduction to algebra. It involved blackboard work and discourse followed by worksheets based on a widely used textbook source. The main approach and initial presentation of the topic was through letters representing a shorthand for words/objects, e.g. 'In a basket there are 10 apples, 5 bananas, 12 oranges and 7 pears → 10a + 5b + 12o + 7p. There were exercises on collecting like terms through addition and subtraction and some work on codes. Directed numbers were revised and one lesson concentrated on the substitution of numerical values for letters in algebraic expressions and their evaluation. The notation 8a was explained in terms of multiplication and repeated addition but the teacher felt more work was required on this aspect. This constituted the pre-formalization work as planned by the teacher.

The pre-formalization interview (PreF) responses

A summary of the pre-formalization interview responses is given in Table 8.2. Those aspects concerned with numerical relationships, i.e. pupils' interpretation of the '=' sign, their appreciation of operating identically to both sides of an equation and an appreciation of inverse operations were little changed from their first interview responses.

Probably the most significant feature of this set of interviews was the emergence of some pupils' intepretation of letters as representing abbreviated words rather than numerical values. It is likely that this is directly attributable to the pre-formalization work. Both Küchemann (1981) and Booth (1984) discuss the difficulties children face with the change from 'letter as object' to letter 'standing for a number' or, more complex still, 'taking on different values in turn from a range of values'.

TRANSLATING SITUATIONS INTO MATHEMATICS

For the item, 'I think of a number, I add 14 and the answer is 32, what is the number?', again only Steve approached this by subtracting 14 from 32, the others using informal methods such as counting on from 14 to 32. Only Ann was able to record the situation in a way reflecting an algebraic equation. She wrote 14+   =32, leaving a gap for the unknown number. For the item involving two variables – this time a length of string 8 m long to be cut into two pieces to tie two parcels – Sally moved towards recording this algebraically, initially recording it as 8 ÷ 2 then, following discussion, replacing this by 8 − $\square$. She went on to suggest a list of numbers to 'pick out' from 1 to 7.

TOWARDS THE NOTION OF A VARIABLE AND ITS SYMBOLIC REPRESENTATION

Pupils were shown the equation 18 + a = 47 and asked to explain the meaning of '*a*'. Ann, Ben and Sally described it appropriately as a numerical value but Dee and Steve regarded the *a* as being an abbreviation for a word as can be seen in the following extracts:

(I: Interviewer; D: Dee)

D: Eighteen add *a* equals 47.
I: What does that mean?
D: Eighteen lots... eighteen lots of *a*... has got to equal forty-seven.
I: So what do you think the *a* means then?
D: Eighteen apples.
I: You reckon it's eighteen apples even though there's a plus and... Is there anything to work out there?
D: Got to work out this bit. (*Indicates with finger.*)
I: What, the gap between the *a* and the equals sign?
D: Mmm...

Steve interpreted *a* in a similar way for $18 + a = 47$.

(I: Interviewer; S: Steve)

I: What does *a* stand for there?
S: Apples, alphabet...
I: And how would you work it out?
S: ...(*Pause*)...
I: Do you understand what there is to work out there?
S: No.
I: No. Supposing you were to find what *a* meant; does it just mean apples or does it mean...
S: It can mean anything.
I: Could it be a number?
S: No.
I: No, it couldn't be a number? It means a thing, does it?
S: Yes.

The interviewer then asked Steve about $18 + \square = 47$ and in this case he identified the $\square$ as representing a number but still maintained that *a* did not stand for a number.

However for the equation $x + y = 10$, Steve gave appropriate numerical possibilities for the two unknowns. Dee still wanted to think of x and y in terms of words. The interviewer asked her:

(I: Interviewer; D: Dee)

I: Can they be numbers?
D: Yes.
I: So if they were numbers, what can they be?
D: 9*x*.
I: 9*x*?
D: Yes... just thinking of a word for *x*. If *x* and *y* were numbers then *x* could be 9*x*.
I: You'd still keep the *x*?
D: Yes.
I: And the same with *y*?
D: Yes, but *y* would have to be one to equal 10. (Dee writes down $9x + y = 10$.)

This item, $x + y = 10$, also brought to light some misconceptions about the conventional meanings of algebraic symbols as held by Ben. He offered an appropriate range of numerical possibilities for *x* and *y* but stated that they could not be equal. For him different letters represented different values. He was asked:

(I: Interviewer; B: Ben)

I: Could one of them (i.e. x or y) be 3½?
B: No.
I: Why not?
B: Because they've got to be whole numbers.
I: Why is that?
B: Because it don't say x...x and a half or y and a half.
I: I see. So if it was going to have halves it would have x and a half, would it?
B: Yes.

The pupils were also asked what the expression '5m' meant in the item 'If $m = 3$ find 5m'. Again Dee interpreted m as a word saying 5m meant '5 lots of mats' but did not think $m = 3$ had any relevance to it. Similarly, Steve thought m stood for metres or months and said that if $m = 3$ then 5m was 15m.

QUESTIONS DIRECTLY RELATED TO THE PRE-FORMALIZATION WORK

Several questions were asked which related directly to the pre-formalization class work. In fact they were taken from the worksheets. All pupils were successful in collecting the terms in the expression $5f + 4g + 2f + g$ although Dee recorded it and read it aloud as $7f\,5g$ without the 'plus'.

For the item '$3p - 5p$' and the item 'If $x = 5$ and $y = 7$ find $x - y$', Ann, Dee and Sally said they could not be done because 5 was more than 3 and 7 was more than 5 respectively. Ben gave the appropriate responses $-2p$ and -2 but Steve gave positive values ascertaining that $5 - 7$ and $7 - 5$ were equivalent.

One interesting point which arose from these items was Ann's difficulty in reading them out. For example, note her comments when she was presented with the following written on a card: 'If $x = 5$ and $y = 7$ find $x - y$'.

(I: Interviewer; A: Ann)

I: Can you read that one out to me? What does it say?
A: Is that one 'f'?
I: If...if...
A: If times equals...
I: That's an x (ex) and if x...
A: If x equals five and y equals seven, x take away y.
I: What does that say (*indicating 'find'*)?
A: Find.
I: Do you understand what it's saying there?
A: No.
I: It says, if x equals five and y equals seven find x minus y.
A: Oh.
I: Does that make sense?
A: Yes...you can't do it.
I: Why not?
A: Because the five's smaller than the seven...x is smaller than y.

SUMMARY

At the end of the pre-formalization work the pupils were still displaying an incomplete grasp of fundamental arithmetical relationships, the understanding of which would seem necessary for meaningful learning of a formal method of solving equations. These included an incorrect interpretation of the '=' sign and hence a dubious notion of the concept of an equation, a lack of appreciation of operating identically to both sides of an equation to maintain equality, incomplete understanding of the concept of an inverse operation and a continued need to work with specific values rather than generalizing for all possibilities. The introduction of algebraic notation had led to serious misconceptions with two pupils, namely that the letters stood for words rather than numerical values, as well as some less serious misunderstandings, e.g. letters only representing integral values and different letters indicating necessarily different values.

The formalization work

The formalization work was comprised of two 70 minute lessons and homework. The aim was to progress from solving linear equations of the form $x + 6 = 10$ and $y - 5 = 12$ by means of a balance model, to developing a three-line written method.

The first lesson introduced the notion of an equation through orally presented problems of the type, 'I think of a number...'. These were readily solved by most pupils who then suggested ways of recording them such as $\Box + 6 = 13$ and $a + 6 = 13$. A balance model was drawn for $b + 2 = 5$ and the teacher explained that the aim was to find the value of b by getting b 'on its own', the plus two being 'in the way' so they needed to 'get rid of plus two to make it nought'. Eventually some pupils suggested taking away two and the teacher pointed out that to maintain a state of balance two must be taken away from the other side also so that $b = 3$. This was shown as follows:

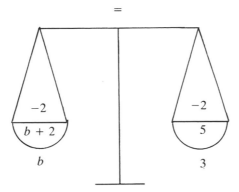

The children copied two examples with drawings of a balance.
The teacher then developed a written method as follows:

$$b + 2 = 5$$
$$b = 5 - 2$$
$$b = 3$$

NB (i) Non-alignment of '=' signs.
(ii) Intermediate stage between lines 1 and 2 where operator works on LHS, e.g. $b + 2 - 2 = 5 - 2$ was deliberately omitted because the teacher found that in the past this had caused confusion.

Thus the formalization did not fully reflect the balance model. The pupils were given a worksheet of equations to be solved by the three-line method, e.g. $5 = y + 1$, $y - 11 = 19$, the balance model now having been abandoned.

It was apparent that pupils experienced difficulties relating to the change in format of some equations, recognizing the required inverse operation and in distinguishing between the commutativity of addition and the non-commutativity of subtraction. The second lesson was aimed at overcoming these problems by reviewing the first lesson's work.

The post-formalization interviews, (PostF) and (D), responses

The immediate post-formalization interviews (PostF) occurred later on the same day of the second formalization lesson. The same items were again asked three months later on the delayed post-formalization interviews (D). A summary of the responses to both sets of interviews is given in Table 8.2. Selected aspects of these are discussed in the next four subsections.

ARITHMETICAL RELATIONSHIPS

All five pupils persisted in their interpretation of the '=' sign as indicating 'finding the answer'.

In both interviews (PostF) and (D) Sally and Steve appeared to appreciate the necessity of operating identically to both sides of an equation whereas Dee was only making some headway on this by interview (D) (see Table 8.3).

Some of the pupils' replies to the 'hidden number' items indicated a greater awareness of the inverse operations of addition and subtraction (see Table 8.2). However it was not until interview (D) that all pupils were progressing towards an understanding of the generalizable nature of addition and subtraction and their complementary relationship and as such the realization that one no longer needed to assign specific values to the 'hidden number'.

TRANSLATING SITUATIONS INTO MATHEMATICS

In the 'I think of a number, I add 19 and the answer is 41...' item, pupils continued to use informal strategies, such as counting on, although Ben and Sally had begun to move towards a more generalizable approach.

Table 8.4 shows pupil profiles of the strategies used and their methods of recording. For example, on interview (D), when asked to record the above item using algebra, Dee replied, '...put 19 apples or something like that, or 41 cars', and wrote down 19A + 14C.

TOWARDS THE NOTION OF A VARIABLE AND ITS SYMBOLIC REPRESENTATION

There was very little change in this aspect. Once again Ben maintained that different letters necessarily represented different values while Dee and Steve continued in the belief that letters represented objects. On both post-formalization interviews everyone, except Ben, showed misunderstandings when responding to the item 'What does $4x$ mean? If $x = 6$, what is $4x$?' Sally could again only see $4x$ as 46 while for 'If $a = 6$ what is $4a$?' Dee wanted to add 4 and 6 together to make it $10a$.

SOLVING EQUATIONS

Presented with the three equations, $x + 5 = 11$, $b - 8 = 3$ and $5 = y + 1$ and asked to read them out, describe their meaning and say how they would work them out, most of the group were unable to refer them to the balance model (see Table 8.6). Only Ben used it appropriately in both interviews but was then unable to progress to the written method. Steve used the balance successfully in interview (PostF) alone. Three months later he could only solve $x + 5 = 11$ informally and $5 = y + 1$ not at all. On interview at PostF the three girls were more successful with the formal method than the balance model. This success was sustained by Sally alone on interview (D) suggesting that Ann and Dee may have temporarily grasped the method as a result of learning the formalization by rote. For example, to quote Ann's attempts to solve $b - 8 = 3$ during interview (PostF):

Table 8.6: Nature of responses for solving equations on Post-formalization interviews (PostF) and (D) – School 16, Class A

	Ann PostF	Ann D	Ben PostF	Ben D	Dee PostF	Dee D	Sally PostF	Sally D	Steve PostF	Steve D
Informal Strategy										
$x + 5 = 11$	✓	✓	✓	✓	✓	–	✓	✓	–	✓
$b - 8 = 3$	×	–	✓	–	–	–	✓	✓	–	–
$5 = y + 1$	✓	✓	✓	✓	✓	–	✓	–	✓	?
Use of balance model										
$x + 5 = 11$	–	–	–	–	×	×	✓?	–	✓	–
$b - 8 = 3$	×	×	✓	–	×	DK	?	×	✓	–
$5 = y + 1$	×	×	–	✓	DK	–	?	–	✓	×
Use of formalization										
$x + 5 = 11$	–	–	✓	–	✓?	×	✓	–	✓	–
$b - 8 = 3$	✓	–	×	DK	✓	DK	✓	✓	✓	✓
$5 = y + 1$	×	×	?	DK	DK	–	✓	✓	✓	DK

Key

✓   Appropriate use of strategy
×   Inappropriate use of strategy
–   Not asked
DK   Don't know

(I: Interviewer; A: Ann)

I: And how would you work that out?
A: Um...say three and I'd count up to eight and that'd be five.
I: And is that what *b* is?
A: Yes.
I: ...Can you show me how you would work that out in class. Today...how you were doing it?

Ann writes: $b - 8 = 3$
$b = 3 + 8$
$b = 11$

I: ...now how did you get from the first line to the second line?
A: You swap them two numbers around.
I: Which two, sorry?
A: Eight and three. And you put three first, then you put eight on the second line and you add them up.
I: And why do you add them?
A: 'Cos if it says take away then you have to add them there.
I: So you've got *b* is eleven now – before you said it was five...so which do you think is right?
A: Eleven.
I: Why?
A: Because I forgot that you had to add it when it says take away.
I: Can you show me how you would do it using the scale pans?
A: I've forgot.

Summary

It was apparent from the outset that most of the pupils had an incomplete understanding of certain arithmetical relationships which may be regarded as prerequisite to learning a formal approach to solving equations. Without exception and throughout the duration of the study pupils had a limited conception of the '=' sign and hence an inadequate notion of an equation. Most pupils lacked an appreciation of operating identically to both sides of an equation and were not conversant with the notion of inverse operators.

It was also apparent from their performance on these aspects that pupils (Ben excepted) were not ready to generalize even at a fundamentally numerical level since they often wished to perform calculations and assign specific values in situations where it was not necessary. Their progress towards the development of structured and more generalizable approaches was hampered by the retention of informal, child strategies, e.g. counting on rather than subtraction. With the exception of Ben it was not until the post-formalization interviews and often not until interview (D) that there was a sign of some maturity in the grasp of these numerical relationships.

The introduction of algebraic notation resulted in the development of some serious misconceptions: in particular the belief that the letters represented words or objects. It would appear that this was as a direct result of some of the teaching based on (mathematically unsound) ideas found in the textbooks used for reference.

All five pupils seemed to have a good grasp of 'container' symbols and an informal mental approach to solving 'I think of a number...' type questions. This would perhaps have been a better starting point for their introduction to algebra in general and equations in particular. The container mode of representation could perhaps be retained indefinitely to ensure the appropriate development of the notion of a variable.

The model of the balance which was used as a precursor to the formalization could be regarded as being the pre-formalization aspect. Most pupils had difficulty with this model seemingly because of their inadequate grasp of prerequisite ideas and perhaps because they did not themselves have the opportunity to work with the balance (in diagrammatic form). Also it will be recalled that the written formal method did not fully reflect the approach with the balance by virtue of omitting the recording of the all-important notion of operating identically to both sides of the equation with the inverse operator.

As noted, none of the five pupils in the interview cohort indicated a working knowledge of a formal method for solving equations at both the pre-teaching and pre-formalization interviews, (I) and (PreF). An indication of the consistent successful use of the taught formalization for solving equations on interviews (PostF) and (D) is given in the 'use of formalization' section of Table 8.6. Only Sally showed an appropriate use of the formalization across the two sets of interviews. Of the other four children only Steve made an appropriate use of the formalization immediately after it was taught (PostF), but three months later none of these four pupils was able to employ it on any of the equations used in interview.

School 3, Class B (aged 12)

As shown in Table 8.1, this was a class (n = 24) of 12-year-olds from the middle ability band. The six children who made up the interview cohort and reflected the spread of ability in this 'middle ability' class were Daley, Darren, Denis, Sally, Steve and Tricia. The programme of work devised by the teacher aimed to develop a formal method for solving equations of the type $ax + b = cx + d$, by analogy with a balance model.

The pre-teaching interview (I) responses

Once again, as with School 16, there were indications that some pupils did not have a full understanding of the '=' sign and hence the concept of an equation. For instance Darren, shown $10 + 6 = 20 - 4$, said, 'That's a two...two sums really'. Later, shown $10 = 16 - 6$, he commented, referring to the LHS, 'It ain't a question, not really, because it's not got an add or a take away sign and a 10'. As before, the '=' sign was seen as indicating an answer to be found rather than in terms of equality of value. Steve also made inappropriate use of the symbol in recording his strategy when deriving a missing number by 'counting on' from 17 to 31, writing: $17 + 3 = 20 + 11 = 31 = 14$. Later however he displayed a grasp of the possibilities for the RHS of $10+6=$, saying, 'It could be anything, say 30 take away 14, something like that. There's loads. You could go on for ever'. This same wider understanding appeared in his responses to the question concerning the length of liquorice to be cut into two, where he was the only pupil to volunteer lengths involving fractional quantities, once again concluding that, 'You could go on for ever'.

As in School 16, most pupils found difficulty with the principle of operating identically to both sides of an equation to maintain equality and also with the recognition of inverse operators, e.g. thinking of specific values for a multiplied 'hidden' number and restoring equality by subtraction.

The pre-formalization work

A programme of activities was developed by the teacher leading towards a formal method for solving equations of the type $ax + b = cx + d$ using a balance model as analogy. They included the substitution of numerical values for letters, and the solving of simple equations, e.g. $x + 2 = 9$, by 'balancing the scales' accompanied by discussion of the appropriate inverse operation. One activity, concerning the collection of like terms, used letters as a shorthand for words thus:

$$6 \text{ apples} + 2 \text{ bananas} + 7 \text{ carrots} + 3 \text{ more apples} = 9a + 2b + 7c$$

Comments on the difficulties inherent in this 'letter as object' approach have already been made (School 16, Class A).

Table 8.7: Summary of pupil responses – School 3, Class B

Items	Daley I	Daley PreF	Daley PostF	Daley D	Darren I	Darren PreF	Darren PostF	Darren D	Denis I	Denis PreF	Denis PostF	Denis D	Sally I	Sally PreF	Sally PostF	Sally D	Steve I	Steve PreF	Steve PostF	Steve D	Tricia I	Tricia PreF	Tricia PostF	Tricia D
Completing an equation																								
$10 + 6 = \square$ What could you put here? Could you have	✓	–	–	–	✗	✗	a	–	✓	✓	–	–	✓	–	–	–	–	–	–	–	✓	✓?	–	–
$10 + 6 = 20 - 4$ etc.?																								
$3 \times (10 + 6) = 16$ What can you do to the RHS to make it true? Calculate LHS and $+ 32$ to RHS	–	✓	–	–	✓	✓	a	–	✓	–	–	–	✓	✓	–	–	✓	–	–	–	✓	✓	–	–
Find value of LHS then multiply $\times 3$ to RHS	–	–	–	–	✓	–	a	–	–	–	–	–	✓	✓	–	–	✓	✓	–	–	–	?	–	–
Multiply RHS by 3 straight away	–	–	–	–	–	–	–	–	–	✓	–	–	–	✓	–	–	–	–	–	–	–	–	–	–
Inverse operators																								
Operators $\quad ? + 3 \swarrow \to ?$	–	–	–	–	☑	✓	a	–	☑	✓	–	–	✓	✓	–	–	✓	✓	–	–	–	✓	–	–
vary with $\quad$ e.g.: $? - 7 \swarrow \to ?$	–	–	–	–	–	✓	a	–	–	–	–	⊠	–	–	☑	–	–	–	✓	–	–	–	☐	–
interview $\quad ? \times 6 \swarrow \to ?$	–	✓	✓	☑	⊠	⊠	a	–	✗	✗	–	–	✗	–	⊠	–	☑	☑	⊠	–	–	✓?	☐	–
Translating situations into mathematical language and procedures																								
e.g. I think of a number, I add 17 and the answer is 31. What number did I think of?																								
Appropriate generalizable strategy e.g. $31 - 17$	✗	✓	✓	–	✓	?	a	–	✗	✗	?	✓	✗	✗	?	–	✗	✗	✗	–	✗	✓	–	–
Can you write it down – recorded as equation	✗	✗	✓	–	✗	?	a	–	✗	?	✓	✓	✓?	✓	✓?	–	✗	✓	✓	✓	✗	✓	–	–
Towards the notion of a variable and its symbolic representation																								
e.g. I have a long piece of liquorice (6 m) to be cut into two pieces. How long might they be?	✓?	✓	–	–	✓	✓?	a	–	✓?	✓?	–	–	✓?	✓?	–	–	✓	✓	–	–	✓	✓?	–	–
What does $4x$, $3p$ etc. mean?	–	✓	✗	–	–	✓	a	✗	–	✓?	✓	–	–	✓	–	✗	✓	✓	✓	✗	✓	✓	✓	–
$x + 3 = 5$, $18 + a = 47$, x and a interpreted numerically	✓	✓	✓	–	✓	✓	a	✓?	✓	✓	✓	✓?	✓	✗	✓?	–	✓	✓	✓	✓	✓	✓	✓	–
$x + y = 8 \quad$ What can you say about x and y?	✗	✓?	✓	–	✓	✓?	a	–	✓	✓	✓	✓?	✓	✗	✓?	✗	✗	✓	✓	✓	✓?	✗	✗	–
$x + y + z = x + n + 2 \quad$ Is this true? When?	–	–	✓	–	–	–	a	–	–	✓	✓	–	–	✓	✓	–	–	–	✓	–	–	–	–	?

Table 8.7 contd

Solving equations

i) Balance

How many apples in each box

Task description						
Recorded appropriately e.g. $2b + 8 = 4b + 2$.						
Formalization used.						
Take away/crossing out 2 boxes and 2 apples each side.						
Solved by grouping/matching process.						
A boy found 6 loose sweets in his pocket and also 2 bags of the same sweets. These balanced on the scales with 5 bags each containing the same number of sweets. How many sweets in each bag?						
Grouping/matching done mentally.						
Balance drawn and grouping/matching approach.						
Balance drawn and 2 bags crossed out on each side.						

ii) Symbolic

$ax + b = c$ type

$4x + 7 = 15$ (PreF)
$n - 14 = 32$
$3p + 5 = 14$ (PostF)
$7 + 5x = 20$

$ax + b = cx + d$ type

(e) $2x + 8 = 4x + 2$ (PostF)
(f) $4b + 4 = 3b + 8$ (D)

Task description						
'Formalization' done mentally						
Empirical trial and error approach						
Formal written approach						
Balance – crossing out						
Empirical trial and error						

Somebody wrote this down. What is wrong?

$$3x + 8 = 5x + 4$$
$$3x + 8 - 4 = 5x + 4$$
$$3x + 4 = 5x$$

Key

✓	appropriate performance on this aspect
?	dubious grasp
□	specific values tried
×	inappropriate performance on this aspect
–	not asked
a	absent

The pre-formalization interview (PreF) responses

The responses for all four interviews are summarized in Table 8.7. On interview (PreF) Daley was now displaying a greater appreciation of variables. Presented with the 'string into two pieces' problem he spontaneously recognized that fractional quantities were appropriate and that there would be 'millions' of possibilities. Conversely, Tricia limited the possible options to integral values.

Each of the pupils still tended to use a non-formalized approach to the 'I think of a number ...' problem and in solving $18 + a = 47$. Thus, Darren 'just kept adding numbers' in the first case and with the latter counted on.

There was still a tenuous grasp of inverse operators, particularly of '$\times 6$'. Tricia suggested '$\div 6$' and then tested it for specific low values of ☐ but she doubted that it would work for large numbers, e.g. 111.

Solving $4x + 7 = 15$, each one would either substitute on a trial and error basis or initially try subtracting 7 from 15 but then not record it. For example, Sally quickly saw that x was 2, stating that she had just tried it. Asked to find some other way to work it out she suggested as one step $15 - 7$, realizing that the result would then be '4 times 2'. (All done in her head.)

The formalization work

There were two lessons aimed at developing a formal method for solving equations of the type $ax + b = cx + d$. This format was introduced by means of a balance drawn on the board showing boxes of apples and loose apples (see Figure 8.1).

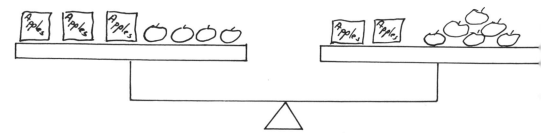

Figure 8.1: Use of the balance in School 3, Class B

The teacher emphasized the importance of keeping it balanced – taking the same amount off each side by erasing extraneous apples and boxes. However some pupils instead used a matching/grouping strategy whereby they would group the four apples on the RHS to match those on the LHS and the remaining two would be seen as equivalent to the contents of the third box on the LHS. The balance model was recorded as $3b + 4 = 2b + 6$ in which the teacher explained that b stood for 'box' (rather than the number of apples in a box). The following formalization was presented:

$3b + 4 = 2b + 6$ erasing 4 apples and then
$ 3b = 2b + 2$ 2 boxes from each side, the result of the
$ b = 2$ action and not the action itself being recorded.

The balance model only reflected situations involving additions and the teacher talked in terms of what could be got rid of. Situations involving subtraction were introduced in symbolic form, e.g. $2b - 1 = b + 2$ or $9x - 6 = 10x - 10$. Checking by substitution was mentioned in passing.

The pupils were interviewed after the lesson and again three months later. Their responses are summarized in the next section and in Table 8.7.

The post-formalization interviews, (PostF) and (D), responses

Following the formalization work the pupils sometimes described letters as standing for words, e.g. *b* for box, rather than numerical values. There were instances of inappropriate use of algebraic notation for translating situations into symbols and vice versa. For example, Tricia (interview (D)) recorded her solution 'one box contains 4 apples' as $1b = 4a$. There were also occasions when ax was interpreted as meaning $a + x$.

Some pupils' tenuous grasp of the meaning of the '=' sign seemed to lead to a misunderstanding of the symbolic format of an equation and the nature of the required task: some thought they had to find the answer to each side of the equation and that a variable on one side need not necessarily take on the same value as the identical variable on the other side – for them the crucial point being that whatever the values of the variables the LHS of the equation should work out to the same 'answer' as the RHS.

The children's approaches to solving the equations seemed to vary according to the type of equation under consideration and the mode of presentation. The balance diagrams usually elicited a 'crossing out' or 'grouping/matching' strategy and the algebraic symbolization usually invited a mental version of a 'formal' approach or a trial and error strategy. On the whole the pupils did not employ the formal written approach for solving the equations nor did they indicate a meaningful grasp of the connection between this and the 'balance' analogy.

School 17, Class A (aged 11–12)

As shown in Table 8.1, this was a class (n = 22) of 11- to 12-year-olds identified as the top set of three. A summary of pupils' (n = 6) responses for each set of interviews is given in Table 8.8.

The pre-teaching interview (I) responses

The six pupils were asked similar questions to those already described. Although all six were from a top ability set, with prior experience of algebra, some still appeared to experience difficulties or had not completely grasped various fundamental ideas.

Only one pupil, Sandra, interpreted the '=' sign as meaning 'is the same as', the others describing it in terms of a result or answer. However, by interview (D) Sarah had developed some concept of equality saying, '...they both mean the same (referring to both sides of an equation) but it's a different way of putting it...on each side'. All six showed an appreciation of inverse operators for addition and subtraction but several had difficulty with multiplication and division. For example, Stuart suggested multiplying by '− 6' as the inverse of '× 6' and put forward '× 2' as the inverse of '÷ 4'.

Four of the six used a generalizable strategy in the 'I think of a number...' problem, Anthony and Stuart recording it as $14 + 17 = 31$. None of the pupils could record the 'liquorice' question as an equation in generalizable form; they could only represent this with specific values, e.g. $6 \div 2 = 3$ and $4\frac{1}{2} + 1\frac{1}{2} = 6$.

Each of the pupils referred to letters as representing numerical values though Mena, when asked about x and y in $x + y = 8$, commented, 'They've been changed into letters...the x and the y...like they were numbers before'. Stuart had difficulty with 'Find $4x$ if $x = 2$', interpreting it as '2 to the power of 4'.

Anthony, regarded as one of the more able, had problems with x and y in the equation $x + y = 8$, stating that, '...in equations you don't have zeros. Zero always means one.' Asked for an example, he said, 'If you put 12 lots of zero...the answer would be 12'. Later, on interview (D), he explained, '...the p by itself, if there's no number with it, it always equals one'. He appeared to have confused the coefficient of p with its value.

Table 8.8: Summary of pupil responses – School 17, Class A

Items	Anthony I	PreF	PostF	D	Matthew I	PreF	PostF	D	Mena I	PreF	PostF	D	Sandra I	PreF	PostF	D	Sarah I	PreF	PostF	D	Stuart I	PreF	PostF	D
Interpretation of '=' sign — What does '=' mean? [Response indicating equality]	×	×	?	–	–	DK	–	a	×	?	–	DK	✓	✓	–	✓	×	×	–	?	×	×	a	a
Operating identically to both sides of an equation — 3 × (10 + 6) = 16 What must you do to RHS to make it true?								a	✓	–	–	–	✓	–	–	–	✓	–	–	–	✓	–	a	a
Appreciation of inverse operators e.g. ☐ + 3 → ☐	✓	✓	–	–	✓	✓	–	a	✓	✓	–	✓	✓	✓	–	✓	✓	✓	–	–	✓	✓	a	a
☐ − 7 → ☐	✓	✓	–	–	✓	✓	–	a	✓	✓	–	✓	✓	✓	–	✓	✓	✓	–	✓	✓	✓	a	a
☐ × 6 → ☐ (Operators may differ on each interview.)	✓	✓	–	–	DK	×	✓	a	✓	✓	–	✓	✓	✓	–	✓	DK	×	✓	✓	×	DK	a	a
☐ ÷ 4 → ☐	✓	✓	–	–	×	×	✓	a	✓	✓	–	✓	✓	✓	–	✓	✓	✓	✓	✓	×	×	a	a
Translating situations into mathematical language and procedures (and vice versa) i) Length of liquorice (string) to be cut in two — How long might the 2 pieces be? (Appropriate numerical value.)	✓	✓	✓	✓	✓	✓	✓	a	✓	✓	–	✓	✓	✓	✓	✓	✓	✓	✓	✓	✓	✓	a	a
Can you write it down in some way? (Recorded as a general equation.)	×	–	×	?	DK	×	DK	a	×	×	DK	DK	×	×	×	×	DK	×	×	×	×	×	a	a
ii) I think of a number, I add 17 and the answer is 31. What was the number? (Different numbers for different interviews.) (Appropriate generalizable strategy.)	✓	✓	✓	✓	✓	✓	✓	a	✓	✓	–	✓	✓	✓	✓	✓	x?	✓	✓	✓	×	×	a	a
Can you write down the situation in mathematical language? (Recorded as equation.)	?	×	✓	✓	DK	?	✓	a	×	✓	–	×	×	✓	×	✓	×	×	?	×	?	×	a	a
iii) Write a way of saying 'a number which is 7 more than, 4 times q'.	–	–	×	✓	–	–	✓	a	–	✓	DK	DK	×	–	✓	×	–	✓	✓	×	–	–	a	a
iv) Write down 'a number such that when it is trebled and 4 is added the result is 24'.	–	✓	✓	×	–	–	x?	a	–	–	✓	×	–	–	✓	✓	–	–	✓	✓	–	–	a	a
v) Translate into English 3x + 4 = 5x.	–	–	?	?	–	–	?	a	–	–	×	?	–	–	✓	✓	–	–	?	✓	–	–	a	a

Towards the notion of a variable and its symbolic representation

i) What does 'x' mean? (Response indicates numerical variable)

ii) What does 4x mean? (or some other, e.g., of type ax).

iii) $x + y = 8$ ($p + q = 9$) (x and y interpreted in conventional way).

iv) Can $x = 10$ in $x + y = 8$? ($p = 10$) (Yes for appropriate reason).
    $x + x = 8$ ($p + p = 9$) $x = 4$ only ($p = 4\frac{1}{2}$ only).

Understanding of terminology

i) What is an unknown?

ii) How many unknowns in $3x = 14 - 4x$?

iii) Give an example of an equation.

iv) What is meant by solving an equation?

Solving equations

$18 + a = 47$ Solved empirically $47 - 18$.
                 Solved empirically counting on from 18.

$4x + 7 = 15$ Solved empirically (appropriately)
                 Written formal approach (appropriately).

$2p - 3 = 5$
$3x = 14 - 4x$ } Formal approach 'trick', change side, change signs.
$3y - 4 = 6 - 2y$} Formal approach – same to both sides.

Method A
$$2g - 7 = 13$$
$$2g - 7 + 7 = 13 + 7,$$
$$2g = 20, \quad \frac{2g}{2} = \frac{20}{2}$$
$$\therefore g = 10 \text{ (judged correct)}$$

Method B
$$2g = 13 - 7, \quad 2g = 6, \quad g = \frac{6}{2}$$
$$\therefore g = 3 \text{ (judged incorrect)}$$

Connections: 'Seesaw'   Balance

Key
✓   Appropriate performance on this aspect
✗   Inappropriate performance on this aspect
DK Don't Know response
−   Not asked
a   Absent

The pre-formalization work

The pre-formalization work consisted of one 70 minute lesson. Five months previously, the class had been introduced to equations of the type $ax = n$. This work was revised, the teacher stressing terminology, e.g. 'equation', 'unknown', 'solve'. These were used in discussion of equations devised by both teacher and pupils. The class also took notes and worked through examples such as $3p = 6$, $5l = -5$, $5y = 16$. In some sense the method of solution given in the teacher's notes involved a formal aspect. He wrote:

$4q = 20$ Q. What have I done to $4q$ to get q?
$q = \dfrac{20}{4}$ A. Divided by 4.
                 NB If one side is divided by 4 then the other side has to be
$q = 5$ divided by 4.

The teacher discouraged the recording of q as $1q$. At no time, during the lesson or subsequently, was 'dividing both sides' actually recorded. On subsequent occasions the move from $ax = n$ to $x = \frac{n}{a}$ was written on the board and sometimes described as, '$4q$ equals 20 so q equals 20 divided by 4, therefore q equals 5'.

The pre-formalization interview (PreF) responses

As can be seen in Table 8.8, many responses were essentially similar to those from interview (I). Matthew and Stuart still had difficulty in deciding the inverses of '× 3' and '÷ 5'. Sarah knew them but said she had used specific values for the 'hidden numbers' whereas she just knew the inverses of '− 6' and '+ 7' without having to try values.

Stuart continued to interpret $4x$ inconsistently. So, on being asked to solve $4x + 7 = 15$, he gave the answer as 4:

(I: Interviewer; S: Stuart)

I: How did you get that?
S: I added 4 and 7 together...and there was 4 left over to make 15 so x is 4.

The pupils were asked to make up an example of an equation. All their responses were of the form $ax = n$. The equations and their solutions appear in Table 8.9. Mena and Stuart each indicated that dividing ax by a made a go to zero – just leaving x.

The children were given the equation $4x + 7 = 15$. Nobody solved it by a correct formal method, which had yet to be taught, though Sandra and Stuart made unsuccessful attempts, as follows:

Sandra: $4x + 7 = 15$ then $x + 7 = \dfrac{15}{4}$
           $x = 15 - 7$ $= 3\frac{3}{4}$
           $x = 8$

Stuart: $4x = 15$
           $x = \dfrac{15}{4}$
           $x = 3\frac{3}{4}$

Anthony, Sarah and Sandra could solve it empirically. Thus, Sarah, indicated as one of the least able of the group, was asked to describe her strategy and replied:

(I: Interviewer; S: Sarah)

S: Well if you have 15 and you take away 7 you get 8 left over and if there's 4 lots of x – you say how many times can 4 go into 8 – and it goes twice: 2 will go into 8 four times.
I: Mmm...so...
S: So x is worth 2.

Sarah had performed all this mentally. She was the only pupil to have acknowledged, on interview (PreF), that it was possible for p to equal 15 in the equation $p + q = 10$ recognizing that q would be −5.

Table 8.9: The nature of pupils' responses to the item 'Can you give me an example of an equation?' School 17, Class A

Pupil	Equation given by pupil and pupil's method of solution	Extract from interview where pupil explains solution
Anthony	$4p = 40$ $p = \dfrac{40}{10}$	A: I divided $4p$ by 4 to get p. Then I divided the other side by 4 to get ..10 and then I did that division...40 divided by 10 equals 4. I: Why did you do 40 divided by 10? A: Because whatever I do to one side I must do to the other...I divided $4p$ by 4...so I must divide 40 by 4, which is 10, so you put the 10 underneath the 40 then you do that division sum.
Matthew	$4q = 2$ $q \quad \dfrac{2}{4}$ $\therefore q \quad 8$	I: You started off with $4q = 2$. What did you do next? You got just q...how did you get that? M: Take the 4 away. I: ...And then you've got 2 over 4. What have you done there? M: Can't explain it
Mena	$5q = 25$ $q = 5$	I: How did you do that? M: Divide 5 by 5 and you've got nothing left and...5s into 25 go 5. I: Why did you divide by 5? M: Don't know.
Sandra	$3x = 9$ $x = \dfrac{9}{3}$ $\therefore x = 3$	S: I've divided x by 3 so I divided x by 3 on that side. 3s into 9 go 3 so x equals 3. I: You divided the 'x by 3'...now why are you dividing the 9 by 3? S: So that it balances.
Sarah	$2x = 20$ $x = \dfrac{20}{2} \div$ 10	I: Now can you tell me what you've done? S: You put an x there and you say – what have you done to $2x$ to get x? – and you've divided it by 2, so whatever you do to that side you must do to this side – so you divided 20 by 2. I: Because first of all you didn't have the division sign did you? You just put it in as an afterthought?
Stuart	$4q = 20$ $q = \dfrac{20}{4}$ $q = 5$	I: Now can you explain to me what you've done? S: I've divided the 4 by 4 and brought the q down so I've got to divide this side by 4 and I've brought it down and worked it out and it's 5, q equals 5. I: Mmm...why did you divide it by 4? S: To make it go to nought. I: Make what go to nought? S: Four.

The formalization work

Four 70-minute lessons were spent on the formalization work aimed at developing a written method of solving equations particularly of the type $ax + b = n$ and $ax + n = bx$. The teacher introduced a 'seesaw' model as an idea of balance and explained that in order to solve equations it was desirable to aim at reducing them to the familiar format of $ax = n$ which the teacher emphasized was the balanced form. So, for example, he described the equation $3p - 2 = 7$ as having something 'funny', 'wrong', 'different about it', and continued, 'I'm going to get shot of this minus two. I'm going to lose it ... How can I get rid of that minus two? It's throwing it all out of balance...it's all wrong. I want to get shot of it.'

Eventually the model presented for recording the situation was the following:

$$3p - 2 = 7$$
$$3p - 2 + 2 = 7 + 2$$
$$3p = 9$$
$$p = \frac{9}{3}$$
$$p = 3$$

This method was subsequently refined by the teacher who introduced a 'trick' which was explained as follows:

> ...the trick that we play, if we've something we don't like on this side, we put it on the other side, we change its sign...the trick is a lot faster (i.e. change the side; change the sign.)
> Thus: $4x - 5 = 9$
> $$4x = 9 + 5$$ NB The solutions to equations were not checked by
> $$4x = 14$$ substitution.
> $$x = {}^{14}/_4$$
> $$x = 3\frac{1}{2}$$

The programme of work was completed by translating situations into equations and solving them, e.g. 'when a certain number is multiplied by 6 and 9 is subtracted the result is the same as when it is multiplied by 4 and 11 added. Find the number.'

The post-formalization interviews, (PostF) and (D), responses

On the post-formalization interviews, the pupils were asked questions similar to those posed previously and others more directly related to the classwork. The discussion which follows focuses on three main areas: translation, solving equations and 'connections'.

TRANSLATING SITUATIONS INTO MATHEMATICAL LANGUAGE AND VICE VERSA

'Translation' was regarded by the teacher as being the culmination of the teaching programme although it might also be seen as pre-formalization. The results for 'translation' items are given in Table 8.10. No pupil was able to record the 'string' problem adequately, taking into account all possible lengths of the two pieces. Most pupils could translate the 'I think of a number...' item into an equation but Anthony and Matthew then went on to display certain misconceptions, namely $p + 19 \rightarrow 20p$ (Matthew (PostF)) and $19 + a \rightarrow 19a$ (Anthony (D)). On interview (D) Mena and Sarah both displayed confusion between '5 more than x' and '5 times x'. Sandra (PostF and D) and Sarah (D) were the only pupils to interpret $3x + 4 = 5x$ in a fully appropriate way. Mena (PostF) interpreted the x on the RHS as representing a different value from the x on the LHS, this being in line with her opinion that the equation contained two unknowns.

SOLVING EQUATIONS

Anthony, Mena, Sandra and Sarah made consistently successful use of the 'trick' approach described by the teacher in the formalization lesson. Matthew had difficulty in dealing with situations in which there was no numerical value on the LHS to transfer to the 'correct' RHS. So for $3x = 14 - 4x$ he said the 'trick' could not be used because, '... here you've got to start ...the minus 4...so you haven't got a number besides the unknown...so I can't swap places'. Matthew said the 'trick' could be applied to $2x + 14 = 9x$, adding, '...swap places with 14 and put it in place of $9x$ and put $9x$ where 14 was'. He was able to solve $3x = 14 - 4x$ by the original, longer, method involving the recording of the addition of $4x$ to both sides of the equation though he did consider that progressing from $7x = 14$ to $x = {}^{14}/_7$ involved the 7 moving from one position to the other.

Various pupils had difficulty in explaining this stage. For instance, Sandra talked in terms of dividing p by 2 in $2p = 8$, instead of $2p$ by 2. Mena continued to think of the coefficient becoming zero saying, '... to get 2 to nothing you've got to divide it by 2 so it just leaves you p'. On the whole, the children were able to use the taught method with varying degrees of understanding of the underlying processes.

CONNECTIONS

The children were asked what the connection was between the seesaw model and solving equations. They all mentioned the notion of balance and doing the same to both sides. Sandra's words from interview (PostF) perhaps note some of the difficulties with such an analogy, '... with seesaws... if you haven't got two people that weigh the same one'll go down ... and if you do something to the equation at one side that'll go down as well... so you've got to do it to the other to make it balance'.

Summary

Most of the children in the interview cohort seemed to appreciate the notion of inverse operators though there were some difficulties with those involving multiplication and division. Also, their descriptions of the '=' sign generally referred to 'finding the answer' rather than 'equality'.

There were no instances of children referring to letters used in algebraic notation as words or objects. The teaching had emphasized the numerical nature of these symbols and the fact that they represented unknown quantities, and this appeared to have been successfully learnt. There were a few instances of confusion concerning whether or not different letters necessarily represented different values.

The children displayed a tentative grasp of accurately translating situations into algebraic notation and vice versa. There were sometimes difficulties in appreciating that an expression such as $p + 19$ or $19 + a$ could not be simplified any further, i.e. not $20p$ and $19a$ respectively, nor indeed could $4x + 7 = 15$ be interpreted as $4 + x + 7 = 15$.

The formalization for solving equations particularly with respect to performing the 'trick' (i.e. change side, change sign), was successfully taken on board by the pupils with the exception of Matthew who had misinterpreted its applicability and operation. However there were signs that it was not fully understood in terms of the seesaw model of operating identically to both sides of the equation. This was particularly the case for the format

$$ax = n \rightarrow x = \frac{n}{a}$$

where at no time during the teaching had the pupils been required to record the intermediate step of

$$\frac{ax}{a} = \frac{n}{a}.$$

Some pupils regarded this process as resulting in the coefficient of x being reduced to zero or 'disappearing' rather than one.

The seesaw analogy was appreciated by the children in terms of doing the same thing to both sides to maintain a state of balance. In line with the teaching this was seemingly restricted to addition and subtraction and the children did not indicate any extension of this idea to multiplication and division.

School 15, Class A (aged 13)

As shown in Table 8.1, this was a class (n = 26) in the first year of the upper school of 'top' ability (the top half of the top ability set). Six pupils, who reflected a range of ability in this group were chosen for interview, primarily on an age basis. They were amongst the youngest pupils in this 13+ upper school. All were 13 years old for the duration of the study, which took place at the beginning of their second term in school.

Table 8.10: Pupils' responses to situations requiring translation into mathematical notation and vice versa on interviews (PostF) and (D) – School 17, Class A

Pupil		I have a piece of string 6 m long to be cut into 2.	I think of a number, I add 19 and the answer is 41.	A number which is 7 more than 4 times q.	A number such that when it is trebled and 4 added the result is 24.	$3x + 4 = 5x$
Anthony	PostF	$6 \div 2$ $6-1$; $6-2$; $6-3$	$p + q = 41$	$11q$. 'I saw the number which had to be more than, which is 4 and I added what...how much added...had to add on which is 7...to get 11...then I put the q down to get $11q$...11 lots of q'.	$3w + 4 = 24$	'I have a number, I treble it, add 4 and the result is $5x$'.
	D	$2\overline{)6}$ $a + a = 6m$	$19 + a = 41$. 'Could you add the 19 and the a together to get $19a$ there?' he asks as he writes $19a$.	$4q + 7$	6; $4\overline{)24}$; $24 - 4 \div 3$; $4a = 24$. 'I just thought that the 4 there means 4 lots of "a", so "a" is the unknown and it'd find the number when trebled...so I've put the "a" as the value of what the unknown is'	'A number which is 4 more than 3 times x equals 5 times x'.
Matthew	PostF	Don't Know	$p + 19 = 41$ $20p = 41$ $p = \dfrac{41}{20}$ $\therefore p = 2\tfrac{1}{20}$	$4q + 7$	$q \times 3 + 4 = 24$ $q \times 7 = 24$	'3 lots of x plus 4 equals $5x$...5 lots of x'. (Can't say it any other way.)
	D	Absent	Absent	Absent	Absent	Absent
Mena	PostF	Don't Know	$s + 19 = 41$	Don't Know	$3x + 4 = 24$	'You've got 3 lots of a number, and you've got to add 4 to it and then 5 lots of another number'
	D	Don't Know	$\begin{array}{r} ^3\!41 \\ -\,19 \\ \hline 22 \end{array}$ can't think of another way	Don't Know	Don't know. Asked to write down '5 more than x'; writes $5x$ saying $5x$ means '5 lots of x' and realizes it's different but can't write '5	'3 lots of x plus 4 equals 5 lots of "x"',

Sandra PostF	$2\overline{)6}$; $2f = 6$	$n + 19 = 41$	$q = 7 + 4q$ $q - 4q = 7$ $-3q = 7$ $q = 7/-3$ $\therefore q = 2\frac{1}{3}$ — Unprompted goes on to solve like this	$3p + 4 = 24$ $3p = 24 - 4$ $3p = 20$ $\therefore p = 20/3$ $\therefore p = 6\frac{2}{3}$	'I think of a number, times 3 and add 4 and the answer is 5 times as much as the number first started with.'
Sandra D	$6 - 2 = x$ $6 = 2x$	$41 - 19 =$ $x = 41 - 19$ $x + 19 = 41$	$x + 7 = 4q$	$3x + 4 = 24$	'You think of a number and times it by 3…then add 4, it is the same as 5…5 times the number you first start with.'
Sarah PostF	$\overset{3}{2\overline{)6}}$ described as '2 divided by 6'. Can't think of any other way.	$41 - 19 = 22$ $22 + 19 = 41$	$4q + 7$	$3p + 4 = 24$	'Find a number which when trebled…and when added to 4 and the result is 5x.'
Sarah D	Again $2\overline{)6}$ described as '2 divided by 6'. Can't think of any other way.	41 -19 Can't write it any other way.	$4q \times 7$ '4q times 7'. Asked to write down '5 more than x' writes $5 \times x$ saying '5 times x'	$3x + 4 = 24$	'Find a number that when trebled and added 4 equals 5 times its own number…5 times the number you have to find.'
Stuart PostF and D	Absent	Absent	Absent	Absent	Absent

Background knowledge

All the children except one, Ellie, had previously been introduced to equations in their middle schools. It was assumed that they could substitute values in expressions such as $3x + 4$ and evaluate them. During the first term in upper school they had all met flag diagrams such as:

with the accompanying notation $x \rightarrow 3x + 4$. Brackets had been used for

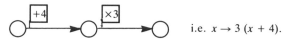

i.e. $x \rightarrow 3(x + 4)$.

They also had experience of listing sets of number pairs belonging to functions and associated graphs. The programme of work for the group was based on the notion of generating functions and solving equations through the use of operators and inverse operators and *not* upon any notion of a balance model.

The pre-teaching interview (I) responses

The responses at interview (I) are summarized in Table 8.11. All pupils appeared to have a good grasp of the notion of an inverse operator within the context of the 'hidden number' items for all four 'rules'. Some confusion was apparent with the 'mapping' notation, e.g. $x \rightarrow 6x - 4$. Thus Daniel described 'maps on to' as meaning 'equal to' and said that $x \rightarrow 6x - 4$ was shorthand for writing an equation; he then referred to $y = 6x - 4$ which he stated was used for drawing graphs. Other pupils were unable to draw a clear distinction between the 'maps onto' notation and the more common notion of equations. The following excerpt from Ellie's interview illustrates her incomplete grasp of the notion of an equation – though it should be noted that she had no previous experience of algebra from middle school:

(I: Interviewer; E: Ellie)

I: Have you come across the word 'equation'?
E: Yes...it's 2 or more things making up to one thing.
I: What do all equations have?
E: An answer.

Asked if $x \rightarrow 6x - 4$ was an equation, she replied; 'No, because you can't find out what that is, the x, but it is sort of an equation'. She described '$\rightarrow$' as meaning 'x goes to' adding: '... you see our teacher said that you should say "goes to" but I said x equals x multiplied by 6 minus 4, well that's wrong, so she said you should use "goes to", but I've forgotton.'

All pupils were unsuccessful in their attempts at recording

appropriately in the form $x \rightarrow \dots$. Mostly they wrote $x \rightarrow x + 4 \times 3$ but correctly indicated that all of the $x + 4$ was multiplied by 3. Ellie had particular difficulties with this, writing $x \rightarrow x \rightarrow 4$ $3x$, appearing to replace the '+' in $x + 4$ by a second arrow. She also confused shorthand notation for $3 \times x$, i.e., $3x$, with the situation in which $x + 4$ was to be multiplied by 3. Additionally she thought that there may be special ways of writing $x + 3$ and $x \div 3$, etc. She did explain however that it was all of $x + 4$ which was to be multiplied by 3.

So, before the onset of the teaching programme all pupils were showing a tentative grasp of the 'maps onto' notation and interwoven with this some displayed 'limited' understanding of the concept of an equation. The symbolic notation of functions where brackets were involved was also causing difficulty.

Table 8.11: Summary of pupils' responses across the four interviews – School 15, Class A

Items	Abe				Andy				Daniel				Ellie				Lesley				Sandra			
	I	PreF	PostF	D	I	PreF	PostF	D	I	PreF	PostF	D	I	PreF	PostF	D	I	PreF	PostF	D	I	PreF	PostF	D
Background knowledge																								
Numerical																								
(1) I have a piece of liquorice (string) 6 m long to be cut into 2 pieces. How long can they be? (Including fractional quantities)	✓	✓	–	✓	✓	✓	–	✓	✓	✓	✓	a	✓	✓	✓	✓	✓	✓	✓	✓	✓	✓	✓	✓
(2) 10 = 16. What must you do to RHS so that it is equal to LHS?	✓	–	–	–	✓	✓	–	–	✓	–	✓	a	✓	–	✓	–	✓	✓	–	–	✓	–	✓	–
(3) 3 × (10 + 6) = 16. What must you do to RHS so that it is equal to LHS?	✓	✓	–	–	–	✓	–	–	✓	✓	–	a	✓	✓	–	–	↗ ✓	↗ ✓	–	–	↗ ✓	✓ ? ✓	–	–
Multiply RHS by 3	–	–	–	–	×	✓	–	–	✓	–	–	a	–	–	–	–	↗ ✓	✓	–	–	↗ ✓	–	–	–
Evaluates LHS first																								
(4) I have a hidden number. I add 3, what must I do next to get back to the hidden number I started with, etc.	✓	–	–	–	✓	–	–	–	–	–	–	a	↗ ✓	–	–	–	↗ ✓	–	–	–	↗ ✓	–	–	–
☐ + 3 →	✓	–	–	–	✓	–	–	–	✓	–	–	a	↗ ✓	–	–	–	↗ ✓	–	–	–	↗ ✓	–	–	–
☐ – 7 →	✓	–	–	–	✓	–	–	–	✓	–	–	a	↗ ✓	–	–	–	↗ ✓	–	–	–	↗ ✓	–	–	–
☐ × 6 →	✓	–	–	–	✓	–	–	–	✓	–	–	a	↗ ✓	–	–	–	↗ ✓	–	–	–	↗ ✓	–	–	–
☐ ÷ 4 →	✓	–	–	–	✓	–	–	–	✓	–	–	a	✓	–	–	–	✓	–	–	–	✓	✓	–	–
(5) Find the missing numbers in two flag diagrams	×	✓	✓	✓	×	✓	✓	✓	✓	× ✓ ✓	✓ ✓	a	×	×	×	×	×	×	×	×	✓	✓	✓	✓
Algebraic																								
(1) Liquorice/string recorded appropriately as an equation (See (1) above).	✓	✓	✓	✓	✓	✓	✓	✓	✓	✓	✓	a	–	✓	✓	✓	✓	✓	✓	✓	✓	✓	✓	✓
(2) I think of a number, add 17 and the answer is 31. Can you write this down in some way? Recorded as an equation: x + 17 = 31 or x = 31 – 17	✓	✓	✓	✓	✓	✓	✓	✓	✓	✓	✓	a	✓	? ✓	✓	✓	✓	✓	✓	✓	✓	✓	✓	✓
(3) What do x, 4x, (6x) mean? Appropriate numerical interpretation	✓	✓	✓	✓	✓	✓	✓	✓	✓	✓	✓	a	✓ ?	✓ ?	✓	✓	✓	✓	✓	✓	✓	✓	✓	✓

Table 8.11 contd

(4) $x + y = 8$ (I) $x + y = 10$ (PreF)
$p + q = 9$ (PostF) and (D)

a) What can you say about x and y (p and q)
   Appropriate responses relating to understanding of variable – (integral and fractional values)

b) Can $x = y$ ($p = q$) (if not mentioned in a)

c) Can one variable be zero (if not mentioned in a)?

d) Can x (p) be 156 (10)?
   Yes, if y is negative or other appropriate response

c) What can you say about $x + x = 8$, etc.?
   Response appropriate, i.e. $x = 4$ only.

Understanding of functions

(1) What is this shorthand program in words?
$x \to 6x - 4$

a) Appropriate description of '$\to$'
   e.g. 'maps on to' or 'goes to'.

b) What do you call all of this? $x \to 6x - 4$
   Appropriate response e.g. Mapping. Program. Instruction.

(2) Complete $x \to \square$ for:

a)

Appropriate response, i.e. $x \to 3x + 4$

b)

Appropriate response, i.e. $x \to 3(x + 4)$ or
$x \to 3x + 12$

Algebraic equations

(1) What does this mean?
$x + 3 = 5$ (I), $4x + 7 = 15$
or $18 + a = 47$ (PreF)

(2) What's the difference between
$\dfrac{x+2}{4} = 5$ and $\dfrac{x}{4} + 2 = 5$?

(3) What is meant by solving an equation?

(4) What is an operator? Which are the operators and inverse operators in $4x + 7 = 15$ (PreF)
$\dfrac{x}{2} - 1 = 3$ (PostF) and (D)

What are the operators operating on? (PostF) and

(5) a) I think of a number.....
Equation solved by written formalization: I, PreF, PostF and D*

    Mental formalization

b) $x + 3 = 5$ (I)
c) $13 + a = 47$ (PreF)
d) $4x - 7 = 13$ (PreF)

    Generalizable strategy

e) $2(x + 4) = 24$ (PostF and D)

    Informal written approach

    arrow diagram

    Trial and error substitution

    Solution checked appropriately

(6) Look at the worked solution to this equation. Is it correct?

    Inspects and recognizes operators in wrong order.

$\frac{x}{2} - 1 = 3$ Works it out using arrow diagram.

(×2) $x - 1 = 3 \times 2 = 6$ Works it out by written formalization.

(+1) $x = 6 + 1 = 7$ Substitutes $x = 7$ and checks.

$x = 7$

Connections

What's the connection between

$2x + 3 \xrightarrow{-3} 2x \xrightarrow{\div 2} x$

$17 \xrightarrow{-3} \Box \xrightarrow{\div 2} \Box$

    Appropriate response.

and

$2x + 3 = 17$
$(-3)\ \ 2x = 17 - 3 = 14$
$(\div 2)\ \ x = 14 \div 2 = 7$

    Will they always give the same solution?

    Appropriate response

Key

√	Appropriate response	
×	Inappropriate response	
DK	Don't know	
CR	Can't remember	
?	Some doubt or contra-indication	
a	absent	

*The letters above an entry in (5) refer to the items a–e.

The pre-formalization work

This account is based on the teacher's notes of two lessons (70 minutes and 35 minutes) each followed by homework. The first lesson revised the notion of 'flags', the class discussing examples such as:

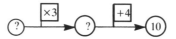

which were solved intuitively and which introduced the inverse operator and associated diagrams, e.g.

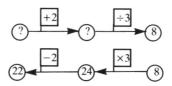

'I think of a number...' examples, which became increasingly complex (e.g. 10 steps), were given orally. Pupils could record these in any way they liked. The homework comprised a worksheet on operators and inverse operators, e.g.

$3(x + 4)$:
Write in operators above arrows

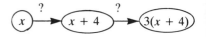

Write in operators needed
to convert expressions to x

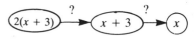

In the second lesson the homework was discussed and a worked example given, as follows:

We can solve an equation such as $2x + 3 = 17$ by using a diagram:

$$2x + 3 \xrightarrow{\;-3\;} 2x \xrightarrow{\;\div 2\;} x$$

We use the same operators on 17

$$17 \xrightarrow{\;-3\;} 14 \xrightarrow{\;\div 2\;} 7 \qquad \text{i.e. } x = 7$$

It is sensible to check the answer by substituting 7 for x in $2x + 3$.
Check $2x + 3 = (2 \times 7) + 3 = 14 + 3 = 17$.

As can be seen, checking was emphasized and similar examples were given as homework.

The pre-formalization interview (PreF) responses

A summary of the (PreF) responses appears in Table 8.11. Some pupils were still displaying an incomplete grasp of the notion of an equation and confusing it with a mapping function. For instance, Lesley initially described $x \rightarrow 3x + 2$ as meaning 'x goes to' or 'x becomes' but then said 'it's an equation'. Andy appropriately described $x \rightarrow 3x + 2$ as an instruction and $4x + 7 = 15$ as an equation where you work out the unknown. He was able to solve the equation first of all by a trial and error approach involving mental substitution of values for x and then later by the written formal approach learned at his previous school, i.e. 'change the side, change the sign'. However when asked to use the 'flag' diagram he wrote:

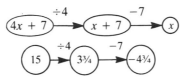

He checked this by substituting $x = 15$ into the LHS $4x + 7$ thus obtaining 67 which he then claimed was the value of the RHS as well. Andy did not seem to realize that his use of the diagram had generated a solution, albeit incorrect, namely $- 4\frac{3}{4}$. Nor did he seem to be aware that he had now obtained two different solutions to the equation. Apart from using the operators in the wrong order he seemed unaware that the vertical pairs of boxes were supposed to represent equal quantities.

On the whole pupils were now able to make appropriate use of brackets for the function

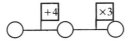

although this was a little tentative in one or two cases. Sandra, for example, wrote $3(x + 4)$ but then maintained that $x + 4 \times 3$ meant the same thing.

One of the significant features of this set of interviews was the employment of a written formalization for solving equations together with frequent mention of the associated verbalization 'change the side, change the sign', emanating from middle school work. Although some pupils mentioned there was a connection with the notion of operators and inverse operators only Daniel explained it at all adequately. Most pupils were making appropriate use of a 'check' during their work. The following extract from Ellie's work illustrates this as well as her informal approach to the use of operators and inverse operators and the way she recorded this. For $4x + 7 = 15$ she said:

> Well first of all I'd subtract the 7 from 15, then that would leave me with 8, I think, yes...then this $4x$ means multiply by 4 so...I'd put the opposite to that, divide by 4, and that would leave 2, then just to make sure I've got it right, I'd put 4 times 2 is 8 plus 7 is 15.

During the course of this she wrote $15 - 7 = 8 \div 4 = 2$.

Thus just prior to the formalization work all pupils with the exception of Ellie showed a working knowledge of a formalized approach to solving equations.

The formalization work

The formalization work comprised two lessons (70 minutes and 35 minutes) and homework. The first lesson revised the homework described earlier, on solving equations by arrow diagrams. There was, as before, particular emphasis on identifying and checking solutions which, the teacher said, might be done mentally. Gradually this lesson progressed towards the abandoning of the arrow diagrams and towards a formal method of solution that was more familiar to most pupils, thus:

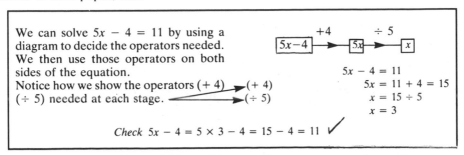

Following a similar example on the board, a worksheet was given and the pupils told to omit the arrow diagrams when they felt they did not need them. During this work some pupils displayed difficulties in terms of their understanding of the concept of the RHS and LHS of an equation and the underlying principle of equating these. For example, Ellie asked whether '73' constituted the LHS of the equation $15x - 7 = 73$! Sandra questioned whether all the equations on the worksheet were 'right' since an arithmetical error on her part had resulted in the LHS not equating with the RHS in the process of checking one of her solutions.

The homework and second lesson concentrated on extending the formal method of solution to equations of various types with particular emphasis on the order of operations involved. Pupils then solved the following four equations:

(i) $3x + 2 = 19$ (ii) $2(x - 5) = 11$

(iii) $\dfrac{x + 11}{6} = 1$ (iv) $\dfrac{x}{5} + 4 = 3$

They could use arrow diagrams if they wished and were encouraged to check their solutions.

The post-formalization interviews, (PostF) and (D), responses

During the three-month period between the two sets of post-formalization interviews the class had engaged in some work on functions, in/out tables and mappings associated with their study of straight-line graphs and gradients. Daniel was absent for the final set of interviews. A summary of the pupils' responses appears in Table 8.11.

EQUATIONS AND MAPPINGS

Following the formalization work there seemed to be a better understanding of the distinction between the idea of a function or mapping and that of an equation (although in this latter respect understanding was still incomplete as will be seen shortly). This distinction was generally described in terms of x taking on any value for the mapping whereas for the equation there was only one value of x which would satisfy the stipulation that the LHS equal the RHS. Only Lesley, on interview (PostF), called the arrow notation an equation judging that the LHS of $\rightarrow$ was equal to the RHS.

Turning now to the children's understanding of the idea of an equation it seemed that some pupils were not clear about this nor what was meant by solving an equation or the solution to an equation. Some pupils frequently talked of solving an equation in terms of finding an answer. On interview (PostF) Abe was asked about the solution to the equation $2(x + 4) = 24$. He commented that he did not remember what finding a solution to an equation meant but the answer was $x = 8$.

One or two pupils did not include checking their solutions as a natural step in the process of solving the equations, although this had been emphasized in the teaching. On interview (PostF) several pupils doubted whether or not the check would always culminate in the LHS being equal to the RHS assuming the solution had been worked correctly. By interview (D) this doubt had mainly diminished.

SOLVING EQUATIONS

Abe, Andy and Lesley who had attended the same middle school all used a formal written approach to solving equations which dated from that time. Consistently throughout the two sets of interviews they generally wrote the following solution for $2(x + 4) = 24$:

$$2(x + 4) = 24$$
$$2x + 8 = 24$$
$$2x = 24 - 8$$
$$2x = 16$$
$$x = \frac{16}{2}$$
$$x = 8$$

On interview (PostF) Abe was able to incorporate into this method aspects of the more recently learnt formalization and also present it diagrammatically as follows:

and then:

$$2\,(x + 4) = 24$$

$(\div 2)$ $\qquad x + 4 = \dfrac{24}{2} = 12$ (Lesley was also able to produce this.)

(-4) $\qquad x = 12 - 4 = 8$

$\qquad\qquad x = 8$

Andy became confused when asked to solve $2(x + 4) = 24$ by the more recently taught approach. He muddled the notion of multiplying out the brackets with the idea of the operator $(\times 2)$.

On interview (D) Lesley again used the earlier (middle school) method for solving $2(x + 4) = 24$ but could not exhibit any depth of understanding of how or why it 'worked'. She talked in terms of numbers moving from one side of the equation to the other and changing their signs. Abe, on interview (D), also described this approach in these terms saying: '...I sent the 8 over to the other side to minus from 24.' Asked why that happened, why it had to change, he replied, 'I don't know [why]. I've just been told it has to....' Also on this interview when Abe was shown a worked solution to $\dfrac{x}{2} - 1 = 3$ (see Table 8.11) and asked to explain it, he said, referring to the operator '+ 1':

(I:Interviewer; A: Abe)

A: It's telling you to add one on the other side.

I: Is it telling you to do anything to the left hand side?

A: Yes, take it away from that side... you're balancing it out; you're doing equal on either side... equal to both sides. You're taking one from that side, so you add one to that side.

Other pupils also were confused with the operators. For instance Ellie on interview (D) said the operators operated on the LHS but not the RHS. She also admitted working out the solutions to equations mentally, then checking them mentally and then writing out the method but preferring to record only the LHS and then doing the RHS in her head, e.g.

$$2x + 3 = 17$$

(-3) $\qquad 2x$

$(\div 2)$ $\qquad x$

$\qquad\qquad x = 7$

She may have felt deterred from recording the RHS because of possible criticism for her non-standard way of doing this, e.g. for $2(x + 4) = 24$ she wrote:

$$2(x + 4) = 24$$

$(\div 2)$ $\qquad x + 4 = 24$

(-4) $\qquad\quad = 24 \div 2 = 12 - 4 = 8$

$\qquad\qquad x = 8$

CONNECTIONS

One of the items on interviews (PostF) and (D) asked pupils to describe the connection between the arrow diagram method and the formal written approach to solving equations (see

Table 8.11). Some pupils could not determine what the equation was which was being referred to in the arrow diagram. On interview (D) neither Abe nor Andy were able to do so. Andy correctly decided, on close inspection of the arrow diagram and the associated written formalization that the top line of the diagram was like the LHS of the equation and the bottom line like the RHS. Lesley, on interview (D) commented that she could see some connection between the arrow diagram and the written formalization but neither had anything to do with her 'change the side, change the sign' rule. Somewhat inconsistently she considered that the equation $2(x + 4) = 24$ could not be done using an arrow diagram but could possibly be solved by the written approach using operators. There was also some uncertainty as to whether the arrow diagram method and the written formalization would generate the same solution.

Summary

The six pupils interviewed all displayed a fairly good grasp of background knowledge in terms of the notion of a variable and the idea of inverse operators. All pupils consistently interpreted algebraic notation in numerical terms although an appreciation of certain conventions was not always present. For example some believed that for $x + y = 8$, x and y must take on different values. Also there were occasions when it was thought that $x \neq 0$ because if it were zero then there would be no need for it to be recorded. There was evidence of an incomplete understanding of the idea of an equation, this being more evident when compared with the notion of a function and the associated mapping notation. However as the study progressed the development of a greater understanding of the distinction between the two ideas was apparent.

One of the most striking features of the approach to solving equations as exhibited by these pupils (except Ellie) was the employment of a previously taught formalization dating back to their middle school days. Although some pupils were able to interpret this approach in terms of the present work their understanding was tentative and incomplete. On occasions their more recent approach although implemented correctly was explained incorrectly by an inappropriate interpretation of the role of the operators which seemed to be distorted in order to tie in with the previously learnt formalization (change side, change sign).

The pupils seemed to have a good grasp of the role of the operators within the context of the functions and mappings in the pre-formalization work but some were not confident in making the transition from this to the idea of an equation and its solution or in fact what was actually meant by solving an equation.

In conclusion then, five of these six pupils already had available to them a formal method for solving equations which they retained throughout the study. Although they were able to employ both old and new methods immediately following the formalization lessons only one of these five reproduced the more recent and mathematically sound approach on the three-month interview (D). The sixth pupil who had no previous experience of algebraic equations adopted the newly taught formalization on interview (PostF), although three months later she had modified it slightly, but appropriately, in order to overcome her difficulties with notation and recording.

Conclusions

At the beginning of this chapter there was a brief discussion of some of the difficulties experienced by children in their learning of algebra (the concept of variable) as found by Küchemann (1981) and Booth (1984). During the present study there were instances of all these areas of difficulty as well as others related more specifically to work on solving equations.

Difficulties at a numerical level

(i) Some pupils, particularly lower attainers, depended on non-generalizable strategies to solve problems.

(ii) Many children had difficulties with the idea of inverse operators in 'hidden number' items, particularly for multiplication, '×', and division, '÷'.

(iii) Inverse operators were tested frequently by the use of specific values for the 'hidden number' and pupils could rarely generalize them to all values.

Algebraic notation

(iv) Fundamental problems arose from the interpretation of letters as representing words/ objects rather than numbers, which seemed to arise as a direct consequence of the teaching – see discussion of School 16, Class A.

(v) Container symbols, e.g. $\square$ and $\triangle$, offset these difficulties since they were always interpreted as numbers.

(vi) The concept of a variable was often incompletely grasped: different letters were seen as necessarily representing different values; a failure to comprehend that a letter could represent zero; and attributing different values to x on different sides of the same equation.

The idea of an equation

(vii) The '=' sign was often misinterpreted as giving the 'answer' to 'sums' rather than as expressing equality: so both $10 + 6 = 20 - 4$ and $6 = x + 4$ might present problems since children frequently wanted to put a simple numerical answer on the RHS.

(viii) Equations of the form $ax + b = cx + d$ were sometimes seen as two 'sums'.

(ix) Even more able, older, children initially confused mapping notation $x \rightarrow 3x + 4$ with an equation (see School 15, Class A).

(x) Specific teaching of the notion of an equation seemed to be beneficial (see School 17, Class A).

(xi) Only one teacher, School 15, Class A, emphasized checking the accuracy of solutions by substitution.

The pre-formalization models

(xii) Balance/seesaw models were limited in scope, since they did not readily represent situations involving subtractions, e.g. equations of the form $ax - b = c$, and were not used to incorporate notions of multiplication and division.

(xiii) The appropriateness of incorporating the concept of mass into the equation solving model might be questioned, pupils sometimes talking in terms of one side becoming lighter or heavier, going up or down.

(xiv) The notion of mass is itself distorted by such representation since the actual mass of objects and containers is ignored in discussion.

(xv) The arrow diagram approach (School 15, Class A) was universally applicable to all operations and being mathematically more sound (than the balance) might later incorporate more advanced ideas such as powers, roots, etc.

(xvi) Extended work and discussion with the pre-formalization models (School 3, Class B and School 15, Class A) seemed to develop a greater facility for operating in the pre-formal mode.

Making the transition to the formalization

(xvii) Methods of solution in pre-formalization work did not always directly match the process of the formal method.

(xviii) Division of, say, $3x$ by 3 sometimes led to the impression that the coefficient of x was then zero, particularly when recording $1x$ was discouraged (see discussion of School 17, Class A).

(xix) Methods of using the balance model for solving equations sometimes bore no resemblance to the formal approach used by pupils.

(xx) A rapid transition from 'getting rid of' actions in the balance model seemed to promote an interpretation based on superficial symbol manipulation and a rote relationship to the 'change the side, change the sign' rule. This led to a diminishing need to understanding the underlying rationale and process.

The use of the formalization

On the whole, with the exception of those pupils from School 15 with prior experience of solving equations, the use of a formal approach did not emerge until after the formalization lessons. On interviews (PostF) and (D) a minority of pupils from each of the classes in Schools 3 and 16 made successful use of the formalization whereas for the classes in Schools 15 and 17 the majority did so. The distinguishing features between the classes in the two pairs of schools were:

(a) School 3, Class B and School 16, Class A were middle band and average/below average ability while School 15, Class A and School 17, Class A were top ability sets.
(b) Pupils in the cohorts from Schools 15 and 17 used appropriate generalizable strategies at a numerical level and had a more complete grasp of inverse operators.
(c) The pre-formalization work for the pupils in Schools 3 and 16 involved drawings of balances and some inappropriate interpretations of letters as objects. With pupils in Schools 15 and 17 the approach was more mathematical in the pre-formalization stage (School 17, Class A, the teacher mentioned the notion of a seesaw and balance as a background idea, but no drawings were involved) and at all times throughout the programmes of work algebraic notation was consistently interpreted in terms of numerical values.
(d) The 'change the side, change the sign' rule was a shorthand method that the pupils in the interview cohort from Schools 15 and 17 readily took on board and retained (for addition and subtraction) although this was not extended in any meaningful way to also apply to multiplication and division.

So although the more able pupils (interviewed) from Schools 15 and 17 could successfully implement a formal approach to solving equations it did not necessarily imply a complete understanding of the procedure. It is also worthy of mention that on several occasions pupils, from all groups, who were identified by their teachers as being some of the most able in their group displayed a less complete grasp of certain aspects, than some judged to be among the less able.

Chapter 9
Ratio: Enlargement

Rod Clarkson

Introduction

This chapter is concerned with the topic 'Ratio' and in particular 'Enlargement'. Ratio and proportion was one of the topics in the 'Concepts in Secondary Mathematics and Science' (CSMS) project (Hart, 1981) and also ratio was investigated further in the subsequent research project 'Strategies and Errors in Secondary Mathematics' (SESM) (Hart, 1984).

Some of the aspects of ratio noted in the above research that relate to this peice of work are that, (i) 'the methods used by children to solve problems vary with the problem presented', (ii) 'most children see ratio as an additive operation and essentially replace multiplication by repeated addition', and (iii) 'in enlarging figures there is the danger of being so engrossed in the method to be used that the child ignores the fact that the resulting enlargement should be the same shape as the original' (Hart, 1981).

Some of the main considerations in any treatment of enlargement are exemplified by the progression of learning experiences, including the development of appropriate vocabulary, briefly outlined below, based on book D of the SMP 'Lettered' series (1969).

— Making patterns with squares (equilateral triangles, rhombuses) of different sizes to show pattern lines. (See Figure 9.1.)
— Centres of enlargement. Where pattern lines meet.
— Similarity. Figures are similar when they can be arranged to form patterns with pattern lines.
— Scale factors.
— Enlarging shapes by means of a centre of enlargement, pattern lines and a scale factor. The distance from the centre of enlargement to a vertex of the shape is measured, multiplied by the scale factor, and the new measurement is made along the pattern line to mark the new vertex.
— Positive scale factors less than 1.
— Negative scale factors.

After completing such a sequence, the child should be able to take any shape and enlarge it by a given scale factor, from any centre of enlargement.

The teachers who participated in this research prepared their own scheme of work. On the whole, however, they found it difficult to delineate the stages of development in the topic, partly because of the complex nature of the topic, and partly because of the unhelpful treatment of the topic in the texts consulted. This contributed to the difficulty the teachers encountered in identifying the 'formalization' and distinguishing it from the preparatory work.

The sample

Four classes from four different schools participated in the investigation into 'enlargement'. The nature of these classes is outlined in Table 9.1. The pupils were in the 10–12 year age range, with the exception of one child, who was also in the interview sample, who was over 12.

Table 9.1: Details of classes participating in the ratio: enlargement research

School/class	Type/age range	Class/size	Year/pupil age	No. interviewed
18/A	Junior/7–11	Mixed Ability/10	4th/10–11 yrs	6
19/A	Junior/7–11	Mixed Ability/10	4th/10–11 yrs	6
20/A	Secondary/11–18	Band 1 of 3/25	2nd/12–13 yrs	6
21/A	Secondary/11–18	Mixed Ability/6	1st/11–12 yrs	6

The mathematics curriculum for each of the classes would normally have included work concerning enlargement. Each teacher chose for the interviews those pupils whom they judged to reflect the spread of ability across their particular class. In some cases the topic was taught only to a group within the class. In School 18 it was convenient to extract a small group for administrative reasons, in School 19 the teacher judged the group to be ready for the topic, and in School 21 the pupils were following an individualized learning scheme.

The interviews

The progress of the pupils was monitored, by means of interviews: before the scheme of work began (I); before the formalization lessons (PreF); immediately after the formalization lessons (PostF), and some three months after the teaching of the topic (D). The main findings of the research on ratio will be drawn from School 18, Class A with the other groups used to support and extend these results.

Each set of interviews is discussed in terms of two categories, 'Recognition of enlargement/scale factors' and 'Construction'. The first is concerned with the pupil's judgements of what constitutes an enlargement and how one might determine a scale factor. For example, in interview item 3 (see Figure 9.2, page 194), the children were asked to determine which, if any, of the photograph frames would be suitable if the original photo was made bigger. They were also asked to explain their answers.

The second category is about what methods a child uses to enlarge a shape, using a pencil and ruler. An example of this is interview item 2 (see Figure 9.2, page 194). The children were asked to make the quadrilateral on squared paper twice as big.

The scheme of work

Each teacher was asked to consult a variety of materials and to produce a scheme of work, which was then discussed with the researcher. The teacher then decided at what point the formalization stage would be reached.

In looking at the schemes of work the researcher made some interpretations of what might be the prerequisites. Three of the four schemes of work involved measurement in practical enlargement tasks. An ability to measure accurately was therefore necessary. Although the teachers were aware that they were introducing new 'technical' terms such as scale factor, centre of enlargement and pattern lines, 'ordinary' words, such as 'times', 'bigger', 'much bigger', 'times as big', and perhaps the word 'enlargement' itself, that might have different meanings for different children, were not generally noted. Some of the 'technical' terms were used in the schemes of work. The interpretation in SMP book D is shown in Figure 9.1.

School 18, Class A (aged 10–11)

This was an inner city junior school, pupils 10–11 years of age. The six pupils interviewed were: Sacha, Perry, Nigel, Stella, Jordan and Claire.

Pattern lines: lines passing through corresponding points, usually vertices, on similar shapes.
Centre of enlargement: the point where pattern lines intersect.
Similar: when shapes have corresponding sides in the same ratio.
Scale factor: the number *n* in the ratio 1:*n* of the lengths of corresponding sides in an enlargement.

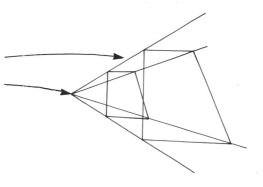

Figure 9.1: Terms used in enlargement

The pre-teaching interview (I) responses

An effort was made during this research to pursue the use and role of language. In both the pre-teaching (I), and pre-formalization (PreF), interviews there was an item to explore the children's understanding of sameness and similarity (item 1, see Figure 9.2).

The children interviewed not surprisingly used both the words 'similar' and 'same' to describe shapes that looked alike in any respect, vaguely the same shape, same number of sides, same area, and some children either included in this, or as a separate category – 'exactly the same'. For example when asked, '…What do you think similar means?'. Stella replied 'Nearly the same, but the other shape's a bit bigger or the length is a bit bigger or the shape is different, but nearly the same'. Jordan's response was 'Well, that's the sort of same shape and they've all got 5 sides. These have got 5 sides and that's got 5 sides…'

Some children classified the shapes they were given to compare in terms of rectangles or five-sided shapes but there was a general vagueness of the use of the terms, and certainly no mathematical interpretation of the word similar. This was the case not only in this group but also in the other three groups (schools) as well.

RECOGNITION OF ENLARGEMENT/SCALE FACTORS

Table 9.2 gives a summary of the results of interview (I) on the recognition and construction aspects of the topic.

When presented with two irregular pentagons drawn on squared paper (item 4, see Figure 9.2) and asked to comment on the shapes, four of the six pupils, on interview (I), counted the lengths of corresponding sides and deduced that one was an enlargement of scale factor 3 of the other. Note for example the comments of Sacha:

(I: Interviewer; S: Sacha)
S: Um…I think that one's 3 times bigger.
I: 3 times bigger? How do you work that one out?
S: Well, the length down there's 3 and here it's 9, so that's 3 times bigger, 4…1, 2… yes it's 3 times bigger there as well, and it's three times bigger there as well.

Perry, whilst also counting lengths, came to a difficult conclusion:

(I: Interviewer; P: Perry)
P: The whole squares…9.
I: The whole squares are 9, are they? And the small one is…
P: 3.
I: So what does that mean?
P: 2 times bigger.

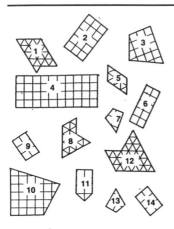

Item 1. Find diagrams which look the same (similar)

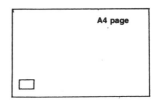

Item 4. Comment on the shapes

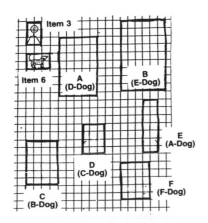

Item 2. Make 'twice as big'

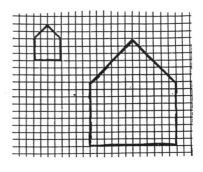

Item 5. Draw '3 times bigger'

Items 3 (person) and 6 (dog). Photograph frames

Item 8. 'T' Shapes

* Notes: 1. Item 7 has not been included in the analysis.
   2. Other diagrams, items 9–13, are shown in Figures 9.4 and 9.5.
   3. All diagrams have been reduced for layout – the reduction scale factor is not consistent across items

Figure 9.2: Diagrams for interview items 1–8*

Table 9.2: Summary of interview responses – School 18, Class A

Type of response Recognition	I	PreF (P)	PostF (J)	D
Absent		P	J	
Can recognize integer s.f.	CJ / S	CJN / SSt	C N / PSSt	CJN / PSSt
Can recognize fractional s.f.	C		S	S
Uses area strategy	N			C N
Uses addition strategy	JN	N / St		N
No counting or measuring	St			

Type of response Construction	I	PreF (P)	PostF (J)	D
Absent		P	J	
Can enlarge on squared paper	CJN / P	✕	✕	CJN / P
Can draw pattern lines		CJN / S	C N / S	JN / S
Can enlarge on plain paper	CJN / PS	S	C N / S	C / S
Uses taught method	✕	✕	N / S	S
No counting or measuring		St	St	
Measuring error			P St	P St

Interviews

Time between: I ↔ PreF ↔ PostF ↔ D
         37 days   9 days   114 days

Key   C   Claire
      J   Jordan
      N   Nigel   arranged | CJN |
      P   Perry | PSSt |
      S   Sacha
      St Stella

Perry interpreted the scale factor as the additional increase in length of the sides of the shape. (In the present research this will be referred to as the 'addition scale factor' strategy. Table 9.5 (p. 217) summarizes the various strategies used.)

Stella guessed that the larger shape was four times as big as the smaller and checked her guesses by drawing four of the smaller shapes to see if they would fit in the larger shape. (Referred to as the 'area' strategy in the table of strategies.)

One of the items given to the children was a sheet of squared paper on which there was a 3 by 2 'photograph', item 3, see Figure 9.2). Other rectangles were drawn and the pupil was asked 'if I made this photo bigger which of these frames would it fit into?'.

Stella did not count or measure but made judgements on the look of the shape. Claire recognized frame C (scale factor 2) as 'double' and frame B (scale factor 3) as '3 doubled twice is 9'. Sacha also described frame C as 'doubling' but rejected two other rectangles as being enlargements of the photograph on the grounds that they were 'not doubling it' and 'more than doubling it'. Frame A (scale factor 2½) was rejected by two children because it had 'got halves' and was 'not a full square'.

In responding to this item, Nigel sometimes used an area strategy, sometimes an addition strategy and sometimes a combination of the two. For example for frame B (scale factor 2):

(I: Interviewer; N: Nigel)

N: Yes, I think it'd fit into that.

I: Why would it fit into that one?

N: It's...this one is 6 times bigger than that.

I: Why is it 6 times bigger?

N: Oh no, it isn't. It's...it's 9 times bigger.

I: Number 2 is 9 times bigger than the photo?

N: Yes.

I: How did you know? What did you do?

N: I imagined that...I got the size of that one...3 up and 2 across and I drew it in my head on those, and I drew it lots and lots of times to see how many times it'd fit in.

For frame D, the rectangle 4 by 3, Nigel first of all considered the area, then used a border strategy, 'It's just one step larger' (see Table 9.5). On returning to this rectangle a little later he looked at the lengths of the sides and decided it was not an enlargement of the photograph. He then immediately changed his mind 'you could make it 1 cm...1 cm square bigger...'cos there's all these spare cm squares'.

CONSTRUCTION

The first item in this category was interview item 2 (see Figure 9.2). The task was to enlarge, on a sheet of squared paper, a given irregular quadrilateral by scale factor 2. The question 'Can you draw this shape twice as big?' was intended to be open to interpretation so as to gauge how the children would interpret the language.

Stella did not count or measure but drew a shape slightly bigger and having the appearance of the original. The remaining five children doubled the left hand and bottom sides of the original to draw two sides of lengths 6 and 4. The two sloping sides of the original diagram then had an aspect of 3-ness and 4-ness about them. Two of the children who interpreted the lengths in this way drew a diagram which preserved the size of the angles. Two of the children, Jordan and Nigel, used a displacement idea to locate the position of the top, right hand corner.

(I: Interviewer; J: Jordan)

I: Now, how do you get that? How do you work that out?

J: Well, that...there's um...that line goes from that corner to that corner, so that's using up 1...1 cm up.

I: Alright, so you're talking about the top sloping line and you're saying that the top sloping line is...what, 1 up?

J: Yes, once. Yes, that's 1 cm and that's...goes down to the bottom, so if that's...it's 3 along, so it's another 3 there.

I: Yes.

J: And so this'll be 6, yes, 6 and 2.

The other item used to assess 'construction' was a rectangle, 3 cm by 5 cm, drawn on plain paper which the children were asked to draw three times bigger (item 5, see Figure 9.2). Again, the question was open to alternative interpretations – and there is no suggestion intended at this time as to what constitutes a correct or incorrect response.

Four of the children carried out this task without any difficulty, by multiplying the lengths of the sides by 3. As in the previous question, Stella did not measure the lengths of the sides and drew a rectangle, approximately 4 cm by 8 cm, to the right of the original rectangle. Nigel, unlike the other children who had drawn a separate diagram, used the original as a guide to start.

(I: Interviewer; N: Nigel)

N: Yes, and that was 3 cm, so I made it 9 cm, by adding 6 cm on.

[He extends the vertical line on left side of the diagram by 6 cm].

I: By adding 6 cm okay, and this one?

N: And this one was 5 cm.
I: Yes?
N: And I made it 15 cm, by adding 10 cm on.

He then drew the top line 15 cm long and completed the drawing to obtain a rectangle 9 cm (height) by 15 cm (width).

SUMMARY

As this was the first set of interviews, and prior to any teaching, the intention was to find out the children's reactions to certain situations. The children were asked to interpret phrases which might result in an enlargement, rather than being asked to carry out carefully specified enlargements.

Before the teaching programme began Stella did not do any kind of measuring or counting but relied solely on the appearance of the items in both the 'recognition' and 'construction' categories. Perry was very reluctant to talk during the interview and so it is not possible to say much as regards his recognition abilities. He did however complete both enlarging tasks. Sacha, Jordan and Claire did not show any consistent strategies other than the linear scale factor strategy.

The pre-formalization work

The pre-formalization work consisted of seven separate lessons, given over a period of one month, and which lasted a total of six and a half hours. The summary given in Table 9.3 is based on the lesson plans and the lesson comment forms filled in by the teacher at the end of each lesson.

It might be argued that lesson 4 (Table 9.3) involves a formalization, at least in a recognition sense. This was not, however, the ultimate goal or formalization as identified by the teacher.

The pre-formalization interview (PreF) responses

Table 9.2 summarizes the results of the interviews on the recognition and construction aspects of the topic.

RECOGNITION OF ENLARGEMENT/SCALE FACTORS

The photograph item of interview (I) was repeated on interview (PreF) but this time with a photograph of a dog and the 'frame' being rotated through 90° and in different relative positions on the sheet (item 6, see Figure 9.2). Stella was still working on visual comparison, although she did recognize B (scale factor 2) 'doubled it'. She counted but her statements did not relate to her judgement as to whether the rectangles were enlargements of the original photo, e.g., 'one more square down', 'B has one more square than F'.

Nigel recognized B (scale factor 2) and E (scale factor 3) but used the border idea for C 'bigger by one square all the way round'.

Sacha, Jordan and Claire all recognized B (scale factor 2) and E (scale factor 3) and everyone rejected A except Claire. She thought A would be suitable and would result in a 'sausage dog', therefore recognizing that A was not right. She was, however, the only child to recognize D (scale factor 2½) 'expanded it by 2½'.

A new item introduced at this stage was four 'T' shapes, A, B, C, D, consisting of squared paper stuck on card and cut out (item 8, see Figure 9.2). B was an enlargement of A scale factor 2, C was an enlargement of A scale factor 3, and D was an enlargement of A scale factor 5. This made possible scale factor 1½ by combining B and C, scale factor 2½ with B and D, and scale factor 1⅔ with C and D.

Four of the children recognized scale factors 2, 3 and 5, but of these four, three said that the scale factor 1½ (B and C) was 'not double'. Stella recognized scale factor 2 but said that the

Table 9.3: Summary of the pre-formalization work – School 18, Class A

Lesson

1 Lengths of Cuisenaire rods were compared and this comparison was expressed in terms of the ratio of the length of one rod to another, e.g. 4:1.

2 The children were given a set of shapes each and were encouraged to compare them and place them on top of one another to identify the two with identical angles.

3 Worksheets were used to transfer drawings from one square grid to a larger square grid and also the children had to decide whether certain shapes were an enlargement of other shapes. For example, comparing pictures of windows of houses.

4 A review of the work done in lesson 3. The children were then given the task of trying to identify the two out of four shapes in a set related by an enlargement, by firstly comparing angles and then seeing whether length and height had increased/decreased in proportion.

5 Teacher then pupils enlarged letters of the alphabet on square dotted paper by scale factors 2, 3 and 4.

6 The teacher gave examples on the overhead projector of how corresponding vertices could be joined to form pattern lines, and that where the lines crossed was identified as the centre of enlargement.

7 The children drew pattern lines on pairs of equilateral triangles and squares to find the centre of enlargement. The group were then given a worksheet which contained seven different shapes each with various enlargements. The children had to study each enlargement and then to estimate the position of the centre of enlargement. This estimate was marked, the pattern lines were then drawn and the centre of enlargement identified and compared with the estimate.

---

scale factor 3 combination (A and C) had been enlarged 4 times. Similarly for the scale factor 5 enlargement (A and D):

> (I: Interviewer; S: Stella)
> I: ... What about A and D then?
> S: It has been enlarged 6 times.
> I: 6 times. Now how did you work that one out?
> S: Because there's 5 down here and one here and if you add that to the 5 here it would be 6 times as big.

CONSTRUCTION

When presented with pairs of shapes that represented enlargements and asked to draw lines on them (items 9, 10, 11, see Figure 9.4, p.203), all of the children, except Stella, joined corresponding points to obtain the centre of enlargement. The four successful children all referred to the 'centre of enlargement' but only Sacha used the phrase 'pattern lines'.

Although the children had not yet been taught the method of how to enlarge a shape using pattern lines, scale factor and centre of enlargement, three of the children were asked to make a quadrilateral, drawn on plain paper, twice as big, using a given centre of enlargement (item 12, see Figure 9.3, p. 200). 'Twice as big' was open to interpretation, as expected.

Jordan could not get round the centre of enlargement problem and did not draw anything. Sacha and Claire, however, used exactly the same method – see Figure 9.3.

SUMMARY

By the end of the pre-formalization teaching Stella was counting, and recognized only scale factor 2. She also used the addition strategy on the 'T's question. Nigel had now abandoned the 'area strategy' but there were still indications of an occasional use of a border strategy. Sacha, Jordan and Claire could all recognize integer scale factors, draw pattern lines and Sacha and Claire could use their knowledge of pattern lines and centre of enlargement to enlarge a shape on plain paper.

Item 12 diagram

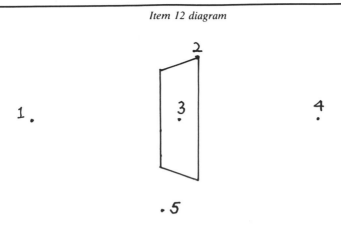

Sacha's and Claire's method using '1' as the centre

First of all they drew in lines from the centre of enlargement through the vertices of the quadrilateral.

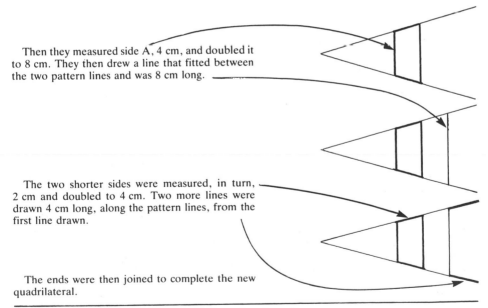

Then they measured side A, 4 cm, and doubled it to 8 cm. They then drew a line that fitted between the two pattern lines and was 8 cm long.

The two shorter sides were measured, in turn, 2 cm and doubled to 4 cm. Two more lines were drawn 4 cm long, along the pattern lines, from the first line drawn.

The ends were then joined to complete the new quadrilateral.

Figure 9.3: Using centres of enlargement, interview item 12

The formalization work

The formalization work took place in two lessons each of 70 minutes duration. The following account of the lessons is based on an analysis of the transcript of the audio tape recording, the notes of the researcher who was observing, and the notes and comments made by the teacher before and after the lessons. The teacher's preparation notes for the first lesson indicated that the aim of this lesson '. . . was to bring together the elements of enlargement already taught to enable the children to enlarge a shape from any arbitrary point using a variety of scale factors'.

On the overhead projector the teacher showed how to enlarge a square of side 4 cm. The method shown to the pupils involved measuring from the centre of enlargement, which was the bottom left hand corner of the square, to the vertices and doubling the distance. The inaccuracy created by the thickness of the pattern lines made the shape look 'crooked', '. . . and in fact you won't have to draw in the pattern lines if you don't want to, you can just like . . . point . . .'

A 'C' was now enlarged on the overhead projector, by scale factor 2, the centre of enlargement being again the bottom left hand corner of the figure. This time no pattern lines were drawn but dots were placed where the new vertices should be. This process was then repeated with a trapezium, the centre of enlargement being near the centre of the shape, and scale factor 3, and a square, but with the centre of enlargement outside the shape, and scale factor of ½.

The children were then given plastic covered workcards with shapes drawn on them. Chinagraph pencils were used to write on the cards, any errors made were easily rubbed out with a sponge. The cards consisted of triangles, quadrilaterals and regular pentagons, two-dimensional representations of three-dimensional boxes, also drawings of a car and a boat with lots of vertices.

The pupils were given the following instructions: 'You may choose your centre of enlargement, but I would like everyone to start off by using scale factor 2 and when you've done some scale factor 2, you may change your scale factor . . . alright, and what I want you to investigate is . . . what is the effect on the final shape . . . of moving your centre of enlargement around the board?'

Some of the children had been absent for the first lesson so in the second lesson the teacher repeated the introduction given in the previous lesson. This time no pattern lines were drawn at all but the term was continually mentioned. In the enlargement of the 4 cm square, some pupils thought that the diagonal distance was also 4 cm. Whilst the teacher was explaining, some of the children continued with the chinagraph work. When everyone was on this exercise the teacher found that the unsupervised group had been enlarging without using a centre of enlargement. That is, they had drawn shapes by doubling or mutiplying the lengths of the sides of the original, and guessing the corresponding angles. The teacher explained why a centre of enlargement was necessary and the children subsequently used a centre of enlargement.

The post-formalization interview (PostF) responses

Interview (PostF) was carried out on the day after the second formalization lesson. Table 9.2 provides a summary of the results for recognition and construction on the three interviews (I), (PreF), and (PostF) as well as interview (D) which is discussed later.

RECOGNITION OF ENLARGEMENT/SCALE FACTORS

The 'T's question (item 8, see Figure 9.2, page 194) was the only item used in this category. All five children recognized scale factors 2, 3, and 5, except Stella, who only managed 2, 'enlarged twice' and 3, 'enlarged by 3'. The scale factor 1½ (B and C) caused a few problems. Claire thought the top had been 'enlarged by ½' but that something different had happened to the bottom of the T shape, concluding 'it's enlarged by 2½'. Perry placed B along the top edge of C and said 'it's an enlargement by ½'. Nigel also thought it was '½ a times bigger' and for the scale factor 2½ (B and D), was in the dilemma he had shown before in not being able to decide if it was an enlargement of scale factor 2½ or 1½, depending on whether he considered the ratio of the lengths of corresponding sides (scale factor 2½), or the ratio of the difference in the corresponding lengths to the length of the side on the smallest T (scale factor 1½).

Sacha managed to get 1½ after considering other possibilities:

(I: Interviewer; S: Sacha)
S: That one is not a whole number enlargement, I don't think it's a ½ either.
I: It's not a whole number enlargement?
S: It isn't by 2... um... ah, it could be enlarged by 1½, I think it is.
I: How did you work that out?
S: Well ½ of 2 is 1 so you've got... that's a whole one so that is enlarged by one which is just going to be the same shape and ½ of that is one and you've got another one on there so it will now be 3 and along here is 6 and there's 6 and a ½ of 6 which is 9, which is 3, and if you add it up it is 9 so it must be 1½, although we haven't done that.

Here she replaced multiplication of 1½ by taking one length and then adding on a half of that length. She rapidly recognized scale factor 2½ and after considering scale factors 2 and 2½ she correctly ascertained that the final item was scale factor 1⅔ '... and across here is 9, so 9 plus ⅔ of 9 which is 6 is 15 and you've got 15 across there...'.

CONSTRUCTION

When the children were asked to draw lines on the pairs of shapes (items 9, 10, 11, see Figure 9.4) to see what kind, if any, of pattern lines they would draw, Perry did not draw any lines at all. Stella on two of the three pairs of shapes picked a 'centre point' arbitrarily and then joined up the 'centre point' to some of the vertices.

Claire drew lines on two of the pairs but on the third she realized that she had not joined up corresponding points, but could not correct it. Sacha and Nigel drew lines through corresponding points that intersected in one point. Of the five children Sacha, Nigel and Claire used the term centre of enlargement but only Nigel used the phrase 'pattern lines'.

The quadrilateral, with various centres of enlargement marked, and drawn on plain paper (item 12, see Figure 9.3), was used to see if the children had assimilated the formalization and could hence enlarge a shape from a given centre of enlargement by a given scale factor.

Stella and Perry both suffered from a handicap in answering this question, as in measuring the lengths of the sides of the shape they started at 1 on the ruler. Therefore a distance measured as 5 was really 4, using scale factor 2 meant that the new distance was not 10 but really 9. Perry did not use any centre of enlargement but measured the lengths of each side and drew a shape that had the appearance of the original. Similarly, Stella drew a shape around the dot marked point 1. Her version of the pattern lines was that she joined up the four vertices to point 1 which she described as the 'centre dot' and 'centre mark'.

Claire chose point 3 as her centre of enlargement and she was asked to enlarge the shape scale factor 2. She drew lines through each vertex to the centre of enlargement and beyond to the other side of the centre of enlargement. She decided that she should have done the enlargement first and then the lines. She tried again with scale factor 2 and suggested point 1 as the centre of enlargement but she used point 2. After completing the diagram, as shown in Figure 9.5, she joined the vertices of her new shape to point 1.

When asked to enlarge the original shape by scale factor ½, with point 4 as the centre of enlargement, she repeated a similar process. She used point 2 as the centre of enlargement again, and when her diagram was complete she drew lines through point 4 to the vertices of her *first* drawing.

Sacha was asked to enlarge by scale factor 2 using point 2 as the centre of enlargement, but she used point 1 as the centre of enlargement instead. She used the method she had displayed previously in interview (PreF), namely, she drew two lines through the vertices from the centre of enlargement, measured the sides of the original, doubled and fitted her new lines on or between the pattern lines.

She then used point 4 for the centre of enlargement and scale factor one-half. She drew lines from the centre of enlargement through the four vertices of the original. She measured the

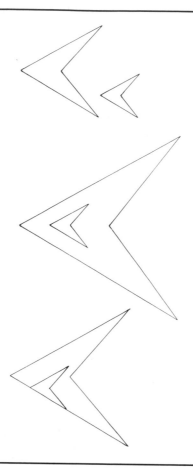

Figure 9.4: Items 9, 10 and 11: drawing pattern lines

longest side and halved it to 3. She fitted the line 3 cm long between the two outside lines, but then had a problem with the line 1 cm long (half of 2).

She ignored the inside lines and could not work out which of the two dots marked she should use. Eventually she decided to use the dot nearest the centre of enlargement and so finished with a shape that was scale factor half the original, but a rotation of 180° of what it should be (see Figure 9.5).

In using point 3 for the centre of enlargement and scale factor 3 she drew the pattern lines right through to the other side of the centre of enlargement. She tried to use her previous method but became confused because of the lines. *Only then* did she use the taught method of measuring from the centre of enlargement to a vertex, use the scale factor and mark the new vertex on the pattern line. However her measurements were inaccurate and she decided to abandon the attempt.

Nigel was the only pupil to use the taught method successfully (but note that Sacha tried). With point 3 as the centre of enlargement and scale factor 2, and also point 4 as the centre of enlargement with scale factor ½, he measured from the centre of enlargement to the vertices, doubled or halved, and put a dot for the position of the new vertex. When all four vertices were marked he joined them up for the new shape. He did not draw any pattern lines. Nigel did not use millimetres and so all his measurements were to the nearest half centimetre. This resulted

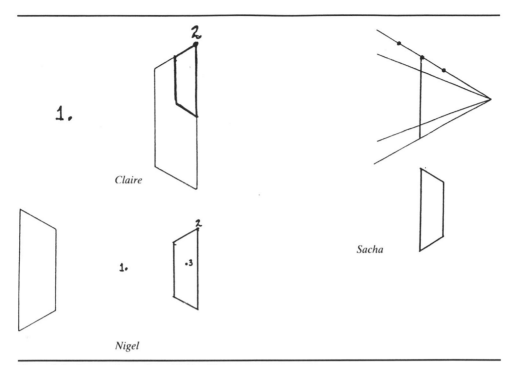

Figure 9.5: Approaches to item 12 (PostF)

in diagrams which he called 'eggy' that is, diagrams that to him did not appear to be sufficiently accurate.

He then tried point 1 as the centre of enlargement and scale factor 1½. In measuring the two distances from the centre of enlargement to the vertices he used an addition scale factor strategy, his length of 6 became a length of 15 and his length of 4 became a length of 10. But as he measured these distances from the original vertex through the centre of enlargement to the other side, his final drawing was of scale factor −1½ (see Figure 9.5).

SUMMARY

In the recognition of scale factors Sacha was the only pupil who had made any gain since interview (PreF). Of Nigel and Stella, Nigel was the only one to now draw pattern lines whereas in the previous interview he had not. The key item in this series of interviews was the practical test of drawing an enlargement given a shape, the scale factor and centre of enlargement. Stella and Perry made a limited attempt, Claire had only partly taken on board the ideas, and Sacha only tried the taught method when her own was giving her difficulty. It was only Nigel who used the taught method and that was with his problems of measurement in starting from 1 on the ruler, and the use of an addition scale factor strategy.

The delayed interview (D) responses

The responses on interview (D) for all six pupils are summarized in Table 9.2, p. 195 (along with the responses for interviews (I), (PreF) and (PostF)).

RECOGNITION OF ENLARGEMENT/SCALE FACTORS

The photograph item (see Figure 9.2) which had been used in interviews (I) and (PreF) was introduced again in interview (D). As on the previous occasion when Perry encountered this item, he gave virtually no information at all. Sacha recognized scale factors 2, 3, and 2½, as did Stella who 'doubled twice' for scale factor 2, 'doubled three times' for 3, and 'just guessed' for scale factor 2½. Jordan also recognized scale factors 2 and 3. Nigel was in his usual dilemma:

(I: Interviewer; N:Nigel)
N: It's enlarged 3 times
I: Enlarged 3 times?
N: ...let me think...um... I don't know what to call this... 9 of them go into... 9 houses go into number 6 and um...the outside is only 3 times higher, so I don't know whether to call it 3 times bigger or 6 times bigger.

In other words Nigel could not decide, in this particular case, whether to use a 'linear scale factor' strategy, or an 'area addition strategy' (see Table 9.5, p.217).

Claire now consistently used an area strategy. For example for the item with linear scale factor 2:

(I: Interviewer; C: Claire)
C: ...um...it would go into it...if you enlarge it...4, I think it is.
I: Why 4?
C: It's 24 there and the photo is 6, and 6 goes into 24...4 times.

The T's of item 8 gave virtually the same results, with the reasons given, and strategies used, as in interview (PostF) three months previously. The only slight difference was that Nigel adopted an area strategy when considering scale factor 1½. In comparing the two areas of 20 and 45 he decided it was 'half the size bigger'.

CONSTRUCTION

When asked to draw lines on the pairs of shapes, (items 9, 10, and 11, Figure 9.4), Sacha, Jordan and Nigel drew in the correct pattern lines as in interview (PostF). Jordan and Nigel even volunteered to guess the position of the centre of enlargement (correctly) before drawing the lines. Claire drew lines through corresponding points but not long enough to form the intersection for the centre of enlargement. Perry and Stella joined up some corresponding points and were performing at the same level as in interview (PostF).

An item encountered for the first time was to enlarge a quadrilateral on squared paper (item 13, see Figure 9.6). This related to a similar item in interview (I), and Jordan used a displacement method of counting squares across and up, in both cases, whereas Nigel used the more common method of doubling the 'lengths' of the sides.

Claire also used the doubling method but she used the original shape as a guide for her enlargement which gave the appearance of using a vertex as the centre of enlargement.

Stella showed a different way to determine the length of a line. In working out the length of the longest side of the new shape, she counted the squares on the left hand side of the original line (which measured 6 m) thus; four whole ones plus two 'halves' makes five, doubled makes ten, but there are two halves so it's really 11 (see Figure 9.6).

(I: Interviewer; S: Stella)
I: So what did you do? You did this line first, didn't you? [*I points to longest line.*]
S: Yes, that's been doubled, that's 4, then 6, then 4, then 1, 2, 3, 4, 5...that'll be 10.
I: Okay.

S: Be 11 actually because it'll be ½... ½...11 so it's ½ there (*points to A, Figure 9.6*) and ½ there (*points to B, Figure 9.6*), it'd be 11.

I: It'd be 11. What do you mean, it'd be a ½ there and a ½ there?

S: 'Cos there's ½ of a square there, ½ of a square there, if you add those two together that'd be a whole one, that'd be 11.

I: So still be 11?

S: Mmm....

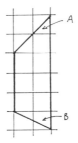

Figure 9.6: Diagram for item 13, enlarge on squared paper [this quadrilateral was placed near the bottom left hand corner of the sheet of A4 squared paper]

The next item used was item 12 from interview (PostF): enlarge a quadrilateral on plain paper, given a centre of enlargement. Four of the children did not use a centre of enlargement. None of them drew pattern lines. Claire used the same method as in the previous question, resulting in an enlargement as shown in Figure 9.5, page 204.

Jordan drew one of the parallel sides, doubled in length, and before drawing the opposite side, he measured the distance between the originals, doubled, and put a dot on his new diagram. As before Perry was having difficulties because he started his measuring from 1 on the ruler. Stella's first attempt at making the shape twice as big resulted in one the same size. Her second attempt might have been better but in measuring one of the sides she started from 1 on the ruler. For her third attempt she was asked to try 1½ times as big. She measured each side correctly, doubled it and added on half a cm so that 4 cm became 8½ cm, 6 cm became 12½ cm, or, the length plus the length again plus ½ cm, was the method used. For the purposes of this research, such an approach is considered to be indicative of an 'addition unit' strategy (see table of strategies in the Conclusions section of this chapter).

Nigel was encouraged to use one of the dots and chose point 4. This meant that he started his new diagram from point 4, instead of anywhere on the page, but did not use the point as a centre of enlargement. Unusually, he asked for a protractor and measured the angle as 60° so that his first new line was like the original. In the process of making his enlargement he thought that all the angles were 60°. Also, at one stage, he used two rulers to try to get his lines parallel.

In the interview (PostF) on item 12 Sacha had only used the taught method when her own method had let her down. In interview (D), three months later, she immediately used the taught method. She was asked to enlarge the original twice as big, and she chose to use point 3 as the centre of enlargement. She measured from the centre of enlargement to the vertex, and then added this distance to itself. She then measured from the centre of enlargement through the vertex and put a dot – just as the teacher had demonstrated. Unfortunately there was an error in one of her additions and so her final drawing was inaccurate.

She was then asked to use point 4 as a centre of enlargement and 1½ times as big as the scale factor. She again used the taught method and, apart from an incorrect addition (7.2 + 3.6 = 10.6), carried out the enlargement successfully.

SUMMARY

The results on this interview show little variation in terms of the recognition of scale factors/ enlargements from those on interview (PostF). On the enlarging task none of the children, except Sacha, used a centre of enlargement or the idea of pattern lines.

Summary

Some of the variation in performance can be accounted for by the difference between the items used; for example, if the shape was on squared or plain paper, or if the shape had right angles or not. This meant that some methods used by pupils would enable them to get the 'correct' answer, whereas others would not.

The high response to the recognition of integer scale factors was, particularly in the earlier interviews, because of 'doubling' to get the scale factor 2. Stella's unwillingness to count or measure was a reflection of an intuitive approach to enlargement.

A variety of different strategies were shown by the children, and these were only affected slightly by the teaching programme. Children's work was often difficult to interpret because besides the particular strategy that they might have been using, they may also have been making a measuring error such as starting at 1 on the ruler. Of the six pupils interviewed, Sacha was the only one who used the taught method on interview (D).

School 19, Class A (aged 10–11)

School 19 was an urban school and the class selected for the research was 4th year juniors, 10–11 years of age. The interview sample was comprised of six pupils; Moira, Emily, Calvert, Derek, Janice and Ahmed.

The teaching programme

THE PRE-FORMALIZATION WORK

The pre-formalization work consisted of eight separate lessons lasting a total of almost seven hours. The first lesson began with the children sorting plastic shapes to find 'the same shape', looking at lengths of sides and sizes of angles, the ideas of similar shape, correspondence and corresponding sides and angles. The second lesson was used to produce a display on enlargement using examples in two and three dimensions. Examples of *Gulliver's Travels* and *Alice in Wonderland* were taken from this display in lesson three to motivate the children to draw themselves and giant versions of themselves for comparison of various lengths. Lesson four continued with this work with a look at the multiplicative aspect of scale factor. Lesson five continued with the same theme as the teacher realized that many of the pupils had not grasped important ideas.

In the next lesson the children used a map of London to experience an enlargement that 'reduced the size of objects'. In lesson seven the pupils were given drawings of two similar houses and asked to compare corresponding lengths. They then drew windows on the drawings in the correct ratio. In the final lesson the children were shown two rectangles and they discussed the relationship between the linear and area scale factors. The children were then asked to draw their own simple shape, like a triangle, square or rectangle, and produce enlargements of scale factors 2, 3, 4 or 5. They then looked at the relationship between area and corresponding lengths.

THE FORMALIZATION WORK

Although only one formalization lesson was planned, three took place. In the first lesson, the teacher reviewed with the class the terms 'corresponding lengths' and 'scale factor', using examples on the overhead projector. The children were grouped in pairs and each pair given one small and one large pinboard, with some rubber bands. One of the children had to put a shape on the small board and the other child made the same shape but larger on the other board. It was after this exercise that the teacher decided to stop the lesson after about 20 minutes' duration.

In the discussion afterwards it became clear that the teacher was preoccupied by the fact that some of the children were not understanding the concepts he was trying to teach. It was then agreed that, as it was the end of term, the formalization lessons would continue at the beginning of the following term. Therefore almost one month later the researcher carried out interviews to verify that the children were at a similar stage as in the previous interview, and the teacher taught two further lessons. In the first of these (lesson 2), the children were given two shapes, one an enlargement of the other, and then asked to place them on paper so that corresponding sides pointed in the same direction/or parallel. They then stuck the shapes down and drew lines through corresponding points to find the centre of enlargement. By taking measurements from the centre of enlargement to corresponding points the children found the scale factor.

The final lesson started with the teacher using an overhead projector to demonstrate how to enlarge a square from a centre of enlargement. The demonstrations used pattern lines and distances from the centre of enlargement to corresponding points. Various examples were given with the centre of enlargement in different positions. The children were then given a shape and asked to choose their own centre of enlargement and enlarge the shape by various scale factors. Some children started work on enlarging their own shapes.

The interviews

The four interviews for the interview sample from School 19, Class A are summarized in Table 9.4.

There were some noticeable aspects in the first set of interviews, (I), namely: The use of the area strategy by Moira, Emily and Calvert; the use of a border strategy, particularly by Derek, and the fact that Emily, Janice and Ahmed were making errors in the way they measured.

When the children were asked the final question in the 'construction' category: a rectangle, measuring 3 cm by 5 cm, on plain paper and asked to make it three times bigger (item 5, Figure 9.2), none of the children drew a rectangle measuring 9 cm by 15 cm. Derek could not carry out the task as the rectangle was near the corner of the sheet of paper, so he redrew the rectangle in the middle of the paper. He then used his border idea as in the previous item mentioned. He measured out from each side 3 cm and put a dot, then drew his rectangle which measured 9 cm by 11 cm (see Figure 9,7).

Calvert measured the shortest side '3 . . . so 3 times 3 makes 9' and drew his new rectangle attached to the original. He then asked, 'Shall I split it in half, or shall I split it into 3 bits here?' He decided to split it into 3 bits, see Figure 9.7. It was not clear whether his new rectangle was 9 by 5, or 12 by 5.

Moira worked on an area strategy. She measured the sides of the original and multiplied to get 15. She then multiplied 15 by 3 to get 45 and then considered squares and rectangles having this area. She finished up with a rectangle measuring 5 cm by 9 cm. Emily also worked on an area strategy and finished with a rectangle 4 cm by 9 cm but via a very different route. She used the physical end of the ruler to start her measuring so that the original rectangle, for her, was 2 cm by 4 cm. The area was therefore 8 and 3 × 8 gave 24 for the area of the new rectangle. She drew a new rectangle 3 cm by 8 cm which was really 4 cm by 9 cm.

Ahmed and Janice started from the 1 on the ruler when measuring. For Ahmed the original rectangle mesured 4 cm by 6 cm. He multiplied each side by 3 and drew his rectangle 12 cm by 18 cm, but because of his measuring error it really measured 11 by 17. Janice also thought the original rectangle measured 4 cm by 6 cm and her new rectangle, like Ahmed's, also had length 17 for the same reasons. Her other dimension, however, was 13, which she arrived at by saying the original was 4 (really 3) plus another 4 (really 3) plus another 8 (really 7). She also used the original as a guide for her new rectangle (see Figure 9.7).

Table 9.4: Summary of interview responses – Schools 19, 20 and 21

Type of response

Recognition

Type of response	School 19, Class A				School 20, Class A				School 21, Class A			
	I	PreF	PostF	D	I	PreF	PostF	D	I	PreF	PostF	D
absent		A			K	K	✕	K	P R	J K		
Can recognize integer s.f.	A J	A C D / E M	C D / E	C D / J	D / K L U	C D J / L U	✕	C D J / L U	P R	J K	D J K / P R	D J K / P
Can recognize fractional s.f.	C D / J	C D	C D	D	K / U	J / U	✕	D J			D	
Uses area strategy	E C / M	E C	C	C	K J / U	J / U	✕	U	S	S	S	S
Uses addition strategy	A D	A J M	J M	A J M	L / U	C D J	✕	C / L	D K / S	D / S	S	R S
No counting or measuring	D / D	D	E	E	C D J		✕	C	J / P R S	S	R	R S

Construction

Type of response	School 19, Class A				School 20, Class A				School 21, Class A			
	I	PreF	PostF	D	I	PreF	PostF	D	I	PreF	PostF	D
absent		A								✕		J
Can enlarge on squared paper	C / M	C / J	C J M	C J M	K	D J / L U	D J / L U	D J / L U	P / J S	✕	D J K / P R	J
Can draw pattern lines	✕		E M	E C / M	✕	U	U	U		✕		
Can enlarge on plain paper		C D / E J M	C D / E J M	A C / J M	C D J K / L U	U	U	U	D J K / P R S	✕		
Uses addition strategy		D / J M	A C / J M	A C / J M	C / K		U	U	K	✕	D / R S	D / R S
Uses taught method		C / E J M	C / E J M	C / M		D / U		D / U		✕	D / R	D K
No counting or measuring	✕	✕								✕		
Measuring error	A / E J	M	E									

Interview

	I ↔ PreF ↔ PostF ↔ D	I ↔ PreF ↔ PostF ↔ D	I ↔ PreF ↔ PostF ↔ D
	59 days 31 days 82 days	16 days 6 days 100 days	13 days 8 days 114 days
		No questions on 'Recognition' were asked on interview PostF	No questions on 'Construction' were asked on interview PreF

Key

School 19
A Ahmed
C Calvert
D Derek
E Emily
J Janice
M Moira

[A C D / E J M]

School 20
C Carey
D David
J Joseph
K Kerry
L Lorna
U Una

[C D J / K L U]

School 21
D Dale
J Jarvis
K Keely
P Patrick
R Ramona
S Sheila

[D J K / P R S]

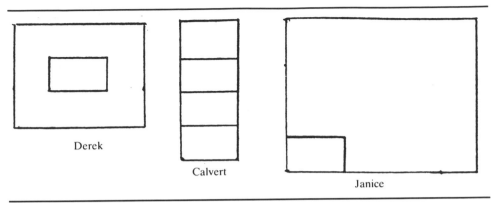

Figure 9.7: Approaches to item 5 on interview (I)

In the second set of interviews (PreF), Derek showed a reluctance to count or measure, but when he did he was successful in recognizing scale factors. Moira moved from an area to an addition strategy. Calvert still used an area strategy but could now recognize scale factors and enlarge a shape on squared paper. Emily consistently used an area strategy in both recognition and construction. Ahmed continued to use a border strategy in all cases.

The strategies of Emily and Ahmed are illustrated in their approaches to item 13 (Figure 9.6), the enlargement of a quadrilateral by scale factor 2.

Emilly: Um... I think that's roughly about 9 squares, ½ squares, so if I wanted to make it 2 times larger, it would be two 9s, 18, and then I would have to copy the shape, which I'm not very good at doing.

She then guessed the area of the left hand part of the original as being 3¾, doubled this to 7½ and then drew a line 7½ cm long. She estimated the right hand half of the original as being of area 5½ but then could not continue as she did not know what to do next.

Ahmed took the lengths of the sides and doubled them, but in spite of making three attempts he was not successful as he was working within a border strategy.

Ahmed: Well if I'm making it two times bigger it has to be something that fits, it can fit into with a border of one centimetre all round.

In the interview (PostF), Moira, Emily, Calvert and Janice adopted a method for enlarging shapes on plain paper and all, except Emily, could enlarge a shape on squared paper as well. Moira and Janice were also using an addition strategy. Calvert again used his displacement strategy as in interview (PreF). Derek, as in interview (PreF), could recognize scale factors, but apart from one occasion could not enlarge any shape, either on plain or squared paper. An example of Derek's difficulties is given below.

When asked to draw lines on the pairs of shapes on items 9, 10 and 11 (see Figure 9.4, page 202) Derek immediately asked, 'Can I put a centre of enlargement?' and after discussing the merits of various positions on item 9, decided none would work and said, 'I'll just draw the lines'. This meant he joined up corresponding vertices on the two shapes without making the lines longer in order to find the centre of enlargement. On items 10 and 11 he guessed where the centre of enlargement was, marked the point and drew lines from the point to the vertices. The degree of inaccuracy of the lines depended upon his judgement of where the centre of enlargement should be.

On the delayed interview (D) all the pupils recognized integer scale factors but only Derek could recognize fractional scale factors (see Table 9.4). Moira, Emily and Calvert could draw pattern lines but Emily could not go any further than this as she did not measure. The preponderance of addition strategies meant that only Moira and Calvert could enlarge the quadrilateral (item 12, Figure 9.3, page 199) on plain paper, and then only with scale factor 2. For her attempts at scale factors 2 and 1½, Moira drew lines from the centre of enlargement, through the vertices, the distance for the particular scale factor. This was successful with scale factor 2 but with scale factor 1½ she used an addition scale factor strategy. She took the distance from the centre of enlargement to a vertex, d, added that distance again, $d + d$, and then added on ½ the distance, $d + d + ½d$, to finish with an enlargement that was scale factor 2½.

Calvert drew his pattern lines first and then measured distances on them. This was correct for scale factor 2, but for scale factor 1½ he used a similar method to Moira. He measured the distance from the centre of enlargement, d, added on half the distance, $d + ½d$, and then added on half of half the distance, $d + ½d + ½(½d)$. So for example with the distance of 6 cm he added on 3 cm and then 1½ cm.

Ahmed did not use pattern lines. He realized that his method had difficulties and made various attempts to make his drawings look right. That is, he tried to give them the appearance of what he thought the finished drawing should be. With the scale factor 1½ he used an addition unit strategy so that the sides of length 2, 4 and 6 were enlarged to lengths of 2½, 4½ and 6½.

Summary

Emily began by using an area stragegy, in the recognition category, on the first two interviews, but did not show this on interview (PostF) and (D) where she was able to recognize integer scale factors. On three occasions during the series of interviews she did not count or measure and on interview (I) made a measurement error, as did Janice and Ahmed. Although able to draw the pattern lines in interview (D) she was unable to use the taught method as she had immediately after the teaching, interview (PostF).

Derek was very good at recognizing integer and fractional scale factors but was unable, except on one specific instance, to enlarge shapes himself. The most notable point to make about the results from this school is the consistency and persistence of the strategies used. Calvert with his area strategy on recognition, and displacement strategy on enlarging on squared paper, and Moira, Janice and Ahmed with their addition strategies on both recognition and construction. On interview (D) only Moira and Calvert could enlarge on plain paper in the limited context of scale factor 2.

School 20, Class A (aged 12–13)

School 20 was an urban secondary school and the class selected for the research was second year, aged 12–13. The interview sample was comprised of six pupils: Lorna, Kerry, Una, Joseph, David and Carey.

The teaching programme

THE PRE-FORMALIZATION WORK

The pre-formalization work consisted of six lessons lasting a total time of approximately six hours. Six worksheets accompanied these lessons, in the first of which the pupils were presented with two irregular quadrilaterals on a coordinate grid. The pupils were asked to measure the lengths of the sides of the shapes and compare, multiply the coordinates of the smaller shape by 2, and draw the new shape. The words 'similar' and 'image' were introduced. The second sheet introduced the terms 'enlargement' and 'scale factor' and the pupils were asked to measure distances from the centre of enlargement to the vertices of a kite. The next sheet required the pupils to step off distances along pattern lines using a compass.

Worksheet 4 was a square on squared paper with one pattern line and one new point marked. The pupils had to construct new shapes of scale factors 2 and 4, and then compare areas. Sheet 5 consisted of a 2 by 4 rectangle on squared paper with its centre of enlargement marked in the middle of the shape and 4 pattern lines drawn. The children were asked to 'Draw the largest similar rectangle possible with centre P', and then draw as many other similar rectangles as they could. The final sheet was a large square with its centre of enlargement in the centre of the shape and 4 pattern lines drawn. The pupils were asked to draw enlargements with scale factors ½, ⅕ and ¹⁄₁₀.

THE FORMALIZATION WORK

The formalization stage was just one lesson of 80 minutes' duration. It began with the teacher reviewing what the class had been working on recently. The terms 'point of enlargement' and 'scale factor' were used and examples of scale factors, including fractional, were given. Two different sized models of men were shown to the class and the children were asked to guess what the scale factor of enlargement was. The two models were placed on a table and a ruler laid on top of their heads so that the centre of enlargement could be found. Measurements were taken by the children from this point to the feet of the two models and eventually it was agreed that the two distances were approximately 28 and 56 cm, giving a scale factor of 2.

The children then worked in pairs on photocopied drawings of the models, first of all with two of different sizes. They then carried out a similar process of sticking their cut outs on a large sheet of paper, to find the centre of enlargement and the scale factor. More men were added to a total of six, showing various scale factors including ½. The children sometimes used a calculator to find 'large distance divided by small distance' for the scale factor.

There was some confusion about whether the distance from the centre of enlargement to the first drawing had to be the same in all cases. This was rectified when a pupil showed that for various positions of the two drawings the ratio for the two distances always remains the same – 2.

The interviews

The results of the four interviews, School 20, Class A, are summarized in Table 9.4, page 208. There were no questions asked in the recognition category in interview (PostF).

In the first set of interviews (I), Lorna and Una were the only ones to be able to enlarge on squared paper and these two together with Kerry and David could recognize integer scale factors. Kelly, Una and Joseph used an area strategy and all the children except David used an addition strategy either on the recognition or construction aspects.

Una enlarged the quadrilateral on squared paper (item 2, Figure 9.2), by first of all using the two sides at right angles and making them 4 and 6 cm, and then the other two sides, of apparent length 3 and 4 cm, to 6 and 8 cm. After correcting her first attempt she achieved the correct diagram. Joseph left the side of length 2 cm to enlarge until last which meant that the angles between the other sides were more difficult to judge (see Figure 9.8).

All the children in interview (PreF) could identify integer scale factors, but none of the fractional scale factors. This was partly due to the preponderance of addition and area strategies.

All five children interviewed on the photograph of the dog (item 6, Figure 9.2 page 194), recognized scale factors 2 and 3. 'F' and 'C' produced comments by the children that implied that they were looking for multiples of 2 or 3, of the lengths of the sides of the original, *only*; for example '5 not 6 for twice as big', 'should be 4 not 5', 'it's an odd number, should be 6', '2 doesn't go exactly into 3'. 'A' provided answers of 'too thin', 'sausage dog' and 'dachshund'.

Because of the teaching programme one might have expected an approach to item 13 (Figure 9.6) to be based on coordinates, however only Carey and Lorna started this way. Carey had difficulty in plotting the coordinates and finished with different points marked with a cross for the 4 vertices of the quadrilateral. Lorna started by finding the coordinates of the vertices of the original shape but abandoned them for another method. Una suggested that

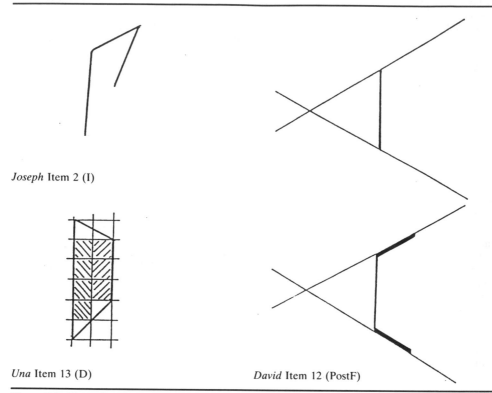

Joseph Item 2 (I)

Una Item 13 (D)   *David* Item 12 (PostF)

Figure 9.8: Examples of approaches to items

$(-1, -1)$ was the centre of enlargement and drew the correct pattern lines through the vertices of the original. She then doubled the lengths of the sides and fitted the new lengths either between or on the pattern lines.

All six children could enlarge the rectangle in the first interview but Carey and Una were the only ones to attempt the quadrilateral of item 12, with Una being successful.

It was not clear from the formalization lesson what exactly the method was that they should use for enlarging a shape. In the interview (PostF), none of the children used any method involving coordinates, and only Lorna considered it. She started enlarging the shape of squared paper (item 13, Figure 9.6), by writing down the coordinates of the vertices and contemplated doubling them for her new diagram, but then said:

(I: Interview; L: Lorna)
L: Um... I don't think the coordinates matter.
I: Doesn't matter – why?
L: Because you just want it twice as big, you didn't say you wanted it in the same sort of place, so if you wanted it in the same place like, it would be 10 or something, 10, 2 or something, but you just want it 2 times bigger so it doesn't really matter about the coordinates.

When faced with the enlargement on plain paper (item 12, Figure 9.3, page 199), David used a mixture of methods. He chose point 1 for the centre of enlargement and, after drawing two other lines, drew the two correct pattern lines. He then measured from the centre of enlargement to the two nearest vertices and doubled to obtain his first line. By doubling the lengths of the two sides lying on the pattern lines he obtained two more lines and joined for the correct completed shape (see Figure 9.8).

A similar method used by Una for scale factor 1½ was: measure the distance from the centre of enlargement to the vertex (d), add on the same distance ($d + d$) and add on half the distance ($d + d + \frac{1}{2}d$).

All the children interviewed at the delayed interview (D) stage could recognize integer scale factors. Joseph and David replied in a similar fashion to the Ts of item 8 (see Figure 9.2). They both recognized scale factors of 2, 3, 5 and 2½ and of the scale factor 1½ David said:

(I: Interviewer; D: David)
D: No, it won't fit into it, 'cos there's um … 2 there and 3 there, it's odd.
I: It's odd, is it?
D: Therefore it'll be either double or ½ the size, it can't be sort of 1½.

Una used an area scale factor strategy. She found the area scale factors of 4, 9 and even 2¼. Lorna used an addition scale factor strategy. She described the scale factors 2, 3 and 5 as being 1, 2 and 4 times bigger.

Lorna, Joseph and David were successful in enlarging on squared paper item 13, by the method of doubling the sides.

Una doubled the lengths of the sides and obtained her new shape, but was not happy with it. In the original quadrilateral the lengths of the two parallel sides were seen by her as the number of whole squares at the side of the line, which gave her lengths of 3 and 4 (see Figure 9.8). Her new diagram, using this method, had lengths of 6 and 9. She therefore changed the position of the top vertex and drew another line so that the offending 9 now had 8 squares to the left of it, a line that was in fact 10 cm long.

Lorna was unable to make any attempt at enlarging on the plain paper (item 12, Figure 9.3). Joseph, David and Carey used the same method of multiplying the length of sides by the scale factor and drawing a shape without taking account of the angles.

Una was the only pupil to be able to draw pattern lines and enlarge on plain paper. When she started from point 4 with scale factor 1½, she drew the pattern lines and her first measurement to a vertex was 6 cm. She then used the scale factor to get 15, which she realized was more than scale factor 2, and so adjusted this to 9. Her method was flawed when she multiplied 7½ by 1½ and obtained 11¾, which made her diagram slightly inaccurate, but otherwise a reasonable attempt.

Summary

The teaching sessions and the formalization lesson all involved some of the elements of centre of enlargement, pattern lines, scale factors, measuring from the centre of enlargement to a point and multiplying this distance by the scale factor. The success in enlarging a rectangle on the first interview changed dramatically on subsequent interviews when faced with the trapezium of item 12. The fact that the formalization lesson did not synthesize a method for enlarging shapes *may* be one of the reasons why only Una was able to make any reasonable attempt at enlarging on plain paper. Other reasons may be that Lorna, Joseph and David had successfully enlarged on squared paper and, particularly Joseph and David, had used this on plain paper – so why adopt another method? The consistent use of addition and area strategies was another feature of the children interviewed from this class.

School 21, Class A (aged 11–12)

School 21, an urban secondary school; the class participating in the research was first year, aged 11–12. The interview sample was comprised of six pupils: Sheila, Patrick, Keely, Dale, Ramona and Jarvis.

The teaching programme

THE PRE-FORMALIZATION WORK

The method of teaching for the class was substantially different from that in Schools 18, 19 and 20. The class normally used SMILE, which is a scheme designed to allow the teacher to set work appropriate for the needs of the individual child. Three boys and three girls were given a special series of workcards to do from this scheme: 0384, 1347, 1388. Worksheets 0384 were concerned with transferring the drawing of a face on to other grids to give examples of stretches, shears and distortions of the original face. Card 1347 asked the pupil to draw small and large versions of trominoes (a shape made by joining three squares edge to edge) and compare their areas. Similarly 1388 was about the comparison of areas of similar shapes, 'When I double the sides of a shape the area becomes...times as big'.

The pupils were allowed sufficient time to attempt this work, a total of 3½ hours in four lessons. After 20 minutes of the fourth lesson the teacher gathered the group together and showed them examples of scale factor 2 and 3 enlargements of a square, giving area scale factors of 4 and 9. The pupils were then asked to 'investigate the effect of enlarging on area change'.

THE FORMALIZATION WORK

In a similar way to the pre-formalization work, the pupils had up to three one-hour lessons to complete the SMILE card 0432. The pupils had to write down the coordinates of various points on the drawing of a boat and then double, or multiply by 3, or add 2, to either the first or second number of the original coordinates and draw the new picture. In addition the teacher also asked them to take a simple shape and multiply both numbers in the coordinates by firstly 2, then 3 and if possible, 4, drawing the new shape in each case and comparing the areas.

The interviews

Table 9.4, page 208 summarizes the results of the four interviews for the interview sample from School 21, Class A. There were no questions asked in the construction category in interview (PreF).

In the first set of interviews, Sheila, Patrick, Ramona and Jarvis refused to count or measure on the 'Photograph Frame' – item 3 (see Figure 9.2). Dale said of 'D' that it was 'one size bigger', and that 'if you put it in the middle...then you've got bits left over, round it'.

Dale made various attempts at trying to enlarge the quadrilateral in item 2 (Figure 9.2). He had difficulties because he started with the top line instead of either of the two lines at right angles to each other. In getting his correct diagram, Jarvis located the top right hand vertex by means of the displacement method of 1 across and 2 up which he corrected to 2 across and 2 up. Sheila also started with the two lines at right angles, but drew her lines of 4 and 6 cm near to the original, so that her final shape surrounded it (see Figure 9.9).

Keely used an addition scale factor strategy for item 2, (D):

(I: Interviewer; K: Keely)
 I: How long is that line?
K: 9.
 I: And how did you get that?
K: I did 3 lots of 3.
 I: You're making the shape twice as big aren't you?
K: Yes.

She completed her diagram which was correct for scale factor 3.

As in the interview cohort for School 20, Class A, all six children enlarged the rectangle on plain paper with scale factor 3 (item 5), by using a linear scale factor strategy.

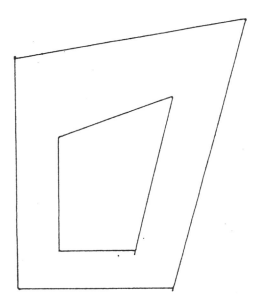

Figure 9.9: Sheila's Approach, item 2, (I)

In the dog photograph (item 6, Figure 9.2), interview (PreF), Keely and Jarvis both recognized scale factors 2 and 3, and both rejected the scale factor 2½ for similar reasons: '5 is an odd number', '2s don't go into 5'. Keely rejected the remaining rectangles, ''cos none of them have got twice size, 3 size or 4 sizes bigger'.

On the Ts of item 8 (Figure 9.2) Dale recognized scale factors 2, 3 and 5 but in each case he changed his mind to 1, 2 and 4. Sheila used an area strategy. She put 'A' on top of 'B' and found that there were three lots of five squares left over so it was '3 times bigger'. For the scale factor 3, Sheila finally decided that if 'A' was on top of 'C' it was 8 items bigger and if it was not on top, it was 9 times.

Considering the emphasis of the teaching programme, it was surprising that Sheila was the only pupil to use an area strategy.

Item 13 (Figure 9.6), the quadrilateral on squared paper with the coordinate axes marked, was used in interview (PostF). Sheila used an addition strategy for the enlargement scale factor 2, '3 to 6 to 9', but her final drawing was not correct for scale factor 3 as the angles were not correct. When encouraged to use the coordinate axes she remembered the boat, of the formalization work, but was unable to do anything. Jarvis finished with the correct diagram by doubling the sides, and he also used the displacement method of 4 across and 4 up. When asked about the axes he thought they might be used to help count the lengths of the sides of the shape.

Patrick, Dale and Ramona all doubled the lengths of the sides, with just Dale being successful in getting the correct diagram by this method. Patrick realized that his first drawing was wrong, and then used the numbers on the axes to locate the positions of the vertices, without using the coordinates in a formal manner. Ramona and Dale wrote down the coordinates and doubled them, and Dale used the term 'coordinates'. Keely was the only pupil who started by using the method of the formalization. 'Can I do it by writing the coordinate out?'.

Ramona recognized the scale factor 2 in the Ts of item 8 (Figure 9.2) on the final interview (D). For the scale factors 1½ and 2½ she used an addition unit strategy by looking at the difference in the lengths of certain sides, getting 'one times bigger' and '3 times bigger'. Sheila put the 'A' on top of the 'B' and counted in fours, then corrected it to fives, around the edge. Her area addition strategy resulted in it being 3 times bigger.

None of the pupils used the formalization method when enlarging the quadrilateral, on squared paper with coordinate axes, of item 13. Sheila used an addition scale factor strategy, so that for example the side of length 3 became 9, but her drawing was still incorret for scale factor 3 as two of the angles were wrong. The only pupil to achieve the correct result for scale factor 2 was Jarvis, who used a displacement method of 4 across and 4 up, and 4 across and 2 down, to locate the position of the two right hand vertices.

Summary

Various aspects of the pupils' performance from the interview cohort from School 21, Class A are particularly noticeable. Four of the children worked without counting on the first interview (I), and both Sheila and Ramona repeated this on subsequent interviews. The inability to recognize fractional scale factors was not surprising considering the lack of exposure to this aspect in the teaching programme. Three of the six children could use the formalization method on the interviews immediately following the formalization 'lessons', but no one adopted this method on the delayed interviews (D). The pupils did show their consistency of approach in other ways. Jarvis used his displacement strategy and Sheila her area strategy on various occasions, but the predominance of the use of an addition strategy, not only in the recognition but also in the enlarging aspects, was clearly shown.

Conclusions

An anlaysis of the summary tables for the four schools, on both the recognition and construction aspects, reveals some consistent patterns. Some children start the teaching programme already using an addition or area strategy (see Table 9.5 for a description of the different 'strategies'), whilst others adopt one or the other during the programme of work. The number of children consistently using one or more of these strategies varied between one out of the six interviewed in School 18, Class A, to five of the six interviewed in School 19, Class A, with three out of five, and four out of six in the interview cohorts in the other two schools.

This adoption of strategies that inhibit success at the (proposed) formalization is quite likely one of the main reasons why only four of the 23 pupils interviewed exhibited the taught method in the final interview (D). This compares with the 11 pupils who used the taught method immediately after the formalization lessons. The level of performance of the children varied considerably, not only over the period of time of the research, but also between the two major categories of recognition and construction, and also from item to item.

The variation in performance can be attributed to other aspects of the teaching of enlargement. While participating teachers were asked to list the prerequisite knowledge and skills they assumed the children would have relevant to the topic to be taught and upon which they were intending to build the teaching programme, they ignored this aspect during the teaching and instead concentrated on producing and following a particular scheme of work.

This will often lead to difficulties. For example, if a child is unable to measure correctly, let alone accurately, then the resultant diagram after an enlargement will be 'wrong', and the measurement error often difficult, if not impossible to detect (see for example the children of School 19, Class A on interview (I), item 5).

The predominance of integer scale factors in the teaching modules, coupled with the lack of certain prerequisites, could well account for the relatively poor performance on recognizing and using fractional scale factors. Another aspect of the teaching which received little attention was angles and their invariance in enlargement. This could help explain the variation

Table 9.5: Strategies employed by children for ratio:enlargement

Strategy	Description	Example
linear scale factor	multiply the lengths of the sides of the original shape by the scale factor to find the lengths of the sides of the new shape.	School 18, Interview (I), Sacha on item 4, page 193
addition scale factor	use of the increase in length of the side of a shape to determine the scale factor. For example 3 cm increased to 9 cm is scale factor 2.	School 18, interview (I), Perry on item 4, page 193
area	takes the area of the original, say 5, and the area of the new shape, say 20, and uses them to obtain a scale factor of 4.	School 19, interviews, page 207
area addition	combination of the two above. From the areas 5 and 20, the difference is 15, so the scale factor is 3.	
addition unit	in fractional scale factors when the child will add on as with an addition scale factor strategy and then add on a further fraction of a cm. For example a s.f. of 1½ will make a length of 4 cm be 8½ cm, 6 cm be 12½ cm.	School 18, interview (D), Stella on item 12, page 205
border	particularly on item 3, regards the original as being in a corner or the centre of the frame and then considers the 'gap'.	School 18, interview (I), Nigel on item 3, page 195; School 19, interview (PreF), Ahmed on item 13, page 208
displacement	On item 2, using the horizontal distance 3, and vertical distance 1, from the top left hand corner to the top right corner, in order to locate the position of the top right hand corner of the new shape. Similarly on item 13.	School 21, interview (PreF), Jarvis on item 2, page 214

in pupil performance related to whether the shape was regular or irregular, it had right angles or not, or it had been drawn on squared or plain paper.

The two major strategies, i.e. related to aspects of addition and/or area, are highlighted by their consistency of use. The addition strategy occurs both in using a scale factor to work out a new measurement, and in the way shapes are drawn or interpreted as having a border around the edge. The use of an area strategy reflects the doubt in some children's minds as to whether an enlargement is concerned with a linear or area scale factor. It seems clear from this work that the relationship between the two should be made explicit in the teaching programme.

The four teachers involved in this research were all very experienced and highly regarded by their colleagues, and yet they all found the topic difficult to teach. This may be attributable to some or all of the following factors: a lack of an overall perspective of what is meant by an enlargement and what may be appropriate stages of development; the difficulty of defining a formalization stage; limited (or no) consideration of prerequisites in the teaching programme; failure to take account of what ideas and strategies the children had *before* the start of the teaching programme.

Chapter 10
Summary and Implications

The CMF research

Each of the preceding chapters, three to nine inclusive, presents findings from the Children's Mathematical Frameworks (CMF) research specific to a particular mathematical topic. These have direct implications for the teaching of the particular topic (for example, equivalent fractions or area of a rectangle) and for teaching 'related' mathematical topics such as number operations involving place value, operations with fractions, measurement (formulae), and more generally for the learning of methods or procedures for performing mathematical tasks, as illustrated by the chapters on ratio/enlargement and equations. Note that in terms of the specific topics, the research team has selected certain interview items for inclusion in an Appendix to this book (available by post from the authors). We feel these items could be helpful in working with children – as an aid to understanding the nature of their thinking in the development of the mathematical topic, and in this regard may be particularly useful in method work in the initial training of teachers (primary, middle or secondary) or in INSET. The reader may well wish to extend the ideas which provide the bases for these questions, i.e. design similar items which focus on such things as prerequisites, the intended role and the child's interpretation of the role of concrete materials/representations, the child's *understanding* of the formal mathematics, etc., for use with children studying other related topics.

As each of the preceding chapters includes a summary of the key points or findings from that chapter, it is not our intention to repeat those points here. However, the information from these seven topic areas has as its common basis the fact that the children were being asked to move in their thinking to accepting, understanding and using a mathematical generalization or method, usually involving some form of symbolism. The common feature in the teaching scheme was the provision of concrete or 'materials based' experiences which were to provide the foundation for learning, and understanding, the more formal mathematics, which was then presented in what for the purposes of the CMF research were called the 'formalization' lesson(s). Table 2.1 (Chapter 2) provides a summary of the formalization in each of the seven topic areas.

The data collected in the research include interviews with 150 children on each of four occasions – prior to the teaching, (I), just prior to the formalization lesson(s) (PreF), immediately after the formalization lesson(s) (PostF) and, approximately three months later, the delayed interview (D). The data also include observations of 30 'formalization' lessons, in 25 classrooms from 21 schools, and teacher-prepared schemes of work for each class or group for each of the particular topics.

The main findings as reported for each topic were in terms of (a) the difficulties many children had moving from the concrete or pictorial representations to the more formal (general) aspects of mathematics and the inability to link these stages of the teaching/learning process together later, (b) the crucial influence of the lack of some prerequisite skill or knowledge, (c) the influence of incidences of 'unsound approaches' or unintentional errors in the teaching, and (d) the differences in understanding exhibited by children who had been provided with the same set of instructional experiences (a feature identified in the earlier research of CSMS and SESM, see Chapter 1, and also noted in the report of the Cockcroft Committee of Inquiry, 1982).

This information taken as a whole provides the research team with a basis for putting forth a number of hypotheses (supported by the data) about the nature of the children's thinking and, in particular, the difficulties experienced, and misconceptions held, by many of the children in their learning of some of the more formal aspects of school mathematics. This then is the purpose of the present chapter. In particular, we put forward our interpretations of the CMF work across the mathematical topic areas. These findings, or interpretations, are first categorized and presented in a listing of 'key points' relative to 'the learner' (the child), 'the teacher', and 'the curriculum'. This is followed by some general points relative to the mathematics being studied – number, measurement, and algorithms (i.e., the presentation of a technique or procedure to be followed in solving a particular type of mathematical problem). The final section makes reference to these summaries in a discussion of the implications for teaching.

Findings: some general points

The suggestion that one can separate the findings into three somewhat unique subsets, the child, the teacher, and the curriculum, is an over-simplification as items under any one of these will also have direct implications for the other two. On the other hand, one can focus on what the research results have to say about, or to, each of these 'partners' or components in the teaching and learning of mathematics – and this is the approach taken in developing the lists presented in the following three sections. The 22 points noted also provide the basis for the final section in this Chapter – Implications for Teaching. The section on 'The mathematics', is an attempt to generalize more in terms of the mathematical areas included in the research – number, measurement (geometry) and algorithms – but still focusing on the participants in the teaching/learning situation.

The child

1. Some children failed to show any understanding of certain prerequisite knowledge necessary for meaningful learning of the formalization to take place (e.g. not appreciating the relevance of multiplication to finding the number of dots in a rectangular array in 'area of a rectangle'). This sometimes lasted for the duration of the study.
2. Children sometimes came to the start of the teaching programme with an incorrect method (e.g. indiscriminate subtraction of a smaller number from a larger number).
3. At the outset some children already possessed a sound strategy, but this may have been at variance with the algorithm (e.g. working from left to right when using an informal method of substraction in mental arithmetic).
4. When working at the pre-formalization stage the approach adopted by the children often differed in terms of order, manner, or significance from that demanded by the formalization (e.g. visual grouping of objects on one side of a balance in terms of matching them to the arrangement on the other side as a method of solving equations rather then the removal of identical amounts from both sides).
5. By and large children from the same group (interview cohort) appeared to take the formalization on board at different times (of those who actually made this step) – e.g. see the performance across the four interviews in Chapter 4, Equivalent Fractions.
6. In specific topics, alternative methods were retained by the children to suit different examples (e.g. see ratio/enlargement for integer scale factors and non-integer scale factors).
7. Even after three months some children who were able to use the formalization (for certain topics), were deficient in their understanding (e.g. in place value, subtraction, the decomposed number was often judged to have changed value).
8. After the formalization had been taught, or three months later, the practical or pre-formalization work which led up to it was often forgotten or not seen as significant.

9. In specific topics it was difficult, if not impossible, for the child to reconstruct the experience with materials if the formalization was forgotten or not used (e.g. in equivalent fractions the symbolic notation for a fraction needed to be understood in order to recall its diagrammatic representation – see also number 11 below).
10. Children who used a formalization successfully often could not return to or remember the pre-formalization mode or experiences which led up to it.
11. The children found it difficult to use the materials to build up a solution to a problem (yet this was expected of them in the use of materials in the pre-formalization work), but if they understood (or thought they understood) the more formal aspects of the mathematics they could on occasion use the materials to explain their reasoning to the interviewer (e.g. see Joe's incorrect reasoning and explanation of addition of fractions in Figure 4.2, Chapter 4).
12. Across most topics a pattern emerged in the use of the formalization. One or two pupils from the interview cohort (of six) employed the formalization in some form from the outset. One or two did not use the formalization at all (throughout the study) and the remaining one or two may or may not have used it 'sucessfully'.

The teacher

13. It was possible to identify assumptions/errors made by teachers which led to or compounded children's difficulties (e.g. using centimetre squares or cubes for measuring length and expecting children to give measurements in centimetres and not square centimetres or centimetre cubes; also the drawing of inaccurate diagrams for fractions and for the enlarged shapes in ratio).
14. Often in the formalization lesson, the teacher made the transition from one mode to another by using both modes in parallel or by reference to each 'mode' separately. It was also the case that for many children the pre-formalization work/experience was *not* an immediate precursor to the formalization. That is, there appeared to be a need for work which linked these stages more closely (e.g., in area of a rectangle pointing out that the length indicates the number of squares which *will fit* in a row and the width indicates how many rows there *will be*).
15. When presenting the formalization, teachers sometimes distorted the mathematics involved by describing the steps in the procedure/algorithm in terms of superficial symbol manipulation (e.g. in solving equations talking in terms of 'getting rid of' say a 'minus 3').
16. The proportion of children whose progress exactly matched that planned in the teaching (or scheme of work) was very small (e.g. for area of a rectangle and for ratio/enlargement this was approximately five per cent or one in 20).
17. In some cases pupils identified by their teachers as being among the most able did not display as high a level of understanding as other members of their interview cohort. Also some pupils, judged by their teachers to be among the least able (often they were described as 'slow') showed evidence of having some of the most sophisticated and meaningful levels of understanding.
18. Some teachers felt it was not always appropriate to teach for the formalization and preferred to place more emphasis on pre-formalization work – it may well be that for some children this only reinforced the notion that their more naive (e.g. counting or 'intuitive') strategies were appropriate for the tasks (problems) they were being asked to do.

The curriculum

19. There was evidence of inappropriate presentations of topics involving mathematically unsound approaches as a result of either textbook material or failure on behalf of teachers to think through the consequences of methods chosen (e.g. introducing variables in equations by using letters to represent names of objects or in the case of ratio presenting both length and area enlargements without an indication as to which is the 'agreed' meaning of the mathematical task).

20. Published materials (among those reviewed and used in the CMF work) seemed to reflect a philosophy of using 'tried and true' approaches without any indication, in the teacher's guide or handbook, as to research findings concerning the difficulties children can experience in following the prescribed approach.
21. Textbook sources often failed to identify relevant knowledge and skills required for learning a particular formalization (e.g. multiplying three numbers together as essential for working with the formula for the volume of a cuboid).
22. Items 1, 3, 4, 8, 10, 11, 14 and 16 in the preceding sections could also be noted here. This highlights further the interconnectedness of the three components – the child, the teacher and the curriculum.

The mathematics

This section presents some selected observations related to specific difficulties encountered by the children when dealing with the mathematics from one of the three domains studied – number, measurement (geometry) and techniques (or algorithms). The ideas presented in this section are not necessarily unique to the particular domain (e.g. the problem associated with lack of prerequisites holds for all three domains), but rather they are noted to emphasize further the importance of considering all aspects of the teaching/learning situation.

The points made in this section are also included in the sections on 'The child', 'The teacher' and 'The curriculum' above. However, the discussion here groups items somewhat differently and hence provides a different perspective and hopefully some insights relative to the teaching of other mathematical topics in the same domain

NUMBER

The information for number comes primarily from the CMF research on place value: subtraction, see Chapter 3, and equivalent fractions, see Chapter 4 (note however that the comments here are also supported by selected results from the other chapters/topic areas).

Three particular points come through as common to the work in number. The first of these is the considerable effect of misconceptions, misinformation, naïve strategies, or 'child methods' which have been assimilated or 'learned' for earlier experiences. Examples include ideas or approaches such as 'one always subtracts the smaller from the larger (misinformation), the use of a pattern to generate equivalent fractions (naive strategy), or the use of a counting strategy to find a difference ('child method').

The second point noted here is the lack of certain prerequisite skills or knowledge. The CMF research demonstrates that it is easy to overlook or assume the existence of some of the more obvious prerequisites. For example, some minimal facility with multiplication and division when working with equivalent fractions (otherwise the child is left trying to complete tasks using only the operations of addition and subtraction).

The final point to be noted here is the difficulty children experience in attempting to attach new meaning to representations which use the familiar symbols. Examples here include (a) the coding used when decomposing in subtraction, i.e. the use of 'small numerals' to keep track of what is happening, actually changes the 'top' number; (b) when working with three-digit subtraction, one moves to acting on the single digits and hence loses the idea of the number itself, and (c) the notion that 1/2 'is the same as' 6/12 when it is clear that '1' is not the same as '6' nor is '2' the same as '12' (not unexpectedly the integers in the fractions are viewed as whole numbers).

MEASUREMENT (GEOMETRY)

Comments here are based largely on the data and results from the work on circumference (Chapter 5), area (Chapter 6) and volume (Chapter 7), with some support from the measurement tasks required in the work on enlargement (Chapter 9).

Firstly, the effect of the lack of certain prerequisite skills and knowledge (and misconceptions) is well documented in the problems of actually physically measuring lengths with a ruler (the common errors related to the failure to properly place the zero point). In addition, in the case of volume, one can point to the problems caused by the lack of familiarity with the multiplication of three numbers and the inability to link the work with earlier work on area (but when one looks at what happened in area, Chapter 6, this is not surprising).

Other points of particular interest in the domain of measurement are the problems linked to

(a) focusing on extraneous information (e.g. the perimeter when working with area).
(b) dependence on pictorial representations with units shown (e.g. squared paper in area and enlargement).
(c) problems with vocabulary, particularly in regards to units of measure – cm, cm^2, and cm^3, (or square cm and cubic cm) – and the linking of these with the context of length, area or volume. The problems of language in enlargement are also quite acute – note the use of vertex, pattern lines, centre of enlargement, make 'bigger' or 'similar' or the 'same shape', etc.

TECHNIQUES AND ALGORITHMS

The implications of the work on equations (Chapter 8) and ratio/enlargement (Chapter 9) provide us with many valuable insights relative to the difficulties children experience when learning a new and often complex procedure for doing some mathematical tasks. Of probably the most significance here is the difficulty that children have in linking the formal rule to that used prior to the teaching or in the pre-formalization work. This difficulty is compounded further by the fact that the transfer is seldom a direct match of the technique used previously and that being taught as the formalization. For example, note the work in equations (Chapter 8) where what the children were doing with the balance was *not* analogous with the formalization of 'do the same to both sides *and* end up with the final state being that of the unknown on one side set equal to a number of units or counters on the other side (of the equals sign).

Another example similar to that noted above is illustrated in the children's attempts at performing substraction of two/or three-digit numbers. When using Unifix cubes one can subtract in, say, the 'tens' column first and return to it later if necessary when doing the subtraction for the 'units' column. This is not easy to do or represent when working with the formal algorithm. A similar statement can be made in regard to linking the formal algorithm to the 'counting on' procedure commonly used in mental arithmetic – there is really little or no match between the two procedures. (This is not meant to imply that any of these procedures is 'wrong' but rather is intended to acknowledge the availability of a number of alternative procedures one of which might well be that typically applied by a particular child.)

The situation involved in the learning of a technique for enlarging a shape using pattern lines and centre of enlargement has the feature that firstly the new technique does not link to either the somewhat 'intuitive' idea of 'measure and construct the new shape somewhere on the page' or to the idea that one can merely extend the sides of the original shape (which is typically rectangular) from one of the corners. There is a further complication in that the pupils fail to see why any new procedure is needed and there is little appreciation that the new procedure provides a technique for enlarging more complex shapes and further, that the technique in fact describes precisely, given the centre of enlargement, the positioning of the enlarged shape.

COMMENT

This discussion has not attempted to bring out all of the important findings relative to the mathematical domains. The reader will quite likely identify other considerations from the discussions in the sets of chapters for each domain.

Implications for teaching

As noted in item 12 (above, p. 220), it seems clear that on average the teacher can expect to find that about two of six, or if we extrapolate this result to larger groups, that prior to the teaching up to one-third of the children already have, or have almost, achieved the formalization which is to be taught. Note, however, that this estimate is only an *estimate* as, for example, in the case of equations and ratio the 'success rate' even after the teaching was extremely low. For these children one must ask about the appropriateness of the full scheme of work which they are often given – might it be more appropriate and effective to change development in the teaching to move more rapidly to the formalization or rule, with time then spent afterwards on justification of results (i.e. more emphasis on justification and less on 'discovery')?

Of the remaining two-thirds of the children, about half (one third of the whole group) have some chance of benefiting from the work; the remaining third make little or no progress. This is generally due to a lack of key prerequisites (e.g. the inability to perform linear measurements leads to numerous errors in finding areas or in producing enlargements, when the task is to be done on other than squared paper). It may also be due to the often quite tenacious adherence to some misconception(s) or 'child methods' (e.g. it is difficult to convince a child of the need to 'decompose' if the child already 'knows' that when you subtract a larger number from a smaller you get zero as an answer). It seems clear that this group of learners needs special attention and in particular a greater emphasis on 'diagnostic teaching' – i.e. a consideration on the part of the teacher of errors and misconceptions – and initial work on at least getting the learner to acknowledge the limitations of his or her ideas. Attention to this area requires some very careful thought on what might 'be going wrong'. The task here for the teacher is formidable. On the other hand there is a quite reasonable research base available in this area, with the potential to provide considerable assistance to teachers. We note for example the work of the APU (DES, 1980, 1981, 1982, and the Cambridge Institute of Education appraisal, 1985), the research of CSMS and SESM (see Chapter 1), and the book *Children Learning Mathematics: A teacher's guide to recent research* (Dickson, Brown and Gibson, 1984), as well as the availability of diagnostic assessment instruments such as the ILEA *Checkpoints Assessment Cards* (1979) and the *Chelsea Diagnostic Tests* (Hart *et al.*, 1985). On the other hand, it is clear that the implementation of teaching approaches which take into account the learner and the literature base will require resources – in particular time for teachers to assess and then to prepare and organize such teaching.

To return to the 'middle' group, we wish we could say that this was the 'third' for whom the lessons, in the CMF research, were clearly appropriate. Unfortunately, this is not what happened. Even though in some classes or interview cohorts it appeared that this subgroup was performing the algorithm or generalization successfully, upon probing (in interview) it became clear that even in the best of circumstances only about half of this group were successful in terms of *some* understanding. Many of the children in this 'middle' group seemed to fix on some aspect of the development (i.e. some point in the sequence of lessons in the scheme of work prior to the actual formalization), and to rely on this when asked to use the rule/formalization in subsequent tasks. For example, relying on the practical work for finding the circumference of a circle (or cylinder) rather than using the formula. Teachers need to be more conscious of this phenomenon and to include careful observation and questioning in their teaching. More attention needs to be given in monitoring how children are progressing. It may not be necessary to go through all stages in the development of a particular topic in the scheme of work, but when a child 'stops' or 'is stuck', the teacher must consider ways of helping the child over or 'around' the particular hurdle or block.

In all the cases noted above, the message is one of establishing a dialogue with the child. The importance of asking the right questions and listening cannot be overemphasized. We suggest that the skill of 'interviewing' would be an extremely important addition to a teacher's repertoire of classroom skills and techniques.

The lessons in the CMF research appear to be based on the assumption that (most) children in an age group (class or subgroup) are expected to take on a particular formalization at some selected point in time during their study of mathematics. This assumption must also be questioned. Would an alternative be to consider the possibility that there might be levels of mastery of such material? For example, wouldn't it be appropriate for some children to stay, at least 'for the time being', with a (correct) counting or measuring strategy for area (volume) or circumference, *as long as they appreciate that the strategy is limited* (or won't always work, and possibly when it won't work)? The more general use of the formula might come at some later time, after the learner has acquired the fundamental concepts and relationships upon which the new learning depends. This of course will require skill and insight on the part of the teacher. It is also the case that the teacher must have available materials which provide for maximum flexibility in use – to handle the wide range of attainment which exists in classrooms (see the Cockcroft Report, 1982).

The CMF research certainly does not simplify the task of the teacher. In fact, as noted above, the research indicates that the task of teaching mathematics effectively requires considerably more effort than is usually acknowledged by those both inside and outside the profession. Note the very commendable efforts made by the highly committed and motivated teachers who participated in the CMF research – and yet many of the pupils still experienced considerable difficulty in dealing with the mathematics, both in the pre-formalization and formalization stages. In some ways this may seem depressing. On the other hand, the insights gleaned from the 'Chelsea' (now King's) programme of research, which has focused on children's understanding of particular aspects of mathematics and the methods and strategies they employ when dealing with mathematical tasks, provide us with guidance as to a way forward which emphasizes *the important and exciting role the teacher has to play in this endeavour*.

References

ASSOCIATION OF TEACHERS OF MATHEMATICS (1967). *Notes on Mathematics in Primary Schools*. Cambridge: Cambridge University Press.

BIGGS, E. and MACLEAN, J. (1969). *Freedom to Learn*. Canada: Addison-Wesley.

BOOTH, L. (1984). *Algebra: Children's Strategies and Errors*. Windsor: NFER-NELSON.

BROWN, M. (1981). 'Place Value and Decimals'. In: HART, K. (Ed) *Children's Understanding of Mathematics: 11–16*. London: John Murray.

CAMBRIDGE INSTITUTE OF EDUCATION (for the Department of Education and Science) (1985). *New Perspectives on the Mathematics Curriculum*. London: HMSO.

COLLIS, K. (1975). *Cognitive Development and Mathematics Learning*. Chelsea College, Psychology of Mathematics Education Workshop.

COCKCROFT COMMITTEE OF INQUIRY INTO THE TEACHING OF MATHEMATICS IN SCHOOLS (1982). *Mathematics Counts*. London: HMSO.

DEPARTMENT OF EDUCATION AND SCIENCE (DES), ASSESSMENT OF PERFORMANCE UNIT (APU): MATHEMATICS (1980). *Mathematical Development: Primary Survey, Report No. 1*. London: HMSO.

DEPARTMENT OF EDUCATION AND SCIENCE (DES), ASSESSMENT OF PERFORMANCE UNIT (APU): MATHEMATICS (1981). *Mathematical Development: Primary Survey, Report No. 2*. London: HMSO.

DEPARTMENT OF EDUCATION AND SCIENCE (DES), ASSESSMENT OF PERFORMANCE UNIT (APU): MATHEMATICS (1982). *Mathematical Development: Primary Survey, Report No. 3*. London: HMSO.

DEPARTMENT OF EDUCATION AND SCIENCE (DES), ASSESSMENT OF PERFORMANCE UNIT (APU): MATHEMATICS (1980). *Mathematical Development: Secondary Survey, Report No. 1*. London: HMSO.

DEPARTMENT OF EDUCATION AND SCIENCE (DES), ASSESSMENT OF PERFORMANCE UNIT (APU): MATHEMATICS (1981). *Mathematical Development: Secondary Survey, Report No. 2*. London: HMSO.

DEPARTMENT OF EDUCATION AND SCIENCE (DES), ASSESSMENT OF PERFORMANCE UNIT (APU): MATHEMATICS (1982). *Mathematical Development: Secondary Survey, Report No. 3*. London: HMSO.

DICKSON, L., BROWN, M. and GIBSON, O. (1984). *Children Learning Mathematics: A Teacher's Guide to Recent Research*. Eastbourne: Holt, Rinehart and Winston.

FITZGERALD, A., LIVINGSTONE, K. and PURDY, D. (1981). *Mathematics in Employment 16–18: Report*. University of Bath.

GLENN, J. and STURGESS, D. (1980). *Towards Mathematics. A Primary Teacher's Guide*. Huddersfield: Schofield and Sims.

HARGREAVES, J. (1982). *Nuffield Maths 5 Teacher's Handbook*. London: Longman.

HART, K. (Ed) (1981). *Children's Understanding of Mathematics: 11–16*. London: John Murray.

HART, K. (1984). *Ratio: Children's Strategies and Errors*. Windsor: NFER-NELSON.

HART, K., BROWN, M., KERSLAKE, D., KÜCHEMANN, D. and RUDDOCK, G. (1985). *Chelsea Diagnostic Tests*. Windsor: NFER-NELSON.

HOWELL, A. and FLETCHER, H. (1978). *Mathematics for Schools*. London: Addison-Wesley.

INNER LONDON EDUCATION AUTHORITY (ILEA) (1979). *Checkpoints Assessment Cards.* ILEA Learning Materials Service.

KARPLUS, R., KARPLUS, E., FORMISSANO, M. and PAULSEN, A.C. (1975). *Proportional Reasoning and Control of Variables in Seven Countries.* Lawrence Hall of Science, University of California, Berkeley.

KERSLAKE, D. (1986). *Fractions: Children's Strategies and Errors.* Windsor: NFER-NELSON.

KÜCHEMANN, D. (1981). 'Algebra'. In: HART, K. (Ed) *Children's Understanding of Mathematics: 11–16.* London: John Murray.

LATHAM, P. and TRUELOVE, P. (1980). *Nuffield Maths 3 Teacher's Handbook.* London: Longman.

LATHAM, P. and TRUELOVE, P. (1981). *Nuffield Maths 4 Teacher's Handbook.* London: Longman.

ALBANY, E. (Ed) (1982). *Nuffield Primary Maths 5–11.* London: Longman.

PIAGET, J. and INHELDER, B. (1967). *The Child's Conception of Space.* London: Routledge and Kegan Paul.

SCHOOL MATHEMATICS PROGRAMME (SMP) (1969). *Book D.* Cambridge: Cambridge University Press.

SEWELL, B. (1981). *Use of Mathematics by Adults in Daily Life.* Leicester: Advisory Council for Adult and Continuing Education (ACACE).

SKEMP, R. (1971). *The Psychology of Learning Mathematics.* Harmondsworth: Penguin.

WILLIAMS, E. and SHUARD, H. (1970, 1973, 1980, 1982). *Primary Mathematics Today.* London: Longman.